MULTICULTURAL EDUCATION SERIES

JAMES A. BANKS, *Series Editor*

(continued)

REACHING AND **TEACHING** **STUDENTS** IN **POVERTY**

Strategies for Erasing
the Opportunity Gap

SECOND EDITION

WITHDRAWN

Paul C. Gorski

TEACHERS COLLEGE PRESS
TEACHERS COLLEGE | COLUMBIA UNIVERSITY
NEW YORK AND LONDON

Published by Teachers College Press, 1234 Amsterdam Avenue, New York, NY 10027

Copyright © 2018 by Teachers College, Columbia University

Cover images: Row of pencils by DNY59, last pencil by NickS, both via iStock. Graph paper by Rawen713, via Deviantart.com.
Permissions acknowledgments appear at the ends of Chapters 4 and 5

Library of Congress Cataloging-in-Publication Data

Names: Gorski, Paul, author.
Title: Reaching and teaching students in poverty : strategies for erasing the
    opportunity gap / Paul C. Gorski.
Description: Second Edition. | New York : Teachers College Press, [2018]
Series: Multicultural Education Series | Includes bibliographical references and
    index.
Identifiers: LCCN 2017039599 (print) | LCCN 2017040675 (ebook) | ISBN
    9780807776728 (ebook) | ISBN 9780807758793 (paperback : acid-free paper)
Subjects: LCSH: Children with social disabilities—Education—United States. | Poor
    children—Education—United States. | Educational equalization—United States.
    | Poverty—United States.
Classification: LCC LC4091 (ebook) | LCC LC4091 .G595 2018 (print) | DDC
    371.826/94—dc23
LC record available at https://lccn.loc.gov/2017039599

ISBN 978-0-8077-5879-3 (paper)
ISBN 978-0-8077-7672-8 (ebook)

Printed on acid-free paper
Manufactured in the United States of America

25 24 23 22 21 20 19 18   8 7 6 5 4 3 2 1

For Ma and Grandma.
I am me because you are you.

Contents

Series Foreword

Since the publication of the first edition of this engaging, compassionate, and informative book, the negative effects of poverty on education have remained serious and intractable, although some progress has occurred. Fewer children are living in poverty and more parents have jobs. However, a substantial poverty rate among children persists. In 2015, one out of every five children in the United States lived in poverty (21%) (Annie E. Casey Foundation, 2017). However, the rates for children of color were substantially higher than the rates for the total population and for Non-Hispanic Whites. The poverty rates for these groups were 36% for African Americans, 34% for American Indians, 31% for Hispanics, 13% for Asian and Pacific Islanders, and 12% for Non-Hispanic Whites (Annie E. Casey Foundation, 2017).

Progress has been made in the high school graduation rate of U.S. students. Eighty-three percent of U.S. high school students graduated on time in 2014–15. However, the graduation rate varied across ethnic and racial groups, as these percentages indicate: American Indians/Alaska Natives (72%), African Americans (75%), Hispanics (78%), Non-Hispanic Whites (88%), and Asian/Pacific Islanders (90%) (McFarland, Hussar, de Brey, & Snyder, 2017, p. 215). Although the high school graduation rate for U.S. students is notable, only a third of Americans had a four-year college degree in 2015. The large percentage of U.S. children who live in poverty, and the comparatively low percentage of U.S. students who are college graduates compared to nations such as Canada, Japan, Ireland, and South Korea (Organisation for Economic Co-operation and Development, 2017), indicate why the effective and creative ways to educate students living in poverty described in this book are timely and needed.

This book makes a unique, original, and significant contribution to the scholarly literature on educating students who are born and grow up in low-income communities. In the 1960s most books that dealt with educating poor students described their cultural deficits and the ways in which their family and community values and behaviors caused their low academic achievement (Bereiter & Engelmann, 1966; Bloom, Davis, & Hess, 1965; Riessman, 1962). A number of books in contemporary times also describe the deficits and problems of the cultures of low-income students (Payne,

2013; Thernstrom & Thernstrom, 2003). Gorski's book is refreshing and empowering because it emphasizes the resilience of low-income students and families and explains why educators need to identify and examine their attitudes, beliefs, and behaviors toward low-income students in order to change their perceptions of poor students and create equitable classrooms and schools in which low-income students can learn and flourish.

Gorski describes how difficult it is for teachers and other educators to change their beliefs, attitudes, and behaviors toward low-income students and their families and become "equity-literate educators." This is an ongoing and difficult process because of the stereotypes and misconceptions of poor people that are institutionalized and perpetuated in the mainstream media and in the national culture writ large. Gorski describes movingly and compellingly how he internalized and had to "unlearn" many of the popular stereotypes and misconceptions about poor people even though he grew up in a home with a father from an urban working-class family and a mother from a poor Appalachian family. He uses this telling and powerful personal example to underscore how deeply embedded stereotypes, misconceptions, and negative attitudes toward poor people are within American society and how hard they are to overcome. Gorski reports research that indicates that most Americans believe that poor people are poor because of their "own deficiencies" and that the problems they experience result from their own behaviors because "America is a land of opportunity for all."

Gorski believes that schools can make a difference in the lives of students and that teachers can become transformative educators if they examine and change their attitudes and beliefs about poor students and families and replace their deficit conception of the poor with a "resilient" conception. A resilient conception of poor students and communities describes the ways in which they survive harsh conditions and environments, show tremendous compassion toward other people, give generously to charity, and cooperate and share with the people in their communities. Gorski thinks that these characteristics of low-income people can help to humanize us all.

Gorski draws upon several decades of research to deconstruct many myths, misconceptions, and popular educational practices that undercut rather than enhance the educational achievement of low-income students. He describes how popular educational "lists" that describe the cultural characteristics of poor students —such as the widely disseminated and popular list authored by Ruby Payne (2013)—are detrimental because they essentialize low-income students and conceal the tremendous cultural differences among low-income population groups. Gorski compellingly describes the myriad differences that exist among population groups that are victimized by poverty and insightfully illustrates how "class is experienced in multiple lenses."

There are a number of excellent books that describe the wide social-class gap between the rich and the poor in the United States and the structural and economic factors that cause this growing and alarming gap (Anyon, 1997; Kozol, 1991; Stiglitz, 2012; Weis, 2008). Gorski's book is unique because although he describes the structural factors that perpetuate inequality in U.S. society, he primarily focuses on what teachers and other educators can do in schools now to create more equitable learning environments for low-income students. He derived his recommendations by reviewing research that had been conducted over several decades. Consequently, his book has a strong empirical foundation, which greatly enriches it. He points out, for example, that many schools are implementing strategies that are designed to improve the academic achievement of low-income students but have the opposite effect. Examples include eliminating art, music, and physical education programs, while research indicates that these programs improve student academic achievement, especially among low-income students. Another example is the widespread practice of teaching low-level math and literacy skills in schools with a high incidence of poverty, while research indicates that students in high-poverty schools learn best when they are taught high-level conceptual and reasoning skills.

This book will encourage teachers and other educational practitioners to rethink their attitudes, values, and beliefs about poor students and families and to critically examine many of the practices designed to increase the academic achievement of low-income students that have the opposite effect. Reconceptualizing and rethinking the ways in which low-income students are educated and implementing thoughtful ways to create classrooms and schools in which they will experience educational equity will greatly benefit the increasing population of students from diverse groups who are now enrolling in the nation's school. Students of color and immigrant students are disproportionately poor, and most of them attend schools in low-income and racially segregated communities.

Teachers and other educators need to become knowledgeable and skilled in educating students who live in poverty because of the growing population of students from diverse racial, ethnic, linguistic, and religious groups in the United States who live in low-income communities. Although students in the United States are becoming increasingly diverse, most of the nation's teachers are White, female, monolingual, and view themselves as middle-class. Race and institutionalized racism are significant factors that influence and mediate the interactions of students and teachers from different ethnic, language, and social-class groups (G. R. Howard, 2016; T. C. Howard, 2010; Leonardo, 2013). Social class is also a significant factor that influences and mediates teacher-student interactions. The growing income gap between adults (Stiglitz, 2012)—as well as between youth who are described by Putnam (2015) in *Our Kids: The American Dream in Crisis*—is another significant reason why it is important to help teachers understand how categories related to race, ethnicity, and class influence classroom interactions and student learning and to comprehend the ways in which these

variables influence student aspirations, behaviors, and academic engagement (Suárez-Orozco, Pimentel, & Martin, 2009).

American classrooms are experiencing the largest influx of immigrant
students since the beginning of the 20th century. Approximately 21.5 million
new immigrants—documented and undocumented—settled in the United
States in the years from 2000 to 2015. Less than 10% came from nations
in Europe. Most came from Mexico, nations in South Asia, East Asia, Latin
America, the Caribbean, and Central America (Camarota, 2011, 2016). The
influence of an increasingly diverse population on U.S. schools, colleges, and
universities is and will continue to be enormous.

Schools in the United States are more diverse today than they have been
since the early 1900s, when a multitude of immigrants entered the United
States from Southern, Central, and Eastern Europe (C. A. M. Banks, 2005).
In 2014, the National Center for Education Statistics estimated that students
from ethnic minority groups made up more than 50% of the students in prekindergarten through 12th grade in U. S. public schools, an increase from
40% in 2001 (National Center for Education Statistics, 2014). Language
and religious diversity are also increasing in the U.S. student population.
The 2012 American Community Survey estimated that 21% of Americans
aged 5 and above (61.9 million) spoke a language other than English at
home (U.S. Census Bureau, 2012). Harvard professor Diana L. Eck (2001)
calls the United States the "most religiously diverse nation on earth" (p.
4). Islam is now the fastest-growing religion in the United States, as well as
in several European nations such as France, the United Kingdom, and the
Netherlands (Banks, 2009, 2017; O'Brien, 2016).

The major purpose of the Multicultural Education Series is to provide
preservice educators, practicing educators, graduate students, scholars, and
policymakers with an interrelated and comprehensive set of books that
summarizes and analyzes important research, theory, and practice related
to the education of ethnic, racial, cultural, and linguistic groups in the
United States and the education of mainstream students about diversity.
The dimensions of multicultural education, developed by Banks (2004) and
described in the *Handbook of Research on Multicultural Education* and in
the *Encyclopedia of Diversity in Education* (Banks, 2012), provide the conceptual framework for the development of the publications in the series.
The dimensions are content integration, the knowledge construction process, prejudice reduction, equity pedagogy, and an empowering institutional culture and social structure. The books in the Multicultural Education
Series provide research, theoretical, and practical knowledge about the behaviors and learning characteristics of students of color (Conchas & Vigil,
2012; Lee, 2007); language minority students (Gándara & Hopkins, 2010;
Valdés, 2001; Valdés, Capitelli, & Alvarez, 2011); low-income students
(Cookson, 2013); and other minoritized population groups, such as students who speak different varieties of English (Hudley & Mallinson, 2011)

and LGBTQ youth (Mayo, 2014). The book by Cookson (2013) in the series, *Class Rules: Exposing Inequality in American High Schools*, complements this book because it describes how social class influences teaching and learning in high schools.

The Second Edition of this book includes several new features that strengthen it. Reflection questions and exercises have been added to each chapter. Other new features include a new chapter on the dangers of the deficit perspective and "grit" approaches for addressing educational disparities, and a new chapter on leadership strategies. The statistics and references throughout the book have been updated, as well as the poverty quiz.

This caring, incisive, and visionary book can help teachers and other school practitioners to rethink their attitudes, beliefs, and behaviors toward poor students and families, as well as to deconstruct popular and detrimental stereotypes and misconceptions about them. It provides educators with the conceptual arguments and empirical information needed to reject some of the harmful educational recommendations that are being made for teaching low-income students and to identify effective ones that are grounded in research. This book is a powerful, informed, and elegant treatise for the rights of all children—including our nation's most neglected and marginalized group of students—to be educated, respected, valued, and affirmed.

—James A. Banks

REFERENCES

Annie E. Casey Foundation. (2017). *Kids count data book: State trends in child well-being*. Baltimore, MD: Author.

Anyon, J. (1997). *Ghetto schooling: A political economy of urban educational reform*. New York: Teachers College Press.

Banks, C. A. M. (2005). *Improving multicultural education: Lessons from the intergroup education movement*. New York, NY: Teachers College Press.

Banks, J. A. (2004). Multicultural education: Historical development, dimensions, and practice. In J. A. Banks & C. A. M. Banks (Eds.), *Handbook of research on multicultural education* (2nd ed., pp. 3–29). San Francisco, CA: Jossey-Bass.

Banks, J. A. (Ed.). (2009). *The Routledge international companion to multicultural education*. New York, NY, and London, England: Routledge.

Banks, J. A. (2012). Multicultural education: Dimensions of. In J. A. Banks (Ed.), *Encyclopedia of diversity in education* (vol. 3, pp. 1538–1547). Thousand Oaks, CA: Sage Publications.

Banks, J. A. (2016). Approaches to multicultural curriculum reform. In J. A. Banks & C. A. M. Banks (Eds.), *Multicultural education: Issues and perspectives* (9th ed., pp. 151–170). Hoboken, NJ: Wiley.

Banks, J. A. (Ed.). (2017). *Citizenship education and global migration: Implications for theory, research, and teaching*. Washington, DC: American Educational Research Association.

Bereiter, C., & Engelmann, S. (1966). *Teaching disadvantaged children in the pre-school*. Englewood Cliffs, NJ: Prentice Hall.

Bloom, B. S., Davis, A., & Hess, R. (1965). *Contemporary education for cultural deprivation*. New York: Holt.

Camarota, S. A. (2011, October). A record-setting decade of immigration: 2000 to 2010. Washington, DC: Center for Immigration Studies. Retrieved from cis.org/2000-2010-record-setting-decade-of-immigration

Camarota, S. A. (2016, June). *New data: Immigration surged in 2014 and 2015*. Washington, DC: Center for Immigration Studies. Retrieved from cis.org/New-Data Immigration-Surged-in-2014-and-2015

Conchas, G. Q., & Vigil, J. D. (2012). *Streetsmart schoolsmart: Urban poverty and the education of adolescent boys*. New York, NY: Teachers College Press.

Cookson, P. W. Jr. (2013). *Class rules: Exposing inequality in American high schools*. New York, NY: Teachers College Press.

Eck, D. L. (2001). *A new religious America: How a "Christian country" has become the world's most religiously diverse nation*. New York, NY: HarperSanFrancisco.

Gándara, P., & Hopkins, M. (Eds.). (2010). *Forbidden language: English language learners and restrictive language policies*. New York, NY: Teachers College Press.

Howard, G. R. (2016). *We can't teach what we don't know: White teachers, multiracial schools* (3rd ed.). New York, NY: Teachers College Press.

Howard, T. C. (2010). *Why race and culture matter in schools: Closing the achievement gap in America's classrooms*. New York, NY: Teachers College Press.

Hudley, A. H. C., & Mallinson, C. (2011). *Understanding language variation in U.S. schools*. New York, NY: Teachers College Press.

Kozol, J. (1991). *Savage inequalities: Children in America's schools*. New York, NY: Crown.

Lee, C. D. (2007). *Culture, literacy, and learning: Taking bloom in the midst of the whirlwind*. New York, NY: Teachers College Press.

Leonardo, Z. (2013). *Race frameworks: A multidimensional theory of racism and education*. New York, NY: Teachers College Press.

Mayo, C. (2014). *LGBTQ youth and education: Policies and practices*. New York, NY: Teachers College Press.

McFarland, J., Hussar, B., de Brey, C., & Snyder, T. (2017, May). The condition of education 2017. U.S. Department of Education, National Center for Education Statistics, Washington, DC. Retrieved from nces.ed.gov/pubsearch/pubsinfo.asp?pubid=2017144

National Center for Education Statistics. (2014). The condition of education 2014. Retrieved from nces.ed.gov/pubs2014/2014083.pdf

O'Brien, P. (2016). *The Muslim question in Europe: Political controversies and public philosophies*. Philadelphia, PA: Temple University Press.

Organisation for Economic Co-operation and Development. (2017). Population with tertiary education (indicator). Retrieved from data.oecd.org/eduatt/population-with-tertiary-education.htm

Payne, R. K. (2013). *A framework for understanding poverty* (5th rev. ed). Highlands, TX: aha!

Putnam, R. D. (2015). *Our kids: The American dream in crisis*. New York, NY: Simon & Schuster.

Riessman, F. (1962). *The culturally deprived child.* New York, NY: Harper & Row.

Stiglitz, J. E. (2012). *The price of inequality: How today's divided society endangers our future.* New York, NY: Norton.

Suárez-Orozco, C., Pimentel, A., & Martin, M. (2009). The significance of relationships: Academic engagement and achievement among newcomer immigrant youth. *Teachers College Record, 111*(3), 712–749.

Thernstrom, A., & Thernstrom, S. (2003). *No excuses: Closing the racial gap in learning.* New York, NY: Simon & Schuster.

U. S. Census Bureau. (2012). Selected social characteristics in the United States: 2012 American Community Survey 1-year estimates. Retrieved from factfinder2. census.gov/faces/tableservices/jsf/pages/productview.xhtml?pid=ACS_12_ 1YR_DP02&prodType=table

Valdés, G. (2001). *Learning and not learning English: Latino Students in American schools.* New York, NY: Teachers College Press.

Valdés, G., Capitelli, S., & Alvarez, L. (2011). *Latino children learning English: Steps in the journey.* New York, NY: Teachers College Press.

Weis, L. (Ed.). (2008). *The way class works: Readings on school, family, and the economy.* New York, NY, & London, England: Routledge.

Acknowledgments

I thank the people whose activism, teaching, and scholarship inspire my activism, teaching, and scholarship. Most importantly, I don't know where I'd be without the love, guidance, and mentorship of Bob Covert, Charlene Green, and Allen Saunders, but I know I never would have written this or any other book about equity and justice. Everything I do is in large part yours.

I thank the Social Justice and Human Rights students at George Mason University with whom I have the privilege to work for keeping me on my toes. I thank my School of Integrative Studies colleagues for opening space for me to pursue my social and economic justice passions and for being amazing collaborators.

I thank the many people who responded to my social media requests for examples of organizations, policies, and practices discussed in this book: Jean Aguilar-Valdez, Dawn Alfano, Laura Angyal, Peter Appelbaum, Suzie Applegate, Wayne Au, Jane Audette, Deanna Barnes, Margarita Bianco, Cyle Bohannon, Sara Bridges, Teresa Bunner, Carmen Cardenas, Samantha Castelblanco, Emily Chiariello, Meg Cline, Sandra Comstock, Nicole Conaway, Adell Cothorne, Erica Dávila, Bob Davis, Geoffrey Davis, Shanti Elliott, Heidi Faust, Shakealia Finley, Bridget Forbes, Kat Fortuna, Tina Franklin, Rubén González, Jon Greenberg, Zaretta Hammond, Haseena Hamzawala, Adam Heenan, Lori Henry, Petya Johnson, Amy Kales, Mary Ann Kornbau, Jori Lyn, Aurora Maria, Julie Marie, Pam Martin, Cynthia Mathis, Lisa McCarty, Kathleen McInerney, Maria McKenna, Melissa Miller, Jennifer McKeown, Zoya Naskova, Shannon Nordby, Samantha Parsons, Leigh Patel, Jennifer Pemberton, Bree Picower, Tunette Powell, Ashley Tuzicka Ray, Jannette Reyes, Kayci Rush, Cindy Schlichte, Chris Seeger, Suri Seymour, Janny Shafer, Ira Shor, Lesley Smith, Taylor Sprague, Laurel Swanson, Sarah Sweetman, Shannon Telenko, Mary Thome, Mary Thompson-Shriver, Sara Tolbert, Michelle Valladares, J-Lynn Van Pelt, José Vilson, Mary Wayland, Zerell Welch, Sunny Wells, Michael White, and Laura Williams.

I thank the good folks at Teachers College Press, especially Brian Ellerbeck, for your patience and support.

Finally, I thank James Banks for inviting me to write this book for your Multicultural Education series. It's an honor.

REACHING AND **TEACHING** STUDENTS IN POVERTY

SECOND EDITION

CHAPTER 1

Introduction

Education is the great equalizer. That's what I heard growing up, the son of a mother from poor Appalachian stock and a father from working-class Detroit. *If you work hard, do well in school, and follow the rules, you can be anything you want to be.* It's a fantastic idea. How remarkable it would be if only it were true.

I've been working with and around educators for the better part of 20 years now, and this I know for certain: Most of us *want* it to be true. We desire an education system that works for every student—not only one that gives everybody a fair shake, but also one that helps make up for the challenges bearing down on students who face the most barriers in and out of school. Many of us celebrate the Horatio Alger education stories: the young woman experiencing poverty who becomes valedictorian, the homeless student who wins a college scholarship, the janitor who works her way through Harvard. We want to believe that schools, of all places, offer equal opportunity for people experiencing poverty, even when the odds are stacked against them.

Unfortunately, schools as constituted today are not the great equalizers they are cracked up to be. Not for most students, at least (Katz, 2015). This, too, I know for certain: Students from families experiencing poverty continue to bear what Jonathan Kozol (2012) called the *savage inequalities* of schooling. The examples are numerous. They are assigned disproportionately to the most inadequately funded schools (Strange, 2011) with the largest class sizes and least experienced teachers (Kids Count, 2016). They are more likely than wealthier peers to be teased or bullied (Carbis, 2015) and to attend schools with fewer extracurricular options (Phillips & Putnam, 2016). They are denied access to the sorts of school resources and opportunities other children take for granted, such as engaging pedagogies (Battey, 2013; Shields, 2014) and arts education (DeLuca, Clampet-Lundquist, & Edin, 2016). By these and almost every conceivable measure, students from families experiencing poverty, the ones most desperate to find truth in the "great equalizer" promise, pay a substantial price for their poverty, even at school. Of course, teachers did not invent these conditions, but often are blamed unjustly for their effects. In fact, teachers in high-poverty schools, along with increasing numbers of their colleagues at *all* public schools, also are denied access to adequate resources.

Complicating matters, as Sue Books (2004) explained, students experiencing poverty "bear the brunt of almost every imaginable social ill" (p. 34) outside of schools, many of which directly or indirectly affect their abilities to do well in school. Starting at birth, youth experiencing poverty have less access than their wealthier peers to a bevy of important resources and services. These include quality preschool (Waldfogel & Putnam, 2016), consistent quality health care (Perrin, Boat, & Kelleher, 2016), and healthy food (Andress & Fitch, 2016). If we're doing due diligence, we should begin this conversation pre-birth, asking which families have access to high-quality prenatal care.

As I consider these realities, what stands out most about the barriers low-income families face is that none of them, *not a single one*, has anything to do with students' intellectual capabilities or desires to learn. They in no way reflect breakdowns in families' cultures, mindsets, grittiness, or attitudes about education. If anything, they reflect just the opposite: the level of society's commitment—*our* commitment—to fulfill the promise of equal educational opportunity.

If you are a teacher, counselor, school psychologist, or school administrator, you might be thinking, *That's awfully sad, but it's a little outside my purview. I have no control over who has health care or high-quality preschool.*

Fair enough. In fact, in today's world of hyperaccountability in education, where high-stakes testing is used to assess not only student learning, but also teacher and administrator performance, educators often are held accountable for not doing what is more or less impossible to do: making up for all of the barriers and inequities students experiencing poverty face starting prior to birth. As schools decrease children's access to nurses, to art and music education, to recess and physical education, and to all manner of other opportunities and resources that improve school performance for youth experiencing poverty, who are least likely to have access to them outside of school, they also limit our abilities to do our jobs in the most effective and rewarding ways.

I believe this is a set-up and a dangerous shift of attention. The testing regimens and test score obsessions have shifted focus away from the savage inequalities of schooling, as well as bigger societal disparities that affect student learning. And they have shifted that focus onto teachers and their unions, school administrators, and other educators. Imagine how patterns of family involvement might change if every parent had access to one full-time job that paid a living wage, or how patterns of student attendance and engagement might change if every student had access to high-quality preventive health care. Consider what it means that these are the most formidable barriers to eliminating educational outcome disparities, yet mainstream conversations about poverty and education are almost always silent on them.

When I sat down to sketch out the first edition of this book, I initially intended to write about that very problem: how we ultimately cannot eliminate educational outcome disparities, such as differences in graduation rates, without addressing these larger societal and socioeconomic disparities. *However*—and this is a big, fat "however"—we all, whether teachers, counselors, social workers, or administrators, have a substantial amount of power to mitigate these barriers. We have the power and, of course, the responsibility to ensure we do not reproduce inequitable conditions in our own classrooms and schools.

I decided to write a book about *that* responsibility, how best to prepare ourselves, as people working in schools and school systems, to create and sustain equitable learning environments for students experiencing poverty. But I decided to do so by making a connection I find sorely lacking in most conversations about poverty and schooling: We cannot understand the experiences of families experiencing poverty, or how they relate to school, or how best to engage them, if we do not understand poverty and economic injustice. I made this decision for two reasons. First, many of the best minds in education have written books and essays that detail with impressive precision the relationships between larger economic inequalities and educational disparities. I find John Marsh's (2011) book, *Class Dismissed*, and David Berliner's (2013) essay, "Effects of Inequality and Poverty vs. Teachers and Schooling on America's Youth," particularly helpful in this regard. One limitation of these exposés, as poignant as they are, is that they never manage to describe how school workers can help create the change for which the authors advocate. Yes, of course, all youth ought to have access to health care. Yes, of course, we should confront economic injustice. I have spent much of my own activist and scholarly energies on these issues. But what should people who walk into classrooms and schools full of students each day do in the meantime?

The other reason I chose to write a book about teaching and leading for equity is that, of the many popular books that do introduce practical blueprints for teachers and school leaders (see especially Jensen, 2009; Payne, 2005; Templeton, 2011), few sufficiently acknowledge the larger societal barriers described by John Marsh, David Berliner, and others. Absent this acknowledgment, so much of the available literature on which educators rely in hopes of developing deeper understandings of poverty misinterprets educational outcome disparities as reflections of the supposedly deficient cultures, mindsets, and grittiness of families experiencing poverty. If we want to fix educational outcome disparities, this argument goes, we begin by fixing students and families experiencing poverty rather than by fixing the inequities they experience. The result tends to be dangerously narrow framings. We see these in so much of the brain-research–based approaches, which often suggest that instructional strategies are suitable responses to lifetimes of inequality. Or we get a list of ubersimplistic practical solutions based more on stereotypes than reality.

I decided to write a book from a practitioner's point of view, but one that takes an "open systems" or "relational" approach. This approach nudges us to understand what happens in school within the context of conditions that exist outside school walls (Flessa, 2007). After all, these external conditions—living in food deserts or working multiple low-wage jobs to try to make ends meet—influence families' interactions with schools, which, in turn, influence our perceptions of families.

Consider the example of family involvement, often identified by educators, policy wonks, and researchers alike as the school success panacea for families experiencing poverty (Dotterer & Wehrspann, 2015; Hill & Craft, 2003). It is all too common for those of us who have not experienced sustained poverty to assume that if parents do not participate in on-site opportunities for engagement, they simply do not care about their children's education. How often have you heard those sentiments in a faculty meeting or teachers' lounge? How often have you thought them yourself? *Those parents never show up for anything. No wonder kids are failing when their parents don't value their education.* Unfortunately, many educators seem to have bought into this stereotype—this false stereotype, as it turns out (Johnson, 2016; Williams & Sánchez, 2012). (More on this in a moment.) Given a limited understanding, it can be easy to interpret lower rates of on-site school involvement as indicative of a culture or mindset of poverty that devalues education. We might respond, as many schools do, by offering parenting workshops or circulating memos about the importance of parent engagement.

How might our perspective change if we step back for a moment and attempt to understand on-site family involvement patterns in relation to the social conditions described by Marsh (2011) and Berliner (2013)? What if we soften our impulse to find fault in communities experiencing poverty so a fuller picture can come into focus, even if there are parts of that picture we don't feel equipped to change? What if we account for the fact that parents experiencing poverty are more likely than their wealthier peers to work multiple jobs and to work evening shifts? They are less likely to have paid leave and, as stands to reason, less likely to be able to afford to take unpaid leave. Finding and affording child care is more difficult for them than for wealthier parents as well, and they are less likely to have convenient transportation options (Jarrett & Coba-Rodriguez, 2015; Robinson & Volpé, 2015). And, of course, parents in low-income families are more likely than wealthier parents to have experienced school as unwelcoming or even hostile (Lee & Bowen, 2006).

Then there is this: Decades of studies show clearly that parents of families in poverty are as involved, or even *more* involved, in their children's educational lives when compared with their wealthier peers when we consider at-home involvement along with on-site involvement (Milner, 2015). Similarly, decades of research shows that people of all economic conditions, all races and ethnicities, whether from rural or urban regions, care deeply about their children's education—that they have the exact same attitudes about the value of schooling as their more economically stable peers (Johnson et al., 2016; Lucio, Jefferson, & Peck, 2016; Noel, Stark, Redford, & Zukerberg, 2013). The issue, these studies suggest, is not that low-income communities don't care about education. The issue, instead, is that we as a community of educators are so desperate to step gingerly around a real confrontation with the inequities harming students that we build initiatives for closing educational outcome gaps around anything—grit, growth mindset, fictitious mindsets of poverty, lies about who does or doesn't value education—other than the actual causes of the gaps.

I wrote this book, in part, to push us past these presumptions and doomed-to-fail initiatives and toward deeper, more empathetic, more holistic and equity-informed understandings of poverty's and economic injustice's effects on students' school experiences. I wrote it to push us past the simplifications and stereotypes that hamper our abilities to be the equity-minded educators and leaders we want to be.

I also wrote it because I believe in the transformative power of educators, perhaps not always as frontline people in the struggle to end global poverty (at least not on our own), but as people committed enough to walk into classrooms and schools full of students, dedicated to do the right thing by each of them despite all the challenges. I believe we want a more complex conversation about poverty than we get from books about grit or mindsets of poverty. More importantly, I know we're capable of digging deeper into questions about what we can do to better facilitate educational opportunity for each family. I believe we can, and must, begin by dropping the deficit views about fixing low-income families, then by equipping ourselves with a more structural view of how access and opportunity are distributed in and out of schools. We begin there. Then, with that structural view, we start gathering tools and strategies based on what works. That, in a nutshell, is what this book is about.

In pursuit of these goals I construct this book around a framework, co-developed by my supergenius colleague, Katy Swalwell (2011), called *equity literacy*. I dedicate Chapter 2 to describing this framework and how it builds upon and differs from other popular frameworks for discussing poverty, equity, and schooling, from *cultural proficiency* to *mindsets of poverty*. The gist, for now, is this: Equity literacy is comprised of the knowledge, skills, and will that enable us to become a threat to the existence of bias and inequity in our spheres of influence. It fosters our abilities to recognize, respond to, and redress conditions that deny some students access to the educational opportunities enjoyed by their peers (Gorski, 2016a). Whereas many popular approaches ask us to focus on culture—the *culture* of poverty, *cultural* competence—equity literacy asks us to keep *equity* at the center of our conversations, to focus on how to create and sustain equitable learning environments free of even the subtlest biases and inequities. This requires different, although in some ways complementary, kinds of knowledge and skills from what those culture-based paradigms require. After all, simply knowing (or presuming) something about a student's culture or having the skills to interact cross-culturally is not the same as knowing how to recognize and respond to subtle class biases in learning materials or inequities in school policies.

Parts of the picture I paint are uplifting and hopeful, partially due to the amazing perseverance of high-poverty communities and partially because of the inspirational capacities of educators to advocate for students. Admittedly, other parts are bleak. The odds are stacked heavily against the most economically marginalized students and families, despite the skills, gifts, and determination they bring to the table. But there is something we can do about it, and we all have a role in that something.

DEFINITIONS AND DISTINCTIONS

Let's start at the beginning, with terminology. Already I've been using words like "students experiencing poverty" and "low-income families." It can be difficult to find any two people willing to agree on what these words and phrases mean. My intention here is not to provide social science textbook definitions for these terms or to debate the widely variable semantic arguments for this or that terminology. Rather, my intention is to describe what I mean by the terminology I use. There is no "correct" definition or terminology. However, our understandings of poverty can be influenced by the language we use.

In this section I describe how I use the following terms: (1) socioeconomic status, (2) poverty and people who are *economically marginalized*, (3) working class, and (4) income and wealth.

Socioeconomic Status or "Class"

When I ask people what poverty means, they usually mention the financial component first. They might say, "Poverty means not having adequate financial resources." Almost inevitably, though, they turn quickly to other sorts of resources, everything from *life attitudes* to *resilience* to *positive dispositions.* Certainly students' life circumstances are affected by more than their families' financial wealth. Support networks, whether through extended family, religious organizations, or community organizations, can be critically important for families experiencing poverty, as they can be for *all* families.

However, I worry that such a broad conceptualization of socioeconomic status clouds an important distinction. In the end, in a capitalistic society, the only resource that *guarantees* consistent access to basic human necessities like food, clothing, lodging, and health care is money. Sure, associating with a mosque, synagogue, church, or some other religious organization may provide people experiencing poverty with a network of people willing to lend a helping hand. It might even help them feel spiritually fulfilled. In other words, it might help people experiencing poverty to feel a little more comfortable or secure or happy *within a state of poverty.* But without greater access to financial resources, they are still in poverty (Katz, 2015). Their access to the most basic life resources remains tenuous.

This is why, when I talk about socioeconomic status, I am referring specifically to students' or families' access to economic resources. I am referring to resources they can exchange for food, clothing, lodging, and health care. Yes, it may be possible for somebody to be spiritually or emotionally "rich" even if financially "poor," and perhaps that richness will provide some comfort through the difficulties of poverty, but they cannot trade spiritual or emotional riches for stable housing or preventive health care. More wealth means more choices, more opportunity, more access (Hout, 2008). This, to me, is the essence of socioeconomic status or "class."

Poverty and People Who Are *Economically Marginalized*

In many countries, governments assign a dollar figure to the financial condition of poverty, commonly called the "poverty line." For example, according to the U.S. government, a family of four earning less than $24,600 per year is in poverty (U.S. Department of Health and Human Services, 2017). What you might not realize is that in the U.S. the poverty line is calculated primarily through a process developed in 1965 to estimate the annual cost of a humble but adequate household diet (Eberstadt, 2006). In many ways that figure, $24,600, like any estimate of a complex condition, is arbitrary. It's an imperfect estimate that probably results in an underestimation of the number or percentage of families who are experiencing poverty (Meyer & Sullivan, 2012), a reality I discuss in greater detail in Chapter 3. I take more of a social science view, not limiting my understanding or use of the term *poverty* to a specific dollar figure.

Instead, extending my understanding of socioeconomic status, I use the term *poverty* to describe a financial condition in which an individual or family cannot afford the basic human necessities described earlier, such as food, clothing, housing, health care, child care, and education. If we want to understand poverty in its fullest complexity, we must see that it's not a culture or mindset, but rather a societal condition attached to several disturbing realities. For example, poverty is related, at least in the United States, to growing wealth and income inequality, to unprecedented concentrations of wealth and income at the tippy-top of the economic pyramid (Fuentes-Nieva & Galasso, 2014; Rios & Gilson, 2016). Understanding poverty also means recognizing that it exists in localities, countries, and a world in which sufficient resources are available to eliminate it. As a human collective, we *choose* the persistence of mass poverty. Maybe we don't choose it with intention, but to some extent we do choose it.

So in addition to referring to people who bear the brunt of this choice as *people, parents, families,* or *students experiencing poverty*, I use the term *economically marginalized people, parents, families,* or *students*. I use this term to emphasize that poverty is a form of marginalization, the result of a series of conditions that deny some people access to resources and opportunities granted to others. This is a departure from the language I used in the first edition of this book. I decided to stop using "poor" to describe people experiencing poverty, as I did in the first edition, largely because I find distasteful the image it elicits of generations of my own family that withstood poverty. I also reduced my use of the term "low-income" because I worry that it obscures causes of inequity. (I still use it occasionally as an alternative to the other terms as a matter of a literary diversification of language.)

The term *generational poverty* often is used to distinguish long-term, sustained poverty that spans generations from *situational poverty,* which might be more temporary (or could become longer-term). This is an important distinction, and can help clarify some of the contextual messiness of socioeconomic status. For example, some individuals spend most of their lives in the working or middle class, but then are laid off or struggle to manage the financial hardships of a health crisis. They might find themselves temporarily experiencing poverty, unable to pay for basic necessities. But they also are much more likely to have attained a greater level of education than people whose families have experienced generations of poverty, making their prospects for finding new living-wage work brighter. On the other hand, whether poverty is temporary or generational, it poses significant challenges to people experiencing it; in either case it constrains access to health care, housing, schooling opportunities and options, and myriad other services and resources. So, generally speaking, I use *poverty* to cover both situational and generational poverty, and specify *generational* or *long-term poverty* when I mean to refer to it in particular. (In Chapter 4 I explain why I prefer the term *generational injustice* to *generational poverty*.)

Working Class

It can be easy, with all the talk about poverty, to forget that working-class families also are denied many of the options and opportunities wealthier families enjoy. I acknowledge this reality at times by referring to working-class families along with families experiencing poverty.

Unlike people experiencing poverty, working-class people generally can afford basic necessities, but only at a subsistence level. They make just enough to get by. As a result, they usually are unable to save money or accumulate wealth. This leaves working-class families in a precarious position, balancing on the brink of poverty. If an adult in a working-class family is out of work for just a couple of weeks or experiences unforeseen car trouble, or if a child in a working-class family develops an unexpected medical condition, the family can find itself suddenly in debt, trying to decide whether to see a doctor or pay the electric bill.

Many people who think of themselves as middle-class actually are working-class. Most teachers are working-class. Imagine, for a moment, what would happen if you lost your job. If that would put you in immediate danger of falling behind on rent, being unable to pay your power bill, or struggling to afford groceries, you probably are in the working class.

Income and Wealth

I refer throughout this book to both *income* and *wealth*, terms that are popularly and incorrectly used interchangeably. *Income* refers to the "annual inflow of wages, interest, profits, and other sources of earning" (Taylor, Kochhar, Fry, Velasco, & Motel, 2011, p. 4), so that *family income* is the annual total of these earned by all members of a single household. *Wealth*, on the other hand, refers to the total value of an individual's or family's assets—bank accounts, property, stocks, automobiles, and so on—after accounting for debt. So when you hear somebody say, "Oprah Winfrey is worth two billion dollars," it does not mean she makes $2 billion a year, nor does it mean she has $2 billion in a savings account at her local credit union. It means that, after accounting for her debt, all her assets combined are worth $2 billion.

TWO IMPORTANT CONCEPTUAL SHIFTS

In the first edition of this book I urged readers to ditch deficit views of broken, deficient people in poverty and to adopt what I called a *resiliency* view. In some ways, resiliency ideology is the inverse of deficit ideology. It gives us the impulse to acknowledge family and community strengths rather than obsessing over perceived deficiencies. Educators with a resiliency view understand the barriers economically marginalized students must overcome in and out of schools, sometimes just to survive a hostile world.

That framing worked well. Then *grit* became all the rage. I discuss the dangers of the grit obsession in Chapter 4. Suffice it to say, for now, that it can be understood as the latest in a long progression of attempts to redefine educational outcome disparities around supposed deficiencies of economically and racially marginalized people rather than the conditions that marginalize economically and racially marginalized people. Suddenly people are using "resilience" and "grit" interchangeably, undermining aspects of resiliency theory that insisted on a reckoning with inequity.

I chose in this new edition to advocate, not for a resiliency view, but for what I call a *structural* view. The structural framing captures the essential elements of the resiliency view but even more vigorously emphasizes the importance of understanding how societal barriers—including barriers students experiencing poverty face outside of schools, like disparities in access to health care and affordable housing—impact student engagement and performance. That way we are focusing intently on fixing barriers and inequities rather than fixing a fictional culture or mindset of poverty.

Also in Chapter 4 I explain the dangers of replacing this focus on addressing inequities with a focus on grit or growth mindset or other approaches that locate the problem to be solved as existing within, rather than as pressing upon, people experiencing poverty.

I made one other notable conceptual shift in this edition. I previously used phrases like "parents and other caretakers" when referring to the families of students experiencing poverty, attempting to account for diversity in family structure. Some children are raised by grandparents or other kin. Others grow up in foster care or in group homes. In this edition I use the word "parent" more generically to describe not just children's biological parents or stepparents, but also whoever else might be parenting children. It is not my intention in doing so to presume a particular family structure, but rather to avoid minimizing the *parenting* roles of whoever is playing those roles in children's lives.

THE REMAINDER OF THE BOOK

In Chapter 2, "Imagining Equitable Classrooms and Schools for Students Experiencing Poverty: An Equity Literacy Approach," I describe the dimensions and key principles of the equity literacy framework. I refer to this framework throughout the rest of the book.

Chapter 3, titled "The Inequity Mess We're In: A Class and Poverty Primer," summarizes basic information about class and poverty and how they operate. For example, I discuss overall and child poverty rates and how they're changing. I also share basic data on how wealth is unequally distributed across identities like race, (dis)ability, and gender, encouraging an intersectional view of poverty.

In Chapter 4, "Embracing a Structural View of Poverty and Education: Ditching Deficit Ideology and Quitting Grit," I highlight the dangers of views related to poverty that ignore big inequities and focus instead on fixing the mindsets or grittiness of students experiencing poverty. I also share why adopting a structural ideology is a critical step toward equity literacy.

In Chapter 5, "The Trouble with the 'Mindset of Poverty' and Other Stereotypes about People Experiencing Poverty," I explain why, despite its popularity, the *mindset* or *culture of poverty* approach to understanding people experiencing poverty leads us to those harmful deficit views. I then review common myths about students and families experiencing poverty that often misguide educational policy and practice.

Next, in Chapter 6, I catalogue forms of inequity and bias with which families experiencing poverty contend—inequities that happen outside school, but play considerable roles in educational outcomes. These include concerns like access to living-wage work, access to high-quality child care, and access to opportunities for recreation and exercise. I titled this chapter "Class Inequities Beyond School Walls and Why They Matter at School."

Chapter 7, "The Achievement—er, *Opportunity*—Gap in School," details ways students experiencing poverty are denied the sorts of learning opportunities and well-resourced learning environments enjoyed by their wealthier peers. Topics include disparities in school funding, differences in access to engaging pedagogy, and class-based bullying.

We begin an exploration of strategies for addressing the opportunity gap in Chapter 8, "Teaching Students Experiencing Poverty in Effective, Equitable, and Even *Data-Informed* Ways: Curricular and Pedagogy Strategies." I identified these strategies during a several-year process of reading and synthesizing more than 3 decades of research from more than 400 sources. It was a grueling but rewarding several years.

In Chapter 9, "The Mother of All Strategies: Nurturing Equity-Informed Relationships with Students and Families," I share what that same body of research suggests about effective ways to craft equitable, sustainable relationships with students and families experiencing poverty.

Chapter 10 is titled "Cultivating School Change through Equity Literacy: Commitments and Strategies for School and District Leaders." It outlines pathways for effective leadership toward equity, including strategies for crafting equitable policy, cultivating equity literacy in staff and faculty, and building an institutional culture around equity.

Next, in Chapter 11, "Expanding Our Spheres of Influence: Advocating Change for the Educational and Societal Good," I discuss potential ways to work for the bigger social and economic changes that support equitable education.

Finally, I wrap things up nice and tightly, but not too tightly, in the Conclusion.

REFLECTION QUESTIONS AND EXERCISES

1. What are some of the challenges and barriers with which students experiencing poverty might contend outside school that could impact their ability to achieve to their fullest capabilities in school? Make a list of the challenges and barriers and discuss their possible impacts.

2. If decades of research clearly demonstrate that parents of economically marginalized families care just as much about their children's education as wealthier parents, why do stereotypes suggesting that they don't value education persist?

CHAPTER 2

Imagining Equitable Classrooms and Schools for Students Experiencing Poverty

An Equity Literacy Approach

Just as I learned growing up that education is the "great equalizer," I also learned that it is impolite to talk about money. I remember being shushed when I was 11 for asking my uncle how much money he made teaching at a community college. It seemed a reasonable question for a child who wanted to be a teacher. I was in my thirties before I knew much about the poverty my mom's mom, my Grandma Wilma, experienced growing up in an Appalachian coal-mining town, and she was always my favorite person in the world. In fact, we never talked about those Appalachian roots within the family, not, as far as I could tell, because anybody was particularly ashamed about it, but because, well, it just wasn't something we were supposed to do. I still feel skittish talking about class and poverty today, even though I teach and write about them all the time.

Figure 2.1. Grandma

I'm not alone. Class and money are taboo topics for many people, often making them difficult to discuss within families or among friends or colleagues (Falls, 2010). This, I think, is one reason the conversations we have in the education world about poverty can feel so imprecise and simplistic. It's why conversations about poverty among educators often seem to focus not on poverty (what causes it, how it represses some of our students), but rather on simple, pragmatic strategies based more on stereotypes than on evidence-informed practice. (*If only* those people *cared about school . . .*)

Another reason people in general and educators in particular might struggle with conversations about class is that many of us were raised to believe that the United States and its schools represent a *meritocracy*, wherein people achieve what they achieve based on effort and worthiness. From this perspective, all achievement is deserved rather than rendered or manipulated. When we tell students they can achieve anything they want if they work hard enough, we're saying, "Hey, this is a meritocracy, so you have just as good a shot as anyone else. Everybody has an equal opportunity." This ideal of meritocracy has a long and complex history in the United States, tied to notions of rugged individualism and self-sacrifice (Falls, 2010).

Plus, the media love a good rags-to-riches story. They are celebrated as the quintessential meritocracy narrative: the child from an impoverished family beats the odds and graduates from college; the working-class administrative assistant starts a small business and makes it big. The trouble is, because the media love rags-to-riches stories, we develop inflated notions of their commonness. You'd think most people spend their lives sprinting up the economic ladder. It's a common misperception. According to a national study of class mobility by the Pew Charitable Trusts (2012), "Americans raised at the top and bottom of the income ladder are likely to remain there themselves as adults" (p. 6).

Of course, if we were living in a society in which financial or other types of success could be predicted by hard work, we'd see a lot more economic upward mobility. We'd see a lot more people, like parents who are working multiple laborious jobs, blasting their way out of poverty and into the middle class, surpassing the wealth and income levels of previous generations of their families. My mom's people were coal miners for three generations, laboring and hacking and coughing up dust. If you think they didn't work hard enough to deserve not to live in poverty, I'm guessing you've never mined coal. Rags-to-riches stories might garner a bigger audience, but rags-to-rags and riches-to-riches stories are far more common.

Why? Because privilege begets privilege. Educators know this. It is at least partially why many (although of course not all) teachers and administrators don't tend to stay in the most underresourced schools and why they choose, instead, to seek work in wealthier schools or districts (Simon & Johnson, 2015). It also is (at least one reason) why merit pay programs are flawed: They fail to account for the difference between teaching privileged students in well-resourced schools, where parents might pool resources and pay to hire an additional teacher or two, where they can afford tutors and academic camps and iPads full of educational programs for their children, and teaching economically marginalized students in poorly resourced schools, where students have just as much potential and parents care just as much, but where they are denied the opportunities and resources their wealthier peers enjoy. In other words, meritocracy assumes a level playing field that simply does not exist.

One danger of accepting meritocracy as reality is endorsing its flip side. If we believe that people achieve what they achieve purely through hard work, so we all deserve our lots in life, what do we believe about people who are experiencing poverty? If we fail to keep one eye on that larger context—who can afford stable housing, preventive health care, professional tutors—it can be easy to assume that struggling or disengaged students who don't score at grade level on standardized tests simply don't work hard enough. Or that they're lazy. Or that their parents don't value education. This could lead us to believe that some students simply don't deserve a fair shake. Isn't that belief quietly undergirding the common perception that equal opportunity already exists and that *those people* or *those people* or *those people* are too lazy or irresponsible to take advantage of it?

The truth is, most of us know to at least some extent that the system is rigged and the odds are stacked against the most economically vulnerable families, not because they don't work hard, but because access and opportunity are not distributed fairly. We know at least in some cases which kids' families can afford the exorbitant costs of tutors, academic camps, and other forms of "shadow" education, not to mention the costs of computers and Wi-Fi and bedrooms full of books. Plus, if like me you've had parents or grandparents or aunts or uncles who worked long, back-breaking shifts as coal miners or custodians or day laborers, you know, like I do, the suggestion that they are experiencing poverty because they don't work hard is ludicrous. Working hard is no guarantee, especially when, on top of poverty, you're denied equal educational opportunity.

Still, the myth of meritocracy persists. So it can be difficult to free ourselves from shaky perceptions about students' work ethics or parents' educational commitments. It can be difficult to free ourselves from the dangerous assumption that educational outcome disparities are *all their fault*. If we allow ourselves to begin with that perception, we set ourselves up for a hollow conversation in which we blame our most marginalized students for the symptoms of the inequities many have faced their entire lives. And when our conversations are hollow rather than robust, they inevitably lead to strategies and initiatives that are hollow rather than robust. That is no path to equity.

INTRODUCING *EQUITY LITERACY*

Here is an example of the hollowness. In my experience, most conversations about poverty and education begin with this point: Students experiencing poverty arrive at elementary school far behind their peers on many measures of school readiness. Especially when it comes to literacy, students from families experiencing poverty enter kindergarten with a significant disadvantage. This has been measured a dozen different ways. We all know it to be true.

The question is, how do we interpret this reality? What sense do we make of it? To what do we attribute this "readiness gap"?

We must understand how the process of interpretation, of naming the problem we're trying to solve, happens, because this process drives the sorts of solutions we are capable of imagining to address these gaps. (We explore the belief systems that guide or misguide this process in Chapter 4.) For many people, the "readiness gap" simply confirms their existing stereotypes. *People experiencing poverty don't care about their children's education. Why aren't they reading to their children?* Without equity literacy, we lean on those stereotypes because we lack the knowledge or will to unhinge ourselves from bias and examine conditions through an equity lens. We are incapable of taking a step back and filtering student disparities through bigger contextual understandings that might help us formulate better solutions. As we will see in Chapter 5, dozens of studies have shown since the 1970s that families experiencing poverty share the same attitudes about the value of education as wealthier families (e.g., Johnson, 2016; Milner, 2015; Robinson & Volpé, 2015). This, too, has been measured a dozen different ways. And yet, schools continue to spend resources on programs and initiatives meant to convince low-income parents to care more about their children's education. "Those parents don't care about their children's education" is a problem that does not exist, so why should we continue crafting initiatives as though it does?

The early childhood literacy gap has many causes, none of which has anything to do with how parents value education. Consider, for example, how the scarcity of living-wage work (discussed in more detail in Chapter 3) forces many economically marginalized parents to string together multiple low-wage jobs to make ends meet. Imagine the dent we could make in the "readiness gap" if every parent had access to one living-wage job so they could spend more time with their kids, reading and helping with homework. A significant proportion of families experiencing poverty speak languages other than English at home, so parents might not have the literacy skills to read to their children in English. They also are less likely to be able to afford literacy-boosting computer games or extensive home libraries. Note that none of this speaks to how much anybody cares. It only speaks to access and opportunity.

Equity literacy is the accumulation of these kinds of bigger contextual understandings essential to our growth as equitable educators and leaders (Gorski & Swalwell, 2015; Swalwell, 2011). I define it as *the knowledge and skills educators need to become a threat to the existence of bias and inequity in our spheres of influence.* When we commit to cultivating our equity literacy, our very presence in a classroom or school threatens the existence of bias and inequity because we have the knowledge and skills to see it and eliminate it. The *knowledge* refers to developing those bigger understandings, strengthening our abilities to recognize the inequities students experience in and out of schools and how those inequities impact their school engagement. It means learning how to apply an equity lens to every decision we make as educators so that we disintegrate those inequities. The *skills* refer to cultivating our abilities to act for equity, to advocate, to prioritize the educational success of students experiencing the most inequity by reshaping policy and practice. But on their own, knowledge and skills are insufficient. Equity literacy requires *will*. Do we have the will to develop and use the knowledge and skills to fight for equity, knowing it will create discomfort for some people? I know many people with the knowledge and skills but not the will. They are no threat to inequity.

The equity literacy framework borrows some of its principles from other models and approaches for thinking about equity in schools. For example:

- The underlying principle of equity literacy is inspired by Gloria Ladson-Billings's (2006) and Verna St. Denis's (2009) warnings about how vague notions of "culture" often are adopted in conversations about education and diversity in ways that mask equity concerns like racism, heterosexism, and economic injustice. Their analyses encouraged the most fundamental principle of equity literacy: that we must attend to "diversity" by making *equity*, not *culture* or *cultural diversity* or *cultural competence*, the center of our conversation and commitments.
- Equity literacy shares resiliency theory's refusal to associate poverty with deficiency rather than focusing on the strengths that allow communities experiencing poverty to persevere through the many barriers they face. It encourages us, like resiliency theory, to recognize and build upon "the processes that could account for positive adaptation and development in the context of adversity and disadvantage" (Crawford, Wright, & Masten, 2006, p. 355). In this way equity literacy also builds on *funds of knowledge*, a concept coined by Luis Moll, Cathy Amanti, Deborah Neff, and Norma Gonzalez (1992) "to refer to the historically accumulated and culturally developed bodies of knowledge and skills essential for household or individual functioning and well-being" (p. 133).

- Equity literacy draws from Diversity Pedagogy Theory (DPT), introduced by Rosa Hernàndez Sheets (2009), and its principle that we, as educators, should develop skills that enable us to foster "optimal learning conditions to enable more children to learn what [we] intend to teach" (p. 11). This means strengthening not just pedagogical skills, but also broader equity skills.
- Also helpful are some elements of *cultural proficiency* as described by Randall Lindsey, Kikanza Nuri Robins, and Raymond Terrell (2009), especially the capacity for self-assessment. It's not enough to familiarize ourselves with a stereotypical culture or mindset of people experiencing poverty so that we can interact more effectively, as the cultural competence framework asks us to do. Cultural proficiency requires us to understand our own biases and how they are tied to privilege and even to societal inequalities, a commitment embedded in the principles of equity literacy.
- Finally, equity literacy is built on an ethic of critical caring (Wilson, 2016). Empathy and compassion are important traits, but they must extend beyond interpersonal relationships with students who are economically or racially marginalized. What value are empathy and compassion if we feel them interpersonally, but are not then compelled to fight racism or economic injustice? Equity literacy is concerned both with fostering stronger relationships between educators and students and with preparing educators to be responsive to matters of inequity like poverty and racism. According to Camille Wilson (2016), this kind of caring "can be an act of resistance that challenges marginalization and systemic educational neglect" (p. 560).

Returning to that underlying principle, what distinguishes equity literacy, broadly speaking, from many other popular frameworks for conversations about poverty and education is its recognition that educational outcome disparities cannot be erased by studying the cultures, mindsets, or dispositions of people experiencing poverty. The issue before us, as we attempt to create more effective learning environments for economically marginalized students, is not *culture*, but *equity*. We can learn everything possible about this or that culture, but doing so will not help us spot subtle bias in learning materials or see injustice at play when schools eliminate arts and music programs, or understand the connection between the scarcity of living-wage work and gaps in parent engagement. So equity literacy, while recognizing culture as one important dynamic among many other school and classroom dynamics, shoves it out of the center of the conversation, replacing it with equity (Gorski, 2016a).

With equity at its heart, the equity literacy framework is comprised of four abilities and twelve principles, described below.

WHAT THE "EQUITY" MEANS IN EQUITY LITERACY

A commitment to equity is a commitment to justice, to a fair distribution of access and opportunity. Equality, often wrongly used interchangeably with equity, refers to sameness, to an *equal* distribution of access and opportunity. Not all equity is created equally, and vice versa.

In other words, a fair or equitable distribution of access and opportunity might not be an equal distribution, and an equal distribution of opportunity might require an unequal distribution of resources, at least in the short term (Levitan, 2016). A few years ago I had a student—I'll call her Tina—who is blind. Posted readings and in-class handouts are useless to her without expensive technologies to scan and either read them to her or translate them into Braille. She also requires flexibility with assignment deadlines. Equality or *sameness* in treatment would dictate that I refuse her these accommodations. Allowing them creates inequalities in how time, resources, and leeway are distributed to students. Equity, on the other hand, takes context into account. My priority is to ensure every student an opportunity to achieve to her fullest capability.

Aside from ramps, elevators, and a Disability Services Office, the university where I teach, like the rest of society, is built to accommodate the conveniences of people with no (dis)abilities or differences, not to accommodate students like Tina. This is an important distinction: Everybody who does not have a (dis)ability receives far more accommodation than Tina. The whole campus, nearly every program and policy, is designed to accommodate them. Only a few are adjusted to accommodate Tina. We make accommodations to try to level the playing field. This can be hard to grasp for those of us who are always accommodated simply by virtue of not being blind or not using a wheelchair. So, as an educator who strives to be equitable, I recognize Tina's individual circumstances and adjust the allocation of resources accordingly. I practice inequality in this case because doing so is equitable and because the results, like Tina having access to readings and being able to participate fully in class, give her the best shot at excelling academically (Mann, 2014).

This is equity work. If inequity is an unfair distribution of access and opportunity, equity efforts must redistribute access and opportunity. Sometimes this means redistributing funding, like we do when we allocate more financial resources to special education or to accommodations for students like Tina. But "access" also can be nonmaterial. Do students experiencing poverty in your classroom or school have access to every learning opportunity, or do extra fees attached to some learning opportunities make them unavailable to a portion of families? How is access to the best and most experienced teachers, the most engaging pedagogies, and the most welcoming school environments distributed? To what extent do students experiencing poverty in your classroom have access to an atmosphere free of biased curricula, humiliating circumstances, and bullying? How is access to the arts distributed among students attending your school or district? Are policies and practices developed with the interests and challenges of the most marginalized families in mind, or do some families have access to school policies and practices that better align with their lives? These are all matters of equity, of the distribution of access and opportunity. A commitment to equity requires us to examine these conditions, recognize ways in which access and opportunity are distributed inequitably, and then adjust policy and practice to redistribute access and opportunity, redressing the inequities. Doing so might not erase the bigger societal inequities with which families experiencing poverty contend, but they ensure at the very least we are not recreating those inequities in our classrooms and schools.

This is a brief and useful way to assess your school's equity efforts. Can you explain how those efforts are permanently redistributing access and opportunity?

Later, in Chapters 6 and 7, I describe the wide range of ways the educational playing field is not level for students experiencing poverty. Then, in Chapters 8, 9, and 10, I describe what we can do in our spheres of influence to adjust that playing field by teaching and leading with equity literacy and by advocating for educational equity for economically marginalized youth.

THE FOUR ABILITIES OF EQUITY LITERACY

With that understanding of equity in mind, we cultivate equity literacy by strengthening in ourselves four interlocking abilities, each illustrated with examples throughout this book. These abilities are:

1. the ability to *Recognize* subtle and not-so-subtle biases and inequities in classroom dynamics, school cultures and policies, and the broader society, and how these biases and inequities affect students and their families;
2. the ability to *Respond To* biases and inequities in the immediate term, as they crop up in classrooms and schools;
3. the ability to *Redress* biases and inequities in the longer term, so that they do not continue to crop up in classrooms and schools; and
4. the ability to *Create and Sustain* a bias-free and equitable learning environment for all students.

Figure 2.2 expands on these abilities.

The *Recognize* ability receives top billing in equity literacy. Why? If we cannot recognize inequity when we see it, how will we respond to it, much less redress it? A weakness in many approaches to addressing poverty and

Figure 2.2. Equity Literacy Abilities

Equity Literacy Abilities	Ability Descriptions
Ability to *Recognize* even the subtlest biases and inequities in schools and society.	The first fundamental challenge for educators preparing to create and sustain equitable education is learning how to recognize, to *see*, the biases and inequities we need to eliminate. Sometimes bias and inequity are so normalized, so drenched in "common sense," that even the most well-intended of us must train ourselves just to recognize them. It takes conditioning, because unless we have experienced poverty ourselves, we might be trying to learn how to see something we are conditioned not to see, such as the link between the lack of living-wage jobs and educational outcome disparities. When we strengthen our ability to *recognize* even the subtlest biases and inequities, we prepare ourselves to: • understand ways school policies and practices unintentionally punish students experiencing poverty or humiliate them by forcing them to "perform" their poverty in school (conditions discussed in Chapter 7); and • reject deficit views that locate the sources of outcome inequalities (like test score disparities) as existing within the cultures or mindsets of people experiencing poverty rather than as barriers and challenges pressing upon families experiencing poverty.
Ability to *Respond To* biases and inequities in the immediate term.	It is not always easy to respond to difficult issues that crop up around us, whether we see a student make fun of another student's clothes, hear a colleague disparage low-income parents, or learn of a new school policy we know will create hardship for students experiencing poverty. Despite the difficulty, the equity-literate educator develops the skill and will to do so. We know how to challenge these conditions in the moment rather than letting them slide. We are prepared, for example, to: • intervene effectively when we find biases or inequities in learning materials, school policies, or student interactions; and • foster conversations with colleagues about bias and equity concerns.
Ability to *Redress* biases and inequities in the long term.	However, responding in the moment is never enough. As we build our equity literacy, we realize that most of the day-to-day situations to which we respond are attached to bigger sets of inequitable conditions. If we identify one classroom practice that unintentionally humiliates students experiencing poverty—the classic example is the *let's go around the room and share what we did on summer vacation* icebreaker—

(figure continues on next page)

Figure 2.2. Equity Literacy Abilities (continued)

Equity Literacy Abilities	Ability Descriptions
Ability to *Redress* biases and inequities in the long term. *(continued)*	chances are there are many others. We *redress* bias and inequity when we follow their symptoms to their roots. If there is a culture in our school of teachers disparaging families experiencing poverty, the issue is not just how to address each disparagement, but instead how to change the institutional culture to end the pattern of disparagement. The *redress* ability helps us shift from interpersonal action to changing institutional culture and structural realities. We cultivate our abilities to: • advocate against inequitable school practices, such as racially or economically biased tracking, and advocate for equitable school practices; and • identify ways to mitigate structural barriers—lack of access to preventive health care and jobs with paid leave, for example—that impede educational engagement for students experiencing poverty by replacing practices that exacerbate these barriers with practices designed to mitigate them.
Ability to *Create and Sustain* a bias-free and equitable learning environment.	Sustaining these efforts can be difficult. It requires us to rethink policies and practices that might have long histories in our schools. People tend to resist that sort of change. Also, when we start redistributing access and opportunity, people who had grown accustomed to an unfair share of access and opportunity generally don't stay quiet. We need to cultivate in ourselves the will to continue moving forward through resistance and all the difficulties of change. We must be willing to: • withstand the challenges of institutional change, perhaps including becoming targets of derision from people unsupportive of the change we are creating; and • consider the interests of the most marginalized students and families in every aspect of our educational work.

education, like the mindset of poverty approach, is their failure even to acknowledge the existence of inequity. If we are unable or unwilling to learn how to see the full extent of the bias and inequity families experiencing poverty face, we render the rest of the abilities meaningless.

I know this is difficult for some educators, especially given the *give me a list of practical strategies* culture in education. But what value are practical strategies if they are based on misunderstandings of the problems we're trying to address? How can we understand the problems if we can't even see them? Consider the example of fundraising programs that require students to compete with one another. Whoever sells the most bad chocolate or ugly candles wins a trip to the theme park. Did you know those programs are humiliating to many students experiencing poverty, whose parents can't afford to buy several boxes of bad chocolate? They are. But year after year thousands of students endure the humiliation because schools full of smart, caring educators either cannot see, or do not have the will to name, or are worried about being socially punished for naming, the problem. The solution is easy: Find a different way to raise money. But that solution will not occur to us if we are unable to recognize the inequity inherent in these fundraising contests.

There is no *Respond*, *Redress*, or *Create and Sustain* without a well-cultivated *Recognize*.

EQUITY LITERACY PRINCIPLES FOR EDUCATORS

The principles of equity literacy, which are also the guiding principles of this book, are the consciousness behind the framework. Each principle is based on research about links between what educators *believe about* and their effectiveness in *working with* students and families experiencing poverty. They are meant to move us beyond a simplistic focus on this or that "culture" or "mindset," beyond a narrow focus on "brain research" or "growth mindset," and toward a more robust and meaningful understanding of what it means to ensure every student has access to the best possible education. I have tailored these principles to speak specifically to class and poverty, the core concerns of this book. However, the values underlying them can be applied to any equity concern.

The principles are summarized in Figure 2.3, and discussed in greater detail below.

Principle 1: People experiencing poverty are the experts on their own experiences. Perplexed teachers or principals often ask me how they can tell whether their schools are equitable. Schools and districts are turning increasingly to expensive assessment initiatives, spending tens of thousands of dollars to survey everybody, conduct focus groups, and make these determinations. My organization, EdChange, used to do these assessments for schools and districts. We stopped doing them after conducting twenty or so because we realized how inefficient they were. We learned that if adults in schools listen to what their most marginalized students are already telling them—if they listen and are willing to believe what their students say—they will know much of what they need to know to create more equitable schools. If they combine this listening and believing with an equity-informed analysis of data they already collect about, for example, who is being suspended or how students are organized into academic tracks, they can scale down the

Figure 2.3. Principles of Equity Literacy for Educators of Students in Poverty

Principle	Commitments Embraced in Schools with Cultures of Equity Literacy
1. People experiencing poverty are the experts on their own experiences.	Educators recognize people experiencing poverty as partners in any effective approach to address class-based school inequities.
2. The right to equitable educational opportunity is universal.	Educators believe every student has a right to equitable educational opportunity and are willing to fight policies or practices that deny this right.
3. Poverty and class are intersectional.	Educators know that class is an intersectional identity and poverty is an intersectional condition, informed by other identities and conditions. We cannot fully understand how class inequities operate without also understanding how inequities related to race, sexual orientation, gender identity and expression, language, immigrant status, (dis)ability, and other identities operate.
4. People experiencing poverty are diverse.	Educators recognize the diversity among people experiencing poverty. Studying a singular "culture" or "mindset" of poverty will not help us better understand individual students or families, and instead could strengthen our stereotypes.
5. What we believe about people experiencing poverty informs how we teach, interact with, and advocate (or fail to advocate) for them.	Educators understand that teaching practices are driven in part by our beliefs. In addition to relying on practical strategies for creating more equitable schools, we are willing to fundamentally change what we believe about poverty, educational outcome disparities, and their relationships with inequity.
6. We cannot understand the relationship between poverty and education without understanding the barriers and inequities people experiencing poverty face in and out of schools.	Educators also are committed to developing deeper understandings of biases and inequities endured by families experiencing poverty in and out of school and how they affect school engagement.
7. Test scores are inadequate measures of equity.	Educators acknowledge that equity or its absence cannot be captured by standardized test scores because test scores, which as much as anything measure prior levels of access and opportunity,

Figure 2.3. Principles of Equity Literacy for Educators of Students in Poverty *(continued)*

Principle	Commitments Embraced in Schools with Cultures of Equity Literacy
7. Test scores are inadequate measures of equity. *(continued)*	cannot capture student experience. Raising test scores is not the same as creating equity.
8. Educational outcome disparities are the result of inequities, of unjust distributions of access and opportunity, not the result of deficiencies in the mindsets, cultures, or grittiness of people experiencing poverty.	Educators understand that educational disparities result not from mindset mismatches or cultural deficiencies, but from inequities. Eliminating disparities requires us to eliminate inequities rather than change students' mindsets or cultures.
9. Equitable educators adopt a structural view rather than a deficit view of families experiencing poverty.	With the understanding that outcome disparities result from inequities, educators reject deficit views that implicitly blame families experiencing poverty for their poverty and embrace a structural view that puts disparities in a bigger context of structural inequity. We reject strategies and initiatives for eliminating disparities focused on fixing economically marginalized people. We focus instead on fixing the conditions that marginalize people.
10. Strategies for creating and sustaining equitable classrooms, schools, and school systems must be based on evidence of what works.	Aware of the magnitude of inequity against people experiencing poverty, educators base policy and practice decisions not on what is popular or easily implementable, but on evidence of what works.
11. Simplistic instructional strategies, absent a commitment to more robust institutional change, are no threat to inequities.	Educators know that creating equitable classrooms and schools requires multiple layers of strategies and initiatives. Instructional strategies represent only one of those layers.
12. There is no path to educational equity that does not involve a redistribution of access and opportunity.	Realizing that inequity is an unjust distribution of access and opportunity, educators also realize that equity requires a redistribution. This might include the redistribution of everything from access to classes with high academic expectations to access to validating school cultures.

pricey assessments. I came to see these assessment projects in some cases as an expensive form of heel-dragging, creating the illusion of doing something for equity while delaying any real "doing."

So when I'm asked how schools can identify their inequities, I say, "Ask your most marginalized students and families and believe what they tell you." Do a smaller-scale formal assessment—a dozen focus groups, a survey—but most importantly, believe what you hear, then put the rest of the resources into professional development and policy change based on what you hear. We must learn to see students' stories and experiences as vital data and account for them in "data-driven decisionmaking." The same is true of our colleagues who experience bias and inequity in our buildings. They are the experts.

Even if you read this book cover to cover, also build equity initiatives in collaboration with the communities of people experiencing the most inequity (Cookson, 2013). Reach out to local community leaders in high-poverty neighborhoods; elicit feedback from parents and students. Of course, we should only do this if we are willing to adjust policy and practice based on what we hear. Moving forward without their expertise ensures a failure to equip ourselves with the knowledge we need to be a threat to inequity.

Principle 2: The right to equitable educational opportunity is universal. All people are entitled to basic human rights, including access to equitable education. No student should be denied the educational opportunities offered her peers because of where she was born or the economic condition of her family or, for that matter, her family's home language or racial identity. Unfortunately, our failure to ensure equitable educational opportunity, as evidenced most clearly by enormous gaps in school funding (Baker, Farrie, & Sciarra, 2016), guarantees that many economically vulnerable youth are denied this basic right.

Our first role as equity literature educators is to identify all the ways this opportunity is not equitably distributed within our spheres of influence. Perhaps your sphere of influence is a classroom. Developing equity literacy will help you identify the equity gaps, the opportunity gaps, in your classroom by strengthening your ability to recognize them. It also will give you the skills to eliminate ways you might unintentionally perpetuate those gaps in your classroom. First you must locate and challenge the biases lingering inside you—biases that might paint some students as more deserving than others because of misperceptions about how much they or their parents care.

Perhaps your sphere of influence is a school district or a whole state department of education. Whatever our sphere, we must agree that this principle of equitable educational opportunity is not merely philosophical. We must be willing to act on this commitment, challenging inequitable policies or practices and implementing strategies for redistributing access and opportunity. We must actively advocate for these rights, not just quietly embrace them.

Principle 3: Poverty and class are intersectional. Poverty does not exist in a vacuum. It is linked inextricably to race, gender identity, (dis)ability, and other identities (DeFilippis, 2016; Milner, 2015; Rivera & Tilcsik, 2016), as depicted in Figure 2.4 and as we will explore more fully in Chapter 3. If we hope to understand and respond to the implications of poverty on the educational lives of students, we must also attend to intersecting barriers. Sure, White people experiencing poverty cope with many of the same barriers as People of Color experiencing poverty, but on average People of Color (whether experiencing poverty or not) are more likely than White people to be assigned to underresourced schools and more likely to experience housing and employment discrimination, undermining crucial opportunities to mitigate economic injustice.

We also should remember that the elimination of class inequities does not guarantee the elimination of racial, religious, or other inequities. Nor does the removal of socioeconomic barriers in school erase the out-of-school barriers with which families experiencing poverty contend. In this sense, conversations about poverty and education should never *replace* conversations about, say, racism or heterosexism or even bigger class disparities, but instead should *complement* those conversations toward a more intersectional and holistic commitment to equity.

Figure 2.4. A Partial List of Intersecting Identities

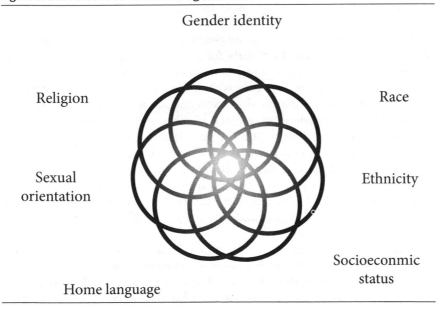

Gender identity

Religion

Race

Sexual orientation

Ethnicity

Socioeconmic status

Home language

Principle 4: People Experiencing Poverty Are Diverse. In Chapter 5 we will explore the trouble with the "culture" or "mindset" of poverty notion, which incorrectly suggests that people experiencing poverty share predictable and consistent values, attitudes, and beliefs; that all we need to know is a person's socioeconomic status to know what she believes. As I discuss in more detail later, that view never made sense to me. Can I assume that my White Presbyterian Appalachian grandmother has the same culture or mindset as equally economically marginalized Somali refugees in Minnesota, or even as equally economically marginalized White urban people?

Like every large and widely dispersed group of people, people experiencing poverty are endlessly diverse (Gorski, 2012; Milner, 2015). They vary by race, ethnicity, and nationality; by religion and language; by political affiliation, vocation, and value system. "There is no single class identity," as Susan Borrego (2008) explains; "class is only experienced through multiple lenses" (p. 2). In fact, most of what economically marginalized people have in common has nothing to do with cultures or mindsets and everything to do with inequities and barriers, which we discuss in detail in Chapter 6.

As a practical, educational matter, this means there is no silver bullet, no magic list of *10 easy strategies for teaching every student experiencing poverty* (Lindsey, Karns, & Myatt, 2010), which makes our pursuit of equitable schools considerably more complicated than a list of "mindset of poverty" attributes can explain. Despite the popularity and marketability of the *10 easy strategies* approach, the most effective solutions are often contextual because barriers and inequities are contextual. We need equity literacy more than we need 10 easy strategies.

Principle 5: What we believe about people experiencing poverty informs how we teach, interact with, and advocate (or fail to advocate) for them. Because our attitudes about poverty and our assumptions about why people are experiencing poverty drive our beliefs about and even our behaviors toward our most economically marginalized students, practical strategies are not enough. As poverty attribution research has shown, for example, our beliefs about who or what is to blame for the very existence of poverty pretty well predicts the extent to which we are willing to battle bias and inequities (Hopkins, 2009; Parrett & Budge, 2012). What we believe about poverty and why it exists even affects our expectations of and attitudes toward low-income students, as J. Gregg Robinson (2007) found in his analysis of data from 400 teachers. Jo Lampert and her colleagues (2016) explain,

> Our perceptions of students, their families, communities, and cultures are inextricably linked to what we have been socialized to perceive as normal. When we consider the mismatch between middle-class teachers and their students in high-poverty schools, what is often perceived as a lack of interest, poor behavior

or poor achievement can simply be a matter of how a teacher understands the common experience. (p. 39)

Complicating matters, low expectations or misunderstandings of students' behavior aren't always a result of rabid bias. Sometimes they come from a well-intended savior syndrome (Dudley-Marling, 2015) or a genuine desire to "protect" from school pressures students we assume, often incorrectly, have awful home lives. So as we develop our equity literacy, we have to remember that good intentions don't do the work for us. Even the most well-intended educators might be doing damage we don't know we're do- ing, damage we never wanted to do, because of belief systems to which we stubbornly cling.

These beliefs are shaped by ideology, by how we are socialized to see and interpret poverty (Bradshaw, 2007; Cookson, 2013). So learning about this or that practical strategy is not sufficient for fostering an equitable learning environment, much less an equitable education system. We also must examine our own class biases by developing deeper understandings of poverty and its effects on youth. It's also why, in addition to describing the sorts of practical strategies that have proven effective in engaging youth experiencing poverty, I focus in this book on challenging common myths about poverty and encouraging readers to develop robust understandings of the experiences of economically marginalized families in and out of schools.

Principle 6: We cannot understand the relationship between poverty and ed- ucation without understanding the barriers and inequities people experiencing poverty face in and out of schools. Research has begun to show how education- al outcome disparities across socioeconomic groups can be traced mostly to poverty itself (Berliner, 2013)—to the barriers and challenges poverty poses in the lives of people experiencing it and to the bigger societal problems that underlie the existence of poverty. These include income and wealth inequal- ity and the many manifestations of this inequality: disparities in access to nutritional food, affordable housing, and other basic needs. Although many of these challenges fall outside our purview as educators and are not fixable solely with educational change, they all play a role in students' and families' engagement in school. So we mustn't limit ourselves to studying poverty and education in ways that omit this larger context. We cannot prepare ourselves to be effective educators for all students if we refuse to understand their lived experiences. We cannot make policy and practice responsive to the barriers and challenges economically marginalized families face if we de- cide that what happens outside school is not our concern. How can we have authentic relationships with students if we don't understand the inequities with which they contend?

This is not to say each of us is responsible for eradicating global pov- erty, for buying every family a car so they can attend family engagement programs, or for single-handedly ensuring passage of living-wage laws. The question is, What can I do *within my sphere of influence* to make that sphere as equitable as possible? Part of this commitment includes finding ways in that sphere to be as responsive as possible to the inequities students experience in and out of school.

Principle 7: Test scores are inadequate measures of equity. I worry all the fuss over standardized test scores has drawn our attention away from a more fundamental conversation about educational equity. Test scores represent one sort of outcome, and not even a very robust one. They don't speak at all to important equity matters such as whether students feel affirmed at school, whether they've been unfairly tracked or disproportionately disciplined, whether they see themselves reflected in the curriculum, whether their parents feel welcome and respected by teachers and administrators, or whether school funding and educational policy are equitable (Au, 2013). I'm reminded of this powerful line from Mistilina Sato and Timothy Lensmire (2009): "Children from poverty are being identified and labeled with grossly overgeneralized, deficit-laden characteristics that put them at risk of being viewed as less capable, less cultured, and less worthy as learners" (p. 365). We can't capture that with a test score.

Throughout this book I refer to studies that use test scores as imperfect proxies for this bigger picture, but I also take a more holistic view of educational equity. Who has access to the most effective instructional approaches? Who has access to school nurses and the most wondrous school libraries? Who has access to schools governed by policy written with them in mind? These questions are bigger than test scores.

Principle 8: Educational outcome disparities are the result of inequities, of unjust distributions of access and opportunity, not the result of deficiencies in the mindsets, cultures, or grittiness of people experiencing poverty. Upon receiving an award for lifetime achievement in educational anthropology, Gloria Ladson-Billings (2006) delivered a speech in which she raised concerns about the tendency in education circles to attribute every possible educational phenomenon to vague notions of culture, especially when it comes to poverty. She explained, "Culture is randomly and regularly used to explain everything . . . from school failure to problems with behavior management and discipline" (p. 104). One problem with this tendency, according to Ladson-Billings, is that the attribution of every challenge or disparity to "culture" almost always results in (or results from) a related tendency to characterize the cultures of students experiencing poverty in stereotypical, and often deviant, ways. She refers to this as the "poverty of culture," a not-so-subtle reminder of the flimsiness of the "culture" or "mindset" of poverty approach.

The other problem with the cultures obsession, as I mentioned earlier in this chapter, is that it can dim our senses to the inequities that underlie disparities in educational outcomes. It can be all too easy, when looking for fault in the families of economically marginalized students, to lose sight of the fact that at almost every stage of schooling they are denied opportunities and access many wealthier people take for granted. We can begin that conversation in preschool, and the quality of preschool to which students from different economic backgrounds have access—if they have any access to preschool at all, which often is not the case for families experiencing poverty.

Because educational outcome disparities result from inequities and not from the cultures or mindsets of people experiencing poverty, we can eliminate them only by eliminating the inequities. We must learn how to spot and critically assess all the strategies and frameworks commonly flung at families experiencing poverty in misguided attempts to fix them while ignoring the inequities. Grit is no threat to inequities, nor is growth mindset (Kundu, 2014; Stokas, 2015). This is not to say that there can't be some room for initiatives meant to help *all students* see themselves as full of potential, but we should be alarmed at how these initiatives always seem to be *replacing* equity initiatives when they are used as detours around direct confrontations with inequity.

Principle 9: Equitable educators adopt a structural view rather than a deficit view of students and families experiencing poverty. This is an ideological stand, but it plays a significant role in everyday educational practice. Researchers have shown that when we adopt a deficit view of people experiencing poverty, attributing poverty to misperceived "deficiencies" in their attitudes, behaviors, or moralities, we are more likely to respond to them negatively, with anger, invalidation, neglect, and a spirit of judgment. When we embrace a structural view, attributing poverty to the hardships and barriers people experiencing poverty face, we tend to lead with sympathy and be more willing to advocate for equitable change (Weiner, Osborne, & Rudolph, 2011). These views are discussed in more detail in Chapter 4. Suffice it for now to say that, to adopt a deficit view, we must pretend all the barriers and inequities that underlie poverty don't exist. We must altogether ignore them. If we ignore them, we can't address them. That is the inverse of equity.

Unfortunately, this reality is of little mitigating consequence against mass perception, which is on the side of the deficit view. Research since the late 1970s shows most people believe the equal opportunity and meritocracy myths and thus believe poverty exists because of the deficiencies of people experiencing poverty (Finley & Diversi, 2010). Research even shows that the deficit view is the dominant view of teachers (Garza & Garza, 2010; Prins & Schafft, 2009). For example, in their study of high school teachers who professed an appreciation for racial and economic diversity, Jean

Patterson and her colleagues (2008) found that the same teachers, while abstractly recognizing inequities with which low-income students contended, still blamed them and their parents for not caring about education or for lacking persistence. This kind of deficit view can weaken our academic expectations and instructional rigor and impact other dimensions of the teacher–student relationship (Lampert, Burnett, & Lebhers, 2016). Mary Amanda Graham (2009), a former school counselor who grew up in poverty, described the effects of the deficit view this way:

> I learned some hard lessons about life. These lessons were taught to me not by my family but rather by system "helpers." I learned that being poor offended people. I learned people had rage and anger toward me and others like me. I learned that people thought being poor equated to lacking intelligence, creativity, motivation and desire. I learned that people felt sorry for me. In the process, I also learned to be weary (and wary) of helpers. (p. 46)

Rejecting the deficit view, equity-literate educators champion a *structural* view of poverty. This view recognizes student and community strengths and funds of knowledge (Gonzalez, Moll, & Amanti, 2005), including the ability not only to persist through poverty's obstacles, but also to demonstrate higher commitments than wealthier people to help others despite poverty's obstacles (Godfrey & Cherng, 2016). Their strengths and funds of knowledge are many, and they can be assets to *all* students if we are inclined to shift our own preconceived notions. For example:

- people experiencing poverty are more prosocial and more attuned to the needs of others than their wealthier peers (Kraus & Keltner, 2009);
- people experiencing poverty are more generous and charitable than people with more economic resources, giving higher proportions of their incomes to charities and causes that help other people (Greve, 2009; James & Sharpe, 2007); and
- on average people experiencing poverty are more kind to strangers, more likely to help others with onerous tasks, and more compassionate than their wealthier peers (Piff, Kraus, Cote, Cheng, & Keltner, 2010).

In addition to recognizing the strengths of people experiencing poverty, people with the structural view recognize the structural barriers that create poverty and, as a result, create educational outcome disparities. When we see a student struggling in school, our initial reaction is to wonder about structural barriers rather than to assume the student or her family is the problem. The structural view helps us interpret what we see through a more sophisticated equity lens so we can develop more sophisticated responses to inequities and outcome disparities. What we might interpret through a deficit view as a child who doesn't want to be in school, who lacks ambition, might well be somebody who has been beaten down by disadvantage (DeLuca et al., 2016). While the deficit view leads us to pile on, the structural view leads us to step back and understand what we see in deeper, more compassionate ways.

Principle 10: Strategies for creating and sustaining equitable classrooms, schools, and school systems must be based on evidence of what works. There is no lack of evidence about strategies that make schools more equitable. Decades of research about effective strategies and initiatives, many of which I describe in Chapters 8, 9, and 10, exist, which makes it strange that so much of what schools do to bolster the achievement of students experiencing poverty appears to be based on precisely the *opposite* of what the evidence tells us to do.

Throughout this book I mention several examples of popular strategies schools adopt despite how they contradict what evidence says we ought to be doing. One example—a particularly illogical example—revolves around art and music programs, which are disappearing from many high-poverty schools. These programs often are downsized or destroyed entirely to save money or to create more time for reading, writing, math, and, sadly, even lessons in test-taking skills. Even in economically diverse schools, students experiencing poverty and other students who are more likely than their peers to perform below the narrow standards of high-stakes tests often are denied art, music, physical education, and other components of a robust education, even if their peers still have access to these experiences.

I suppose this would make perfect sense if we had evidence that some students do not perform as well on standardized tests because they spend too much time learning art and music and not enough time learning reading, writing, and math (and if everyone agreed that standardized test scores ought to dictate what it means to provide a complete education). This might even sound like common sense. But evidence says if this *is* common sense, we're in big trouble. Students, especially students experiencing poverty, who have access to art and music instruction perform better than those who don't on a wide range of academic measures across virtually every subject area (Pogrow, 2006; Tranter & Palin, 2004). Research also shows, in most cases, that student achievement improves at the highest rates not when we extend instructional time, but when we improve instructional quality (Joyner & Molina, 2012).

The equity literacy framework urges us to choose our strategies by considering evidence of what works, not on what's popular, not on our desperation for simplistic practical solutions to problems that are neither simple nor practical. We might consider the results of formal research, but other important sources of data for our data-informed approach include our careful observations and what we know about the communities in which we teach. Being equity-literate means not relying on trendiness. It means having a sense of urgency such that we refuse to spend resources and effort on "commonsense" strategies that do not work or that, like cutting art and music programs, elevate the inequities we ought to be eliminating.

Principle 11: Simplistic instructional strategies, absent a commitment to more robust institutional change, are no threat to inequities. Instructional strategies are important—so important, in fact, that I included a whole chapter of them in this book (Chapter 8). Certainly we should correct the instructional inequities students experiencing poverty tend to face, such as lesser access to engaging pedagogies than their wealthier peers (Milner, 2015; Shields, 2014).

However, correcting these inequities is only part of our bigger task. Making small curricular or pedagogical shifts within a school full of inequitable policy, for example, still leaves us at inequity. The commitment to equity is a commitment to creating change in the institutional culture so that inequitable policies and practices are under constant threat from those of us who can see them and are dedicated to replacing them with equitable and just policies and practices. Instruction is one realm for our equity literacy, but it's not the end-all be-all realm it's often cracked up to be.

Principle 12: There is no path to educational equity that does not involve a redistribution of access and opportunity. This principle takes us full circle, back to the beginning of this chapter. Equity work is fundamentally about identifying how access and opportunity are distributed unfairly and then redistributing them equitably. As mentioned earlier, this might mean redistributing access to material resources, but it also might mean redistributing good pedagogy, the most effective teachers, and access to a bias-free learning environment.

Add-on initiatives can help or bridge us to more permanent change, but our goal should be a permanent redistribution of access and opportunity. For example, many schools attempt to redistribute access to certain extracurricular or even core curricular activities by offering financial support to students who want to participate but whose families can't afford the extra fees, if the students are willing to ask for the help. This might look like equity. However, for some students and families, it can be humiliating to have to perform their poverty by asking, sometimes repeatedly, for help. So while this practice might give them access to this or that activity, it denies them access to a school environment free of humiliation. No student should be forced into deciding whether one form of access is worth the denial of another. The equitable course of action is to eliminate extra fees, to find some other way to raise money, to never distribute access to any educational opportunity based on its affordability.

As in this example, the commitment to redistributing access and opportunity can be difficult because it challenges the very structure not only of public education, but of society. It forces us to rethink common practices like academic tracking. It also forces us to focus on shifting institutional cultures rather than thinking in terms of programs that might mitigate, but don't eliminate, institutional inequities.

CONCLUSION

A variety of frameworks can help us better understand the challenges families experiencing poverty face and the gifts they bear. I chose to build this book around the equity literacy framework because it emphasizes both understanding those challenges and committing to creating an equitable learning environment, even if that means creating it within a larger societal context full of bias and inequity. You will see for the remainder of the book that I indicate at the beginning of each chapter which principles of equity literacy are discussed in that chapter.

Next, in Chapter 3, I provide an overview of patterns and conditions related to poverty in contemporary society. I describe how income and wealth are distributed, how poverty rates are changing, and how poverty is distributed across a variety of identities like race and gender.

REFLECTION QUESTIONS AND EXERCISES

1. What is *meritocracy*? Why is accepting the presumption that it already exists dangerous?

2. How does an *equality* approach differ from an *equity* approach? Describe an example of a school policy or practice that is designed around the idea of equality in such a way that it might reproduce differences in students' existing levels of access and opportunity. How would that policy or practice change if it were designed around the idea of equity instead?

3. What is the relationship between the *Respond* and *Redress* abilities of equity literacy? Describe an example of inequity in a school you have attended as a student. How would you respond to that inequity? How would you redress it?

4. Of the twelve principles of equity literacy, which one resonates with you the most? Which one presents the greatest challenge to your current way of thinking about poverty and education?

CHAPTER 3

The Inequity Mess We're In

A Class and Poverty Primer

> Principles of equity literacy discussed in this chapter include:
>
> **Principle 3:** Poverty and class are intersectional.
>
> **Principle 4:** People experiencing poverty are diverse.
>
> **Principle 5:** What we believe about people experiencing poverty informs how we teach, interact with, and advocate (or fail to advocate) for them.

As anyone who has worked in public education knows, it is impossible to have a worthwhile learning experience without a high-stakes multiple-choice standardized assessment. I'm kidding, of course. Still, we begin an exploration of class and poverty with a brief, decidedly unstandardized quiz. There is no reason you should know the answers to these questions, so be gentle with yourself and use erasable ink. The purpose is not to identify which statistics you've memorized, but to reflect on whether your general perceptions about class and poverty jibe with reality.

POVERTY AWARENESS QUIZ

1. In which of the following region types is poverty growing quickest in the United States (Kneebone & Berube, 2013)?
   a. Urban areas
   b. Rural areas
   c. Suburban areas

2. The median household income in the United States has increased 16% since 1980. During the same period, corporate profits after taxes increased 182%, the average income for the wealthiest 1% of families increased 190%, and the average income for the wealthiest 0.01%

of families grew 322%. What happened to the average income of the poorest 90% during that time (Rios & Gilson, 2016)?

a. Increased 16%
b. Increased 0.03%
c. Decreased 0.03%
d. Decreased 16%

3. According to a report from the Center for American Progress (Spatig-Amerikaner, 2012), schools with 90% White students receive how much more per student funding on average than schools with 90% Students of Color?

a. $733
b. $533
c. $333
d. $3

4. How many children die each day worldwide from poverty-related causes (United Nations Inter-Agency Group for Child Mortality Estimation, 2014)?

a. 2,000
b. 12,000
c. 22,000

5. According to a Kids Count (2016) report, 13% of White children in the United States live in poverty. What percentage of American Indian children in the United States live in poverty?

a. 13%
b. 31%
c. 52%
d. 74%

6. According to a study sponsored by the Pew Research Center (2016), the median wealth of White households in the United States is how many times larger than that of African American households?

a. 3 times larger
b. 13 times larger
c. 23 times larger
d. 33 times larger

7. Since the global financial crisis of the 2000s, which of the following has happened in the United States (Fuentes-Nieva & Galasso, 2014)?

a. The wealthiest 1% of people have received 95% of the financial growth while the poorest 90% of people have gotten poorer.
b. The wealthiest 10% of people have received 95% of the financial growth while the poorest 40% of people have gotten poorer.

c. The wealthiest 20% of people have received 95% of the financial growth while the poorest 20% have gotten poorer.

8. According to the wealth analysis group WealthInsight (as referenced by Rushe, 2012), during President Barack Obama's first term in office, the number of millionaires in the United States:

a. Decreased by 6,500
b. Decreased by 154,000
c. Increased by 49,000
d. Increased by 1,100,000

9. Identify the source of this quote: "We have deluded ourselves into believing the myth that capitalism grew and prospered out of the Protestant ethic of hard work and sacrifices. Capitalism was built on the exploitation of black slaves and continues to thrive on the exploitation of the poor, both black and white, both here and abroad."

a. Martin Luther King Jr., civil rights activist
b. Michael Moore, filmmaker
c. bell hooks, author and educator
d. Eleanor Roosevelt, human rights advocate

10. According to a national study of U.S. parents with children in public schools (Noel et al., 2013), 66% of parents from families not experiencing poverty reported that they always checked to ensure their children did their homework. What percentage of parents from families experiencing poverty reported that they always checked to ensure their children did their homework?

a. 32%
b. 52%
c. 72%
d. 92%

Answer Key: (1) c, (2) b, (3) a, (4) c, (5) b, (6) b, (7) a, (8) d, (9) a, (10) c

In this chapter I provide an overview of class and poverty in the United States, putting the information from this quiz into broader context. We begin by exploring poverty rates, how income and wealth are distributed, and how poverty rates and patterns of income and wealth distribution have changed during the last several decades. We then turn to a different kind of distribution of poverty, looking at how poverty and economic injustice interact with other troubling conditions, such as racism, sexism, heterosexism, and ableism.

Before proceeding, I want to acknowledge what some readers might feel reading about big societal conditions like the quickening spread of poverty into suburban neighborhoods, growing wealth and income inequality, and critical connections between race and class. For some readers the information in this chapter might seem outside educators' spheres of influence. *Sure, you might think, it's unfortunate that child poverty rates are growing, but I don't feel particularly equipped to fight that battle. It's enough of a challenge to come to work each day facing growing class sizes of hungry students and to teach them as well as I can in the face of high-stakes testing pressures.*

I hear you.

I do not intend to suggest that every high school physics teacher or elementary school music teacher should feel responsible for eradicating global poverty. Instead, the goal is to help us understand poverty and how it operates, to demystify it, to cultivate shared understandings of what we and our students are up against. In my experience, conversations about poverty, and frameworks for understanding poverty and education, tend to focus on children and families who are experiencing poverty, on all that needs fixing about "those people." What's often missing from these frameworks are ample understandings of poverty itself—of how poverty operates, of who is most susceptible to it, of why it exists at all in the wealthiest countries in the world. I struggle to imagine how I can be the best educator for every student without knowing at least a little along these lines. I struggle to imagine how I can be effective without pushing myself to reconsider my shaky notions about a society that promises everybody equal opportunity but then refuses to deliver on that promise, even in school.

AN INTRODUCTION TO POVERTY, WEALTH, AND ECONOMIC INEQUALITY

You might remember, following Hurricane Katrina, how U.S. media heralded the dawn of a new era of poverty awareness and antipoverty action. As David Grusky and Emily Ryo (2006) put it,

> there was . . . much journalistic intoning in the immediate post-Katrina period about how the disaster forced the public to rediscover poverty, how it unmasked the human cost of poverty, and how it unleashed a newfound commitment among the public to take on issues of poverty and inequality. (pp. 59–60)

Grusky and Ryo call the popular idea that the aftermath of Hurricane Katrina became a mass revelation about poverty in the United States, previously hidden from the public, the "dirty little secret" (or DLS) hypothesis.

Problem is, when they tested the DLS hypothesis by looking at data on people's awareness of and willingness to act against poverty before and after the hurricane, they learned the whole thing was manufactured by the media. In reality, Katrina had far less impact than people's existing belief systems on their attitudes toward poverty. People who chose not to acknowledge the existence or extent of poverty before the hurricane continued to ignore poverty afterward. Those who blamed people experiencing poverty for their poverty before Katrina held just as tightly to that view in its aftermath. Nor was there an appreciable increase in antipoverty activism or advocacy for economically marginalized people following Hurricane Katrina (Grusky & Ryo, 2006).

This is an important point: We tend to filter information through our existing belief systems. We might be moved by a story about a homeless child or by a YouTube video about catastrophes like the 2015 earthquake in Nepal or Hurricane Matthew in 2016, both of which resulted in death, hunger, or homelessness for thousands of people. We might even support displaced victims with donations or volunteerism. But chances are none of this will alter our views on poverty or our attitudes toward economically marginalized people unless we have the humility to make our views vulnerable to new ideas. The only place to begin is to acknowledge what we don't know, or at least to allow that there's always something more we should know.

I make this somewhat heady point because when it comes down to it, what we believe about poverty and people experiencing it determines what we are willing to do to respond to poverty-related bias and inequity (Hopkins, 2009; Lampert et al., 2016). Unfortunately, what most people believe about poverty is at best incomplete and at worst dangerously biased. We'll dig more deeply into that point in Chapter 4. What is important to consider for now is that sometimes the mythology sounds sweeter than the reality. So we tell ourselves all children have an equal opportunity to achieve whatever they want to achieve even as we send the wealthiest of them, on average, to the most well-funded and well-resourced schools and the most economically marginalized of them, on average, to the most overcrowded, poorly funded, underresourced schools.

The principal purpose of this chapter is not to upend that mythology per se, but rather to provide a basic primer on poverty and how it operates in preparation for the upending we'll do in later chapters. However, I know no honest way to discuss the realities of poverty, wealth inequality, and relationships between poverty and other forms of marginalization without poking at common beliefs about class inequality. So if anything in this chapter rubs against the beliefs you had when you opened this book, remember that the more we know about poverty, the greater our equity literacy and the better equipped we are to support students and families experiencing poverty.

Poverty by the Numbers

A record 47 million people in the United States live in poverty, about 15% of the population (U.S. Census Bureau, 2012). Actually, that figure is based on that government standard for a poverty line income we explored earlier, which is, for example, $24,600 for a family of four (U.S. Department of Health and Human Services, 2017). Another 30 million people are living just above the poverty line, in constant danger of dipping below it (Luhby, 2012a). That's 77 million people at or near the poverty line in the United States alone. In fact, the Center for American Progress (2007) estimates that one in every three people in the United States will spend at least 1 year of their lives in poverty. Many of us are a layoff or medical emergency away.

Complicating matters, many social scientists who study poverty and have examined government methods for calculating the poverty threshold argue that these methods fail to capture the scope and complexity of poverty (Meyer & Sullivan, 2012). The government has used more or less the same method for measuring poverty for 5 decades. The measure, as discussed earlier, is based on a minimal or subsistence standard of estimated food costs. Why food? A 1955 survey showed that families were spending on average one-third of their incomes on food (Blank & Greenberg, 2008). Multiply that subsistence food cost by three and *voilà!*, you have the poverty threshold. Each year hence the threshold has been modified for inflation.

However, the modifications do not account for other significant variables, such as regional cost of living differences. Even more confounding, while the threshold has been adjusted for inflation, it has not been adjusted to reflect new estimates in the average proportion of family budgets spent on food. Today families spend about one-eighth of their incomes on food, not one-third (Blank & Greenberg, 2008). We spend a far greater percentage of our incomes than before on child care, housing, and transportation (Children First for Oregon [CFFO], 2016). As a result, government figures significantly underestimate the number of people who do not have sufficient resources to cover these and other basic needs (Finley & Diversi, 2010).

The poverty rate in the United States was at an all-time low of 11.3% in 2000 according to government estimates. It grew steadily from that point, accelerating between 2007 and the early 2010s during recessions or "financial crises" (Gabe, 2012), and has been in decline since. It dropped to 13.5% by 2015 from 15% in 2012, when it was at its highest point since 1965 (Proctor, Semega, & Kollar, 2016). But again, most social scientists studying poverty believe these are gross underestimates of the percentage of people living in poverty.

Homelessness is on the decline, too, after a sharp increase several years ago following the spree of predatory lending that resulted in record numbers of home foreclosures (Western Regional Advocacy Project [WRAP], 2010). Over 500,000 U.S. people are homeless on any given day (Henry, Watt, Rosenthal, & Shivji, 2016), although homelessness tends to be underreported, too. For instance, people who might be "couch-surfing" or sleeping in cars or tent cities (yes, they *do* exist in the United States) generally are not counted as homeless (Finley & Diversi, 2010). It affects our students, too.

During the 2013–2014 school year 1.3 million people in the United States experienced homelessness at some point; of these, 22.3% were children (Solari, Morris, Shivji, & de Souza, 2016).

The "dirty little secret" about homelessness is who tends to be homeless. For instance, a large percentage of homeless men in the United States are military veterans (National Coalition for the Homeless [NCH], 2009) struggling to readjust to civilian life due to serious injuries or post-traumatic stress disorder. Roughly 40% of homeless youth identify as lesbian, gay, bisexual, or queer (Durso & Gates, 2012). Many left home or were kicked out of their homes due to conflict or abuse related to their sexual orientations or gender identities (Ray, 2006). Additionally, many people with mental health challenges become homeless, especially if their families cannot afford to pay for care at a mental health facility (National Alliance on Mental Illness, 2011). More broadly, people with (dis)abilities are three times more likely than people with no (dis)abilities to experience homelessness (Solari et al, 2016). If, as the saying goes, the measure of a society is how it treats its most vulnerable members, what do these realities tell us about who we are as a society, when disadvantage is punished with more disadvantage?

Child Poverty

Measuring by the official U.S. government's poverty line, about 22% of children in the United States are experiencing poverty. However, as mentioned earlier, the official poverty line underestimates poverty because it fails to account for a variety of factors. If we account for all children living in families unable to afford basic necessities, the estimate nearly doubles to 43% (Jiang, Granja, & Koball, 2017), or almost 31 million children. Nearly 5% of U.S. children live in deep poverty, households in which family incomes are less than half the federal poverty line (Garfinkel, Harris, Waldfogel, & Wimer, 2016).

We can see the growing impact of these poverty rates on schools. By 2013, a majority of U.S. public school students were from low-income families. In 1989, 32% of public school students were eligible for free or reduced-price lunch (Suitts, 2013). Now more than 52% are eligible (Suitts, 2016). Many of these students attend suburban schools previously attended by very few students experiencing poverty, so conditions are changing. The question is, are we as a community of educators able and willing to change at the same pace?

A whole host of variables put some youth at greater or lesser risk of living in poverty, such as their racial identities (or racial injustice, to be more precise) or the region in which they live. We will examine those factors in detail shortly.

Among the most important factors that predict the likelihood that a child will be living in poverty is family structure. Approximately 47.6% of children living in households headed by single mothers are living in poverty, compared with 10.9% of children living in households with two parents (Gabe, 2012). Making matters worse, single mothers experiencing poverty often are targets of a particularly harsh brand of scorn, a trend often traced back to Ronald Reagan's popularization of the term "welfare queen." If we hope to sustain positive partnerships with single mothers, the first step is to refuse to participate in that scorn and instead flex our equity literacy muscles so we can see the bigger picture. For example, many single mothers have made positive and *responsible* choices to leave abusive relationships and raise children on their own, despite potential financial hardships. We might learn to see the high rates of poverty among children being raised by single mothers as a societal failing, as yet another failure by the wealthiest country in the world to care for its most vulnerable citizens. After all, among industrialized nations the United States ranks first in number of billionaires, first in gross domestic product, 28th in infant mortality rates, and second to last (falling between Bulgaria and Romania) when it comes to child poverty (Children's Defense Fund [CDF], 2015).

Income and Wealth Trends

Of the hundreds of essays and books I read while preparing to write this book, one study particularly shook me. Michael Norton and Dan Ariely (2011) asked more than 5,500 people in the United States to estimate how wealth is distributed in the country. Here is my best summary of their findings: Most of us, including economics professors, are clueless. Participants were shown three pie charts, one showing the actual distribution of wealth, one showing Sweden's wealth distribution, and one showing an "equal" distribution of wealth in which every 20% of the population controls 20% of the wealth. Almost every participant got it wrong. Most chose the pie chart in which the wealthiest 20% of people control about 60% of the wealth— Sweden's wealth distribution. At the time of the study the wealthiest 20% of people controlled about 85% of the wealth. Today, the wealthiest 20% of people in the United States control roughly 89% of the wealth (Domhoff, 2012), as illustrated by Figure 3.1.

Even more interesting, though, is what we tend to believe about the wealth controlled by the most economically marginalized people. Most of Norton and Ariely's survey responders believed that the poorest 40% of U.S. citizens control between 8 and 10% of the country's total wealth. Those economics professors flubbed this one, too, guessing about 2%. At the time of the survey, the poorest 40% of people in the United States controlled only 0.3% of the country's wealth (Norton & Ariely, 2011).

Unfortunately, these disparities have grown since 2005 (Wolff, 2012), when Norton and Ariely collected their data, as you can see in Figure 3.2. This is true whether we're talking about wealth—which is net worth (or one's

Figure 3.1. Distribution of Wealth in the United States

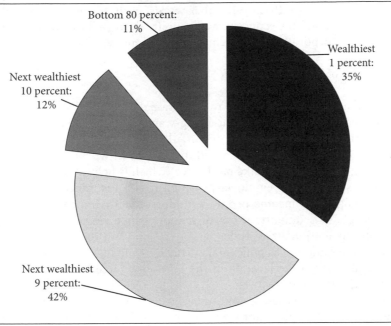

Adapted from G. William Domhoff, "Wealth, Income, and Power" (2012).

assets minus one's debt)—or income. Income inequality has been growing since 1980 and is at its highest level in 40 years. Since the financial crisis of the late 2000s, the wealthiest 1% of people in the United States have reaped the financial benefits of 95% of the financial growth. During the same time the 90% of lowest-wealth people have become poorer (Fuentes-Nieva & Galasso, 2014). In 2011, for example, the income of middle- and working-class people who comprise the middle 60% of the income pyramid *fell* between 1.6 and 1.9%, while the income of the wealthiest 20% of people *grew*

Figure 3.2. Distribution of Wealth in the United States, 1983–2013

	Wealthiest 20 percent	Poorest 80 percent
1983	81.3%	18.7%
1989	83.6%	16.5%
1995	83.9%	16.1%
2001	84.4%	15.6%
2007	85.1%	15.0%
2013	88.9%	11.1%

Adapted from Wolff (2014).

1.6%. The wealthiest 1% of people in the United States saw their incomes grow by 6% (Luhby, 2012b). In other words, even during a "financial crisis" or "recession," the economy works pretty darn well for wealthy people and wealthy corporations and punishes just about everybody else.

The Scarcity of Living-Wage Work

Imagine the dent we could make in educational outcome disparities if every working parent had access to one living-wage job. Imagine the plethora of troubles this one change could quell. All parents could spend more time with their children. They could avoid the anxiety of working multiple jobs. More would have benefits like paid leave (which is helpful for visiting their children's schools) and employer-provided health insurance. Housing stability among lower-income people would drastically improve. This might be the single most important out-of-school change we could advocate for economically marginalized students.

If you're thinking, as policymakers denouncing talk of living wage laws insist, that living wage laws drain the economy, force businesses to close, stunt job growth, and create elevated costs for services and consumer goods, just look at the test cases. Many studies show that when states or localities have increased the minimum wage beyond the federal minimum wage, all the terrible things we're told will happen do not happen (Dube, Lester, & Reich, 2010; National Employment Law Project, 2016; Reich, Jacobs, & Berhardt, 2014). It is all a mess of misinformation, but somehow the misinformation has become common sense—a most regressive brand of common sense.

Speaking of regressive common sense, how often have you heard somebody say that people experiencing poverty ought to have personal responsibility and get a job? Have you thought this yourself? If so, you are ripe for a dose of equity literacy. Most working-age people experiencing poverty *do have jobs*. Often they have two or three jobs, trying to piece together a living for themselves and their families. Many work more than the equivalent of full time. Unfortunately, they disproportionately are working part-time jobs with such low pay that even if they string together 40 hours of work per week across multiple jobs, they do not make enough money to not be in poverty.

The reality is bleak. There are not enough living-wage jobs in the United States for every working adult to have one (Kids Count, 2016). Not even close. About 40% of jobs pay below $15 per hour, a common approximation of a living wage even though a person with a full-time job at that wage would not earn enough to avoid poverty in many parts of the United States. As Ben Henry and Allyson Fredericksen (2015) of the Alliance for a Just Society report, "There are seven times more jobseekers than there are projected jobs paying $15 or higher, leaving workers seeking better wages with few options" (p. 2). Here is the harder reality and a crucial acknowledgment if we hope to understand the barriers bearing down on families experiencing poverty: As long as too few living-wage jobs exist for every working adult to have one, there will be students experiencing poverty who will be at a disadvantage at school. (See Chapter 6 for an exploration of the sources of this disadvantage.) It doesn't matter how hard people work, how much they value education, nor how dedicated they are to their family's well-being. For every seven people at whom we wag our fingers and say *just get a better job*, six have no shot at living-wage work.

So before we join the wave of wagging fingers and "get a job" chants, before we embrace false commonsense narratives about the "lazy poor," we should ask ourselves what part of the picture we might be missing. The answer can open the door to deeper understandings, positioning us to be better advocates for the most marginalized students.

THE UNEQUAL DISTRIBUTION OF POVERTY

Things are about to become more complicated. Poverty doesn't happen in a vacuum, which is one reason simplistic approaches to addressing poverty or supporting economically marginalized students don't work. Poverty and economic injustice are tied to all sorts of other identities and structural inequities, including gender and sexism, race and racism, sexual orientation and heterosexism, even (dis)ability and ableism. Unfortunately, popular models for attending to diversity and equity in education tend to limit our attention to one identity at a time, so we're talking about class *or* race *or* gender identity *or* (dis)ability. The reality is that all these identities and their respective forms of discrimination are intertwined into one big tangled web of injustice. What does this mean when it comes to conversations about poverty and education? It means, if we desire to cultivate a meaningful understanding of poverty, we must simultaneously cultivate understanding about race *and* gender *and* sexual orientation *and* (dis)ability *and* other factors associated with poverty (Cookson, 2013; Hughes, 2010; Luke, 2010).

The gist of the association is this: Poverty is not equally distributed. We've seen how children are affected disproportionately by poverty, especially children being raised by single mothers. But a whole host of other variables matter, too. Consider a race-based example. A legacy of racism is tied to wealth inequality today. Generations of families have been denied opportunities to purchase homes in the most economically desirable neighborhoods, something that still happens. Generations of children in communities of color have been denied access to well-equipped schools, something that also continues today. Consider a regional example, too. People of all racial identities in many parts of Appalachia and people who live on some tribal lands continue to be sent disproportionately to underfunded schools with lackluster technology infrastructure. Women in all regions face gender pay disparities and glass ceilings. These, like poverty itself, are legacies of injustice. They are associated directly with differences in rates of poverty among various groups. Unfortunately, they are just the tip of the injustice iceberg.

It would require an entire book to describe every way poverty is distributed unequally. Rather than embedding an entire additional book into this book, I describe just a few intersectional examples.

Gender

Women attend and graduate from college at higher rates than men today, a reversal that began in the late 1980s (Wang & Parker, 2011). By 2010 women outnumbered men in graduate school, according to the Council of Graduate Schools (2011). This phenomenon has been called the "feminization of higher education," illustrating how much of a social and cultural shift it was. After all, nobody referred to the "masculinization of higher education" during the hundreds of years men dominated college attendance. It's almost as though, as a society, we subtly believe men are *supposed* to have higher attendance and graduation rates than women, so we need to name our surprise when the tides turn, making it sound a little like an infestation: the *feminization* of higher education.

Despite their credentials, women make only 80 cents for every dollar men make in the United States (American Association of University Women [AAUW], 2017). And it's not just that women are in lower-paying professions. Women make less on average than their similarly ranked male colleagues in almost every profession.

According to the National Women's Law Center (Tucker & Lowell, 2016), women are 35% more likely than men to be living in poverty. This is one reason about one-third of female-headed households are in poverty. Race matters here, too. Women in every racial group are more likely than White men to be living in poverty, but African American, Native American, and Latina women are more than twice as likely as White men to be living in poverty.

One of the reasons for the growing disparity in poverty rates, according to Paul Taylor and his colleagues at the Pew Research Center (Taylor, Kochhar, Dockterman, & Motel, 2011), is that men recovered more quickly from the economic recession than women. They explain, "From the end of the recession in June 2009 through May 2011, men gained 768,000 jobs and lowered their unemployment rate by 1.1 percentage points . . . Women, by contrast, *lost 218,000 jobs* during the same period, and their unemployment rate increased by 0.2 percentage points" (p. 1).

Unfortunately, women—especially mothers—still face significant employment discrimination (Rivera & Tilcsik, 2016), exacerbating the threat of poverty for children living in single-mother households. Demonstrating, again, how inequality happens in complex layers, according to the Pew report unemployment rates particularly grew "for Hispanic, [B]lack and Asian women" and for "foreign-born women" (p. 5).

Transgender people also experience employment discrimination. In many states transgender people who are fired simply for being transgender— or, more accurately, for their employers' transphobia—have little legal remedy. As a result, rates of poverty among transgender people are higher than national averages, too (DeFilippis, 2016).

Race

Income and wealth inequality within the United States are among their highest levels when we examine them across race, as illustrated in Figure 3.3. African American and Latinx people are particularly more likely than White people to be in poverty (Kochhar & Fry, 2014). As noted in the quiz at the beginning of the chapter, the median wealth of White households is 13 times greater than that of African American households.

It stands to reason, then, that African Americans, Latinxs, and American Indians are significantly more likely than White people to live in poverty (U.S. Census Bureau, 2016). As you can see in Figure 3.4, when Asian Americans are counted as a single group, it appears they experience less poverty on average than White people. However, this is true only for

Figure 3.3. Median Net Worth of U.S. Households by Race in 2014

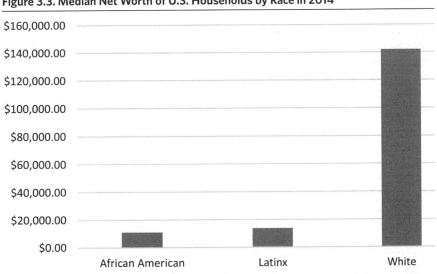

Adapted from Rakesh Kochhar and Richard Fry, *Wealth Inequality Has Widened Along Racial, Ethnic Lines Since End of Great Recession* (2014).

Figure 3.4. Poverty Rates by Race, 2015

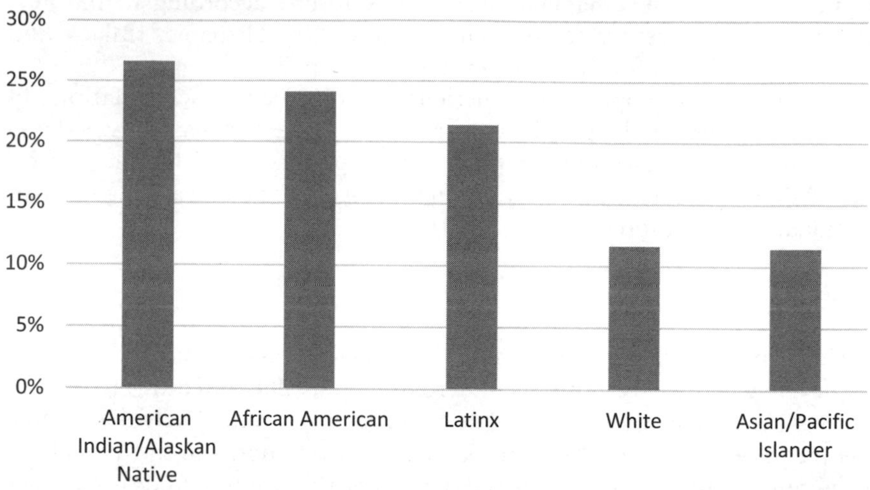

Based on data from the U.S. Census Bureau (2016), *March 2016 Current Population Survey*.

some groups of Asian Americans, partially predictable by region of origin. Hmong people, 26.9% of whom live in poverty, and other people of Asian heritage whose families or forebears came to the United States under duress due to repression, and many of whom were in poverty on arrival, are much more likely to be in poverty now, according to the Southeast Asia Resource Action Center (2011).

As we will discuss more thoroughly in Chapters 4 and 5, when exploring these sorts of data it is crucial to use our equity literacy lenses to check our interpretations. If we accept the meritocracy myth or the false notion that prosperity is directly proportionate to work ethic, it can be easy to interpret racial wealth disparities or uneven poverty rates in ways that confirm biased and inaccurate presumptions. *Of course White families have more wealth than African American families*, we might think, *because* [insert racial stereotype here]. We would need to sacrifice our equity literacy and ignore an astounding amount of evidence about racism to accept such a view, though. For starters, we would have to erase the generations of housing discrimination discussed earlier that has enabled White families to accrue wealth denied to Families of Color (Bonilla-Silva, 2018), disparities in educational opportunity (Leonardo & Grubb, 2013), and decades of mass incarceration policies for nonviolent drug crimes that disproportionately targeted People of Color despite the fact that White people have always been just as likely to use and traffic illicit drugs (Alexander, 2012). We also would have to ignore study after study demonstrating the stubborn persistence of employment racism, including studies that show how responding to want ads with resumes listing stereotypically White-sounding names considerably increases the likelihood of a call back compared with responding with resumes listing stereotypically African American-sounding names, even with comparable work histories and qualifications (Bertrand & Mullainathan, 2003). Equal opportunity is a moral imperative, but grossly unrealized. Research even has shown that Teachers of Color have a harder time finding work than similarly qualified White teachers (D'Amico, Pawlewicz, Earley, & McGeehan, 2017). Taking all this into account, it becomes clear why we simply cannot have a meaningful conversation about poverty and education without also talking about racism.

Sexual Orientation

The public face of the lesbian, gay, bisexual, and queer (LGBQ) community—often White, male, and economically well-off (DeFilippis, 2016)—obscures important realities. It erases the infinite diversity of LGBQ people, obviously. But it also obscures ways many LGBQ people are punished economically because of their sexual orientations—because of people's heterosexist reactions to their sexual orientations.

For example, as mentioned earlier, 40% of homeless youth identify as LGBQ. Many become homeless after parents push them out of their homes—parents apparently more willing to embrace prejudice than their own children. Many LGBQ people of all ages experience harsh discrimination, not only at home and at school, but also in the job market (Christian & Mukarji-Connolly, 2012), challenging the fictitious presumptions of equal opportunity and putting many LGBQ people at risk of poverty.

In 29 states LGBQ people can be legally fired from their jobs for being gay (McDermott, 2014). In fact, scores of popular, effective, even award-winning teachers have been fired after parent complaints about their sexual orientations (Kahn & Gorski, 2016). Imagine the devastating message this sends LGBQ students about their worth.

(Dis)ability

The topic of (dis)ability remains invisible in many conversations about equity despite the plethora of inequities with which people with (dis)abilities contend. In fact, using the underestimating U.S. government poverty line, 27% of working-age adults with at least one (dis)ability are living in poverty, about twice the national average (Erickson, Lee, & von Schrader, 2016). Less than one in four people with at least one (dis)ability works full-time year-round, contributing to the high rates of poverty.

In myriad ways, poverty and (dis)ability are interrelated. People experiencing poverty disproportionately lack access to health care, including preventive and prenatal care; are more likely than their wealthier peers to work dangerous or labor-heavy jobs; and face other challenges that increase the risk of (dis)ability (Palmer, 2011). Meanwhile, as Amartya Sen (1992), Nobel Prize winner in Economics, explained in *Inequality Reexamined*, people with some types of (dis)abilities might be limited in the kinds of employment opportunities to which they have access, which, in turn, could limit their income, which, then, might limit their access to other sorts of opportunities. Moreover, the expenses some people with (dis)abilities incur, such as the cost of adaptive technologies (UNICEF, 2015), increase the likelihood they will struggle to make ends meet. You might imagine that health insurance, for people who have it, would cover those expenses. However, when economist Sophie Mitra and her colleagues (2009) reviewed 8 years of national data on medical expenditures in the United States, they found that people with (dis)abilities spend 50% more *out-of-pocket* on average for health care than people with no (dis)abilities. When it comes to people with (dis)abilities who also are living in poverty, disadvantage begets disadvantage.

Then there's income inequality, which even bears down on people with (dis)abilities who work full-time, year-round. According to Michelle Yin and her colleagues (2014) at the American Institutes for Research, people with (dis)abilities who have high school diplomas earn on average $6,505 less per year than their peers without (dis)abilities. The gap grows with degree attainment, reaching more than $20,000 for those with graduate degrees.

Intersectionally, the poverty rate (based on the U.S. government's low estimates) for women with at least one (dis)ability is 31.9%, while the rate for their male peers is 25.1% (Eichner & Robbins, 2015). This demonstrates, once again, the importance of considering poverty and economic injustice through an intersectional lens.

Region: Poverty Moves to the Suburbs

When it comes to where we live, patterns of poverty are changing in historically notable ways. Since industrialization, many people have considered poverty largely an inner-city problem. In fact, that was never an accurate view. There are high rates of poverty in many city centers, but poverty for decades has been distributed fairly evenly between inner cities and rural areas. Still, many people hold onto the perception that poverty is an urban issue or, more specifically, an urban People of Color issue. This perception is doubly troubling in that it (1) strengthens already ugly stereotypes about urban communities of color, and (2) contributes to the invisibility of low-income people, including low-income People of Color, living in rural areas, small towns, and suburbs (Milbourne, 2010).

Speaking to this invisibility, Marty Strange (2011), policy director for the Rural School and Community Trust, has written, "Rural people remain one of the last groups about whom cultural slurs are considered politically acceptable speech" (p. 9). He goes on to remind us that about 15 million students spanning every racial identity attend schools in small towns and rural areas, and that the poverty rate in those areas is higher than the national average. Neither he nor I would suggest we flip the script completely and prioritize rural poverty while ignoring urban poverty. The point, instead, is to recognize that poverty is everywhere. It's even in schools people presume are filled with "upper-middle-class" students. And increasingly so. It's in every state, from those with large rural populations to those with large cities, as you can see in Figure 3.5.

Poverty in suburbia can be more invisible than poverty in rural areas. George Mason University, where I teach future teachers, sits smack-dab in the middle of Fairfax County, Virginia, the second-wealthiest county in the United States (U.S. Census Bureau, 2013). Adjacent to campus—literally, across the street from Mason's old athletic facility—sits a housing community run by FACETS, a nonprofit that provides homeless families with housing and other services. Many of my students, most of whom grew up in the area, also grew up associating homelessness with Washington, D.C., not Fairfax County. Many are shocked that poverty, not to mention homelessness, exists right under their noses.

In fact, for the first time in U.S. history, poverty rates in suburban areas are growing more quickly than in urban or rural areas. By 2012 the poverty rate in U.S. suburbs had crept past the poverty rate in U.S. cities. Between 2000 and 2014 suburban poverty jumped 65%, twice the poverty growth rate in cities (Kneebone, 2016). Eric Freeman (2010), who has studied this phenomenon in and around Atlanta, calls it the "redistribution of poverty" (p. 678). As urban areas are gentrified, driving up housing costs and property taxes, Freeman (2010) explains, low-income families are

> drawn to the suburbs for the most pragmatic reasons: lower-cost housing and a more plentiful supply of low-wage, low-skill jobs in the burgeoning restaurant, lawn care, home and office cleaning, retailing, health industry, and hospitality trades that have vanished from or moved outside the urban core. (p. 676)

Low-income immigrants increasingly are settling directly into suburban neighborhoods, also because of these job opportunities.

Unfortunately, because many suburban communities are unaccustomed to large numbers of families experiencing poverty, they also tend to lack the sorts of programs and services necessary to support them, as Scott Allard and Benjamin Roth (2010) found in their examination of suburban Chicago, Washington, D.C., and Los Angeles. Similarly, many schools in suburban areas, where teachers and administrators might be unaccustomed to large numbers of families eligible for free or reduced-price lunch, are struggling with the transition.

Figure 3.5. Poverty Rate by State, 2015

State	Percentage	State	Percentage
United States	15.0	Missouri	15.5
Alabama	19.3	Montana	15.4
Alaska	11.2	Nebraska	12.4
Arizona	18.2	Nevada	15.2
Arkansas	18.9	New Hampshire	9.2
California	16.4	New Jersey	11.1
Colorado	12.0	New Mexico	21.3
Connecticut	10.8	New York	15.9
Delaware	12.5	North Carolina	17.2
D.C.	17.2	North Dakota	11.5
Florida	16.5	Ohio	15.8
Georgia	18.3	Oklahoma	16.6
Hawaii	11.4	Oregon	16.6
Idaho	14.8	Pennsylvania	13.6
Illinois	14.4	Rhode Island	14.3
Indiana	15.2	South Carolina	18.0
Iowa	12.2	South Dakota	14.2
Kansas	13.6	Tennessee	18.3
Kentucky	19.1	Texas	17.2
Louisiana	19.8	Utah	11.7
Maine	14.1	Vermont	12.2
Maryland	10.1	Virginia	11.8
Massachusetts	11.6	Washington	13.2
Michigan	16.2	West Virginia	18.3
Minnesota	11.5	Wisconsin	13.2
Mississippi	21.5	Wyoming	11.2

Data from *State of the States Report* by Rachel West and Jackie Odum of the Center for American Progress (2016).

If we aren't willing to adjust our understandings, policies, and practices at the same rate of this change, we simply cannot be effective educators for all students.

CONCLUSION

For some readers, the numbers and percentages filling this chapter might seem far removed from the day-to-day joys and challenges of classroom life. We have plenty to do without adding child poverty to our list of responsibilities. It bears repeating that the purpose of this primer on class and poverty is not to suggest that educators should redirect all our energies to ending global poverty, although I smile when I imagine what we could do if we put some portion of our collective energies toward that goal. Rather, the purpose of equipping ourselves with deeper understandings of poverty rates and wealth distributions is to better understand the challenges bearing down on families experiencing poverty. The problems are big and structural. Even if we can't eliminate them, we can be responsive to them in our teaching and policymaking.

Studying these big patterns also can help us assess what we think we know about poverty against poverty's reality. It can help us consider concepts like meritocracy and equal opportunity from new angles. And with this, we segue into Chapter 4, in which we analyze assumptions and ideologies related to poverty. Most particularly, Chapter 4 challenges us to rethink deficit views and to adopt a structural view of poverty and education.

REFLECTION QUESTIONS AND EXERCISES

1. Why might a government continue to use a formula for determining levels of poverty it knows to be outdated and ineffective? What are possible implications of a government continuously underestimating poverty levels?

2. Why is the belief that people experiencing poverty just need to "go get a job" misguided? How would you respond to a friend or colleague who made such a statement?

3. Identify at least one way poverty intersects with race, gender, (dis)ability, and sexual orientation. What is one other identity around which poverty is not evenly distributed? Describe the relationship between that identity and poverty.

CHAPTER 4

Embracing a Structural View of Poverty and Education

Ditching Deficit Ideology and Quitting Grit

Principles of equity literacy discussed in this chapter include:

Principle 5: What we believe about people experiencing poverty informs how we teach, interact with, and advocate (or fail to advocate) for them.

Principle 6: We cannot understand the relationship between poverty and education without understanding the barriers and inequities people experiencing poverty face in and out of schools.

Principle 8: Educational outcome disparities are the result of inequities, of unjust distributions of access and opportunity, not the result of deficiencies in the mindsets, cultures, or grittiness of people experiencing poverty.

Principle 9: Equitable educators adopt a structural view rather than a deficit view of families experiencing poverty.

Principle 12: There is no path to educational equity that does not involve a redistribution of access and opportunity.

Take a moment to reflect on this question: Why on average do students experiencing poverty not do as well in school as their wealthier peers? Why, despite all the educator workshops on the mindsets of poverty, the brains of low-income youth, grit, and growth mindset do educational outcome disparities persist across socioeconomic status? What comes to mind first? Make a mental note of it.

POVERTY ATTRIBUTION AND THE IMPORTANCE OF IDEOLOGY

Conversations about the "achievement gap" usually are thick with references to parent involvement. These conversations tend to revolve around bemoaning this fact: Parents from families experiencing poverty are less likely than their wealthier peers to participate in family involvement opportunities that require them to visit their children's schools (Noel et al., 2013). Although research has shown that the same parents may be just as likely to be engaged in their children's learning at home (Williams & Sánchez, 2012), their lower rate of at-school involvement is presumed to be one of the core causes, if not *the* core cause, of educational outcome disparities (Barton, 2004; Bridges, 2013). I often hear even from otherwise conscientious teachers how *those parents* are the problem.

There is no debate here. Parents from families experiencing poverty do not visit their children's schools for family involvement opportunities at the same rate as wealthier parents. It has been measured a hundred different ways. It is a fact.

A lot of people and entire organizations are working to change the disparity. The trouble is, many are trying to change it based on misunderstandings about why it exists. They are asking why *those parents* don't value education, why *those families* are unmotivated, why they lack grit, why their mindsets are out of whack. Usually these people and organizations are short on equity literacy. As a result, often they do more harm than good.

If we want to avoid the same fate, we need to ask a different set of questions. We need to know, first of all, that there is a different set of questions to ask. From a policy and practice intervention perspective, we might start by asking ourselves how we should interpret the family involvement disparity. How do our existing belief systems, our existing *ideologies*, influence what we define as the problem to be resolved? After all, how we interpret the disparity drives our understanding of the problem. Our understanding of the problem drives the solutions we are capable of imagining for responding to and redressing the problem. Our choices of solutions determine the extent to which the strategies and initiatives we adopt threaten the existence of inequity or threaten the possibility of equity (Gorski, 2016b). It all tracks back to ideology.

This lands us in a tough spot in the education world, where many of us seem desperate for *five easy strategies for eliminating the achievement gap* and at times reluctant to dig into the ideological muck. Too many of us see practical strategies as *something I can use in my classroom,* but don't see deep understandings of equity issues the same way. Often I'm invited to schools or school districts in hopes that I will provide a list of practical solutions for outcome disparities without delving into the difficult ideological work—into the biases and prejudices and socializations that hamper our abilities to be a threat to inequities. It doesn't work. It can't work. It is impossible to develop meaningful strategies through misinterpretations of the problems we're trying to solve. There is no list of practical strategies that will make us effective educators for students experiencing poverty if our view of them and their families is muddied by the ideological roots of inequity. There is no path to equity literacy without taking stock of our ideologies and, if necessary, shifting them toward views that will help us recognize, respond to, and redress inequities.

When asked why these disparities in on-site family involvement or test scores or other measures exist—why, indeed, poverty itself exists—people tend to attribute them along a continuum between two big ideological positions. On one end of the continuum are people, including educators and policymakers, who see people experiencing poverty as the agents of their own economic conditions. They adhere to a *deficit ideology* (Gorski, 2008; Sleeter, 2004), believing that poverty itself is a symptom of ethical, dispositional, and even spiritual deficiencies in the individuals and communities experiencing it.

This is the dominant view in the United States (Gans, 1996) and, in my experience working with educators in more than 20 countries spanning five continents, a common view among people everywhere who have not experienced poverty. Its adherents are likely to believe that in-school involvement disparities, like other disparities, reflect these deficiencies in people experiencing poverty. Studies suggest that even among educators, the deficit view is the dominant view (Mulvihill & Swaminathan, 2006; Prins & Schafft, 2009). Its remnants are everywhere in education. We can hear them every time a colleague says, or we catch ourselves thinking, despite decades of research demonstrating otherwise (see Chapter 5 for a rundown), that people experiencing poverty do not value education, lack role models, or need more grit.

On the other end of the continuum are people who tend to understand poverty and issues like the family involvement disparity as logical and unjust outcomes of economic injustice and inequity. Adherents to a *structural ideology*, they define gaps in in-school family involvement as interrelated with the inequities with which people experiencing poverty contend. So, by recognizing people experiencing poverty as targets, rather than causes, of these unjust conditions, they might understand lower rates of family involvement as a symptom of in-school and out-of-school conditions that limit economically marginalized parents' abilities to participate at the same rates as their wealthier peers. Acknowledgment of these conditions—families' lack of access to transportation, child care, and paid leave, or schools' tendencies to schedule opportunities for in-school involvement in ways that make little sense for people who often work evenings—is suppressed by the deficit view. The structural view brings them into the light.

To be clear, deficit and structural ideology are at the far ends of a long continuum of ideological positions. They are not a simple binary. Still, I generally can predict the extent to which a school's policies and initiatives related to poverty and educational disparities reflect a deficit or structural view by asking whoever's in charge a single question: *Why, on average, do parents from families experiencing poverty not attend opportunities for family involvement at their children's schools with the same frequency as their wealthier peers?* Based on the response to this question, I often know the effectiveness of the school's policies and initiatives that are meant, at least ostensibly, to eradicate educational disparities across socioeconomic status. This is why, in my view, any evaluation of a school's commitment to equity begins not with an accounting of this or that policy or initiative, but rather with an accounting of the ideological positions of the leadership and staff—the views that underlie the policies and practices those schools are likely to adopt.

It also is why if we want to attend to equity, we must attend to ideology. No set of curricular or pedagogical strategies can turn a classroom led by a teacher with a deficit view of families experiencing poverty into an equitable learning space for those families (Gorski, 2013; Robinson, 2007).

THE DANGERS OF DEFICIT IDEOLOGY

As described earlier, deficit ideology is rooted in the belief that poverty is the natural result of ethical, intellectual, spiritual, and other shortcomings in people who are experiencing it. Adherents to deficit ideology point to educational outcome disparities—differences in test scores or graduation rates, for example—as evidence of these shortcomings (Sleeter, 2004; Valencia, 2009). Low rates of in-school family involvement among parents experiencing poverty or higher relative rates of school absences among students experiencing poverty are interpreted, in their view, as evidence that people experiencing poverty do not value their children's education. People experiencing poverty are deemed the problem. Their attitudes, behaviors, cultures, and mindsets block their potential for success. Deficit ideology is a blame-the-victim mentality.

Sometimes these deficit ascriptions are explicit. Some of the most popular teacher development models related to poverty and education associate a variety of negative attributes with people experiencing poverty. They might paint people experiencing poverty as ineffective communicators, promiscuous, violent, criminally oriented, addiction-prone, and spiritually underdeveloped. Some state explicitly, against decades of research to the contrary, that people experiencing poverty don't value education the way their wealthier peers do (Payne, 2005). We especially should be suspicious of frameworks or approaches that suggest people experiencing poverty share a singular and predictable culture or mindset. As it turns out, economically marginalized people are just as diverse as any other group defined around a single identity. Unfortunately, reality is of little mitigating consequence against ideology. The power and the danger of deficit ideology is that it speaks to popular misperceptions and biases. *People in poverty are broken. Here's how to fix them.*

So we must build institutional change efforts first around ideological shifts. If we believe people experiencing poverty are inherently deficient, no amount of instructional strategies will adequately prepare us to see and respond to the conditions that *actually* underlie educational outcome disparities. As a teacher, can I believe a student's mindset is deficient, that she is lazy, unmotivated, and disinterested in school, *and also* build a positive, high-expectations relationship with her?

Just as importantly, what realities are masked by deficit ideology, and to what are we *not* responding when we respond through a deficit lens? Can we expect to erase outcome disparities most closely related to the barriers and challenges experienced by people experiencing poverty by ignoring those barriers and challenges? Of course not.

Returning to the example of family involvement, the natural inclination of the educator who ascribes to deficit ideology is to believe that parents experiencing poverty show up less often because they do not care, because they do not value education. The logical response to that interpretation is to try to convince people experiencing poverty to care. Across the United States, schools invest time and resources in initiatives designed to solve a problem that does not exist, not only wasting time and resources, but also risking further alienation of the most marginalized families. What we might fail to see are the barriers that make opportunities for family involvement less accessible to families experiencing poverty, so those barriers go unaddressed. Inequity persists.

MEET DEFICIT IDEOLOGY'S COUSIN, GRIT

As advocates for a more sophisticated examination of educational outcome disparities have challenged the deficit view more loudly (Dudley-Marling, 2015; Ullicci & Howard, 2015), an enticing but equally troublesome alternative has emerged. Growing out of the popularity of grit theory (Duckworth, Peterson, Matthews, & Kelly, 2009), the notion that there are personal attributes that enable some people to overcome adversity that could overwhelm others, is *grit ideology*. It differs from deficit ideology in one important way: Unlike people who adhere to deficit ideology, who ignore inequities and other barriers altogether and focus instead on mythical "cultures" or "mindsets" of the targets of those barriers, adherents of grit ideology acknowledge the barriers and inequities. However, rather than responding to or redressing those barriers, they want to bolster the grit of economically marginalized students (Gorski, 2016b).

The most obvious trouble with grit ideology is that of all the combinations of barriers that most impact the educational outcomes of students experiencing poverty, which include housing instability, food insecurity, inequitable access to high-quality schools, unjust school policies, and others, not a single one is associated even slightly with students' grittiness. As Alfie Kohn (2014) notes, adherents of the grit view are grasping for amoral solutions to inequities, which are moral problems. Anindya Kundu (2014), raising a voice of caution against the fascination with grit, explained how the grit view is a cousin to deficit ideology. "By overemphasizing grit," Kundu wrote, "we tend to attribute a student's underachievement to personality deficits like laziness. This reinforces the idea that individual effort determines outcomes" (p. 80). It also ignores that the most economically marginalized students, who show up for school *despite* the inequities and barriers they experience in and out of school, are already the grittiest students.

Like deficit ideology, grit ideology is no threat to educational outcome disparities. In the end, it represents another attempt to sidestep the core causes of those disparities, requiring students to overcome inequities they never should have to bear.

To be clear, the trouble with grit ideology is not necessarily the notion of grit itself. Perhaps it is worthwhile to consider attributes that bolster resilience in everyone: students, teachers, administrators. The trouble comes when we are so intent on finding a simple solution to complex inequities that we apply concepts like grit through a deficit lens in ways they never were intended to be applied. Suddenly we are talking about how to fix students experiencing poverty with grit and not talking about how to fix the conditions that deny students experiencing poverty the access and opportunity afforded their wealthier peers (or how to fix poverty itself). We reinvest in the old *everything is about hard work* bootstraps mentality that masks the barriers we ought to be destroying. Ariana Stokas (2015) nails it:

> [The need for grit] often arises as a way for the individual to cope with suffering and for society to justify social failure through instructing the individual that their condition—poverty, for instance—is related to an intrinsic deficit. It has the potential to indoctrinate the student, through individual metrics such as standardized tests, with the belief that failure is due to an intrinsic lack rather than to systemic inequality. (p. 522)

Replacing the necessary reckoning with systemic barriers with an initiative to cultivate grit is itself an example of deficit ideology and inequitable practice.

While we're exploring the trouble with grit, we might consider other concepts popularly adopted in the perpetual, impossible quest to find an equity panacea without confronting inequity. *Growth mindset* comes to mind. There is a growing body of research supporting some aspects of growth mindset—the notion that if we deemphasize the role of intelligence and emphasize the role of effort in school achievement, students will see intelligence as more malleable than static. They then will believe they *can* grow and improve, and so they *will* grow and improve (Dweck, 2010). The problem is, no matter what mindset students adopt, they only have the access and opportunity provided for them. Their mindset, whatever it might be, is no solution to gross inequities in access to health care, well-funded schools, and engaging pedagogies (Yeager & Walton, 2011). Their mindsets are not the problem. We need a more transformative approach.

THE HOPE OF STRUCTURAL IDEOLOGY

Educators with a structural ideology understand that educational outcome disparities are the result of structural barriers, the logical if not purposeful implication of unfair distributions of opportunity and access in and out of school (Gorski, 2016b; Stokas, 2015). As discussed earlier, this inequitable access tracks most closely to the symptoms of income and wealth inequality (Berliner, 2013)—to poverty and its implications. Outside schools, a lack of access to adequate financial resources might mean students experiencing poverty are coping with some combination of unstable housing, food insecurity, time poverty, and inadequate or inconsistent health care, all discussed in detail in Chapter 6. They likely have less access than wealthier peers to Internet technology, books, tutoring, formal opportunities to engage with the arts, and other resources and experiences that bolster school achievement (Lineburg & Ratliff, 2015). Often students experiencing poverty are even cheated within their schools out of similar levels of access to experienced teachers, higher-order pedagogies, affirming school cultures, arts education, co-curricular programs, and other resources and opportunities their wealthier peers may take for granted (Battey, 2013; Dudley-Marling, 2015). The barriers and challenges are diverse, but they have this in common: They are wholly unrelated to the mindsets or grittiness of families experiencing poverty.

They have this in common, too: As long as they exist, educational outcome disparities will exist. There simply is no way to erase educational outcome disparities while sidestepping inequities. That's why, as Peter Cookson (2013) argues, "We need to reframe the debate from focusing on individuals and personalities and instead focus on restructuring a broken system" (p. 5). Stepping back a couple paces for a wider view, it even can be instructive to consider the possibility that the system is not broken at all. Perhaps it works exactly as it is designed to work, re-creating existing patterns of opportunity, privilege, and disadvantage. When we consider this view, we are forced to look more deeply at the structural roots of outcome inequalities and how those roots are implanted firmly in "commonsense" policy and "tradition" based practice. It requires serious reckoning.

What makes this reality difficult to manage from an educator point of view is that all these out-of-school inequities appear outside our spheres of influence (Gorski, 2012). In fact, neither teachers nor schools are equipped with the knowledge, resources, or time to resolve the scarcity of living-wage work or affordable housing—not in the immediate term, at least. This, in part, is what makes deficit and grit ideology so alluring: They allow us to define problems in ways that call for straightforward and practical solutions. *Teach families the value of education. Cultivate grit in students.* With a structural ideology, we recognize big structural conditions we cannot rectify so easily or practically.

The hope of structural ideology is that even if we cannot fully rectify those conditions, equity policy and practice should be *responsive* to them and not punish economically marginalized students for their implications. We can mitigate even the barriers we cannot eliminate. Returning again to the example of family involvement, rather than blaming parents experiencing poverty for lower at-school involvement rates, the educator with a structural ideology steps back and reflects with greater equity literacy. Do we organize opportunities for family involvement in ways that respond to the challenges economically marginalized families face, perhaps a lack of paid leave, difficulty securing transportation, the inability to afford child care, and the necessity of working multiple jobs? Even if we cannot eliminate these barriers entirely, can we create policy and practice that do not exacerbate them and might even mitigate them? Perhaps we cannot afford to buy every family a car and ensure every family has living-wage work. But we can adjust opportunities for family involvement by taking these barriers into account: providing transportation, offering on-site child care, becoming more flexible with scheduling, making sure each person in the school is trained to engage with parents respectfully. Those moves are within our spheres of influence.

This is equity literacy: knowing that equity requires us to ask these questions and having the will to ask them. Then, with our deeper understandings, equity literacy means shifting policies, practices, and initiatives to be more equitable. A critical early step in this process is to ditch the deficit ideology, quit the grit ideology, and cultivate in ourselves and one another a structural ideology. This is an essential ideological base, positioning us to be a threat to inequity in our spheres of influence.

AN EXERCISE IN STRUCTURAL FRAMING AND LANGUAGE

The concept *generational poverty* never sat right with me. For a long time I couldn't quite put my finger on the problem. Then I thought about the generations of people in my own family who had experienced poverty. When people say *generational poverty*, the explicit intention is generally to differentiate between families whose poverty has spanned generations and families whose poverty is situational: a parent lost a job, a child had a medical emergency not covered by health insurance, that sort of thing. It can be an important distinction, but the distinction means something different through a deficit lens from what it means through a structural lens. The implicit suggestion of "generational poverty" always seemed to me to be a deficit suggestion: the idea that poverty is the result of a set of cultures, behaviors, and attitudes reproduced in families experiencing poverty and passed down from generation to generation. If I interpret generational poverty in this way, I might be easily allured by initiatives designed to interrupt the transference of these cultures, behaviors, and attitudes. If we look more deeply, we see how in a more implicit way the idea that we interrupt poverty by fixing the cultures, behaviors, and attitudes of families experiencing poverty before they can be passed to the next generation is a central (and awful) deficit feature of the culture of poverty or mindset of poverty framework. The language we use in this case lends itself to a deficit view: generational poverty, culture of poverty, mindset of poverty. It frames poverty as a personal failure, not as a social condition attached to a long list of inequitable systems and structures, including public education.

What if, instead of talking about generational poverty, we talked about *generational injustice*? How would it change the way we defined, understood, responded to, and redressed the problem? Suddenly we're not looking at poverty as a personal or cultural failure, focusing on how deficient mindsets are passed from generation to generation, but instead examining how policies, practices, and institutions marginalize generation after generation of some families and communities. We're examining structural conditions. We are making ourselves a threat to inequity.

In my teacher education courses I challenge students who talk about generational poverty to practice reconsidering their ideas using *generational injustice* instead. It's an exercise in noticing what happens to our interpretation, problem identification, and solution strategizing when we shift from a deficit view to a structural view.

In the same way, when I hear participants in one of my workshops talk about the *dropout problem,* I suggest an exercise: *Let's try having this conversation again using the concept of* pushouts *instead of* dropouts. If you think this is only semantics, try it with a group of your colleagues. How does looking at disparities in school completion as a *pushout* problem and not a *dropout* problem change the solutions we're capable of imagining?

Achievement gap, opportunity gap: same thing. Framing matters. This simple exercise can help us tone our equity literacy by consciously choosing a structural view and noticing how our understandings shift.

CONCLUSION

If we think of achievement gaps solely in terms of test score disparities, "dropout" rates, or other symptoms of economic injustice, and not as the *opportunity gaps* they actually are, we likely are embracing a deficit or grit view unconducive to equity. If we seek practical instructional strategies but fail to cultivate in ourselves the ideological shifts necessary to recognize and confront structural barriers (even if we cannot eliminate those inequities altogether), we become conveyors of deficit ideology. It is not easy. I have written about the challenges I face attempting to cultivate these shifts in teacher education students and in myself (Gorski, 2012). Despite the difficulties, this is the only way to position ourselves to be a threat to the existence of inequity. We root the deficit view out of ourselves and our spheres of influence.

Next, in Chapter 5, we identify and challenge the stereotypes and myths that underlie deficit ideology. We also take a deeper critical look at frameworks for understanding poverty that lend themselves to a deficit view, like the *culture of poverty* and *mindset of poverty* frameworks.

REFLECTION QUESTIONS AND EXERCISES

1. Imagine you had a student from a family experiencing poverty who generally did well on quizzes and tests but almost never turned in homework. How might you interpret the student's behavior through each of a deficit, grit, and structural view? Based on those interpretations, what strategies might you develop to address the homework issue?

2. Identify a policy or practice that reflected a deficit ideology in a school you attended or a school at which you have worked—a policy or practice meant to fix something about the cultures, mindsets, levels of grittiness, or values of students or families experiencing poverty. How might you reshape that policy or practice around a structural view?

3. In your opinion, what explains the growing popularity of grit and growth mindset as responses to educational outcome disparities? How does a focus on grit or growth mindset mask the biases and inequities with which students experiencing poverty might contend?

Note: This chapter is derived in part from an article published in *Journal of Education for Teaching* (Gorski, 2016b), 42(4), copyright the Taylor & Francis Group, Informa Group Plc, available online at tandfonline.com/, doi: 10.1080/02607476.2016.1215546.

The Trouble with the "Mindset of Poverty" and Other Stereotypes about People Experiencing Poverty

Principles of equity literacy discussed in this chapter include:

Principle 4: People experiencing poverty are diverse.

Principle 5: What we believe about people experiencing poverty informs how we teach, interact with, and advocate (or fail to advocate) for them.

Principle 8: Educational outcome disparities are the result of inequities, of unjust distributions of access and opportunity, not the result of deficiencies in the mindsets, cultures, or grittiness of people experiencing poverty.

I'm puzzled when I think about how the "culture of poverty" or "mindset of poverty" perspective has come to dominate conversations about poverty and education. I wonder how so many of us bought into a most preposterous presumption: that we can assume anything about people's values, dispositions, or behaviors based on knowing a single dimension of their identities. I imagine Grandma, who grew up rural, Presbyterian, and poor, a White woman speaking her distinctly middle-Appalachian English, standing next to one of the equally economically marginalized, urban, Muslim, Somali youth I had the pleasure of knowing while living in St. Paul, Minnesota. *What,* I ask myself, *do these two people have in common culturally? What can I rightly assume about both knowing only their economic disadvantage?* They and their families do, I concede, have important life experiences in common: a lack of access to health care, for instance, and a lack of access to living-wage work. But these similarities are not *cultural.* Rather, they are social conditions. They are barriers and inequities in spite of which people experiencing poverty must attempt, against considerable odds, to thrive.

The mindset-of-poverty idea is nonsensical because the idea that we can assume anything about a person's mindset or culture based solely on their economic condition is nonsensical. There is as much diversity *within* any identity group, whether "tall people" or "women" or "people with (dis)abilities," as *between* any two groups. But it's ludicrous for a variety of other reasons, too, which we will explore momentarily.

Today, many people associate the culture of poverty or mindset of poverty paradigm with Ruby Payne (2005), the prodigious professional development provider whose book *A Framework for Understanding Poverty* is among the texts most widely read by teachers. However, it was Oscar Lewis (1959) who introduced that term, the "culture of poverty," nearly 60 years ago in his book *Five Families: Mexican Case Studies in the Culture of Poverty*. The basic idea Payne borrowed from Lewis was that people experiencing poverty share unique, consistent, and predictable cultural or mindset traits. People living in poverty, Lewis argued, have a negligible sense of history. The men are violent, often beating their wives. The women are promiscuous, favoring instant gratification. He introduced roughly 70 traits in all, constituting what he called the culture of poverty. Payne borrowed many of these traits and repackaged them as the "mindset of poverty."

Lewis and his scholarship are emblematic of a social science paradigm that gained traction in the late 1950s and early 1960s. In this paradigm, personal and community characteristics—attitudes toward education or propensities toward peace or violence, for example—were driven more by *culture* than *biology* (Rosemblatt, 2009). In some ways, this was a positive development. Lewis rejected the idea that outcome inequalities like differences in IQ were inherent or biological. He suggested instead, as Payne does today, that they result from learned cultural behaviors and dispositions that can be unlearned.

Lewis's "culture of poverty" notion elicited a wide range of responses. On one end of the continuum were Michael Harrington and Daniel Moynihan, who applied it explicitly in their work, often focusing on urban African American poverty (Rosemblatt, 2009). Moynihan applied the culture of poverty concept in the now-famous *Moynihan Report*, originally titled *The Negro Family: The Case for National Action*, which he wrote in 1965 as the U.S. Assistant Secretary of Labor. In the "culture of poverty" tradition, Moynihan suggested that African American poverty could be attributed largely to a "ghetto culture" characterized by single-mother families rather than the lack of employment opportunities in urban centers, as others had argued. The same type of application of Lewis's work survives today in Payne's (2005) mindset of poverty model, which claims that poverty is attributable not to inequities or to an unequal distribution of opportunity or even to educational access disparities—all of which her book fails even to acknowledge—but to what she deems the problematic mindsets of people experiencing generational poverty.

On the other end of the spectrum were Charles Valentine (1968) and William Ryan (1971), who responded vehemently against the culture of poverty model. They argued that attending to a fictitious "culture of poverty" was a diversion, that poverty was the result primarily of the sorts of external factors and repressions we will explore in Chapters 6 and 7. Are you familiar with the phrase "blaming the victim"? William Ryan coined it, *invented* it, in response to the culture of poverty framework, particularly to the way it was being applied to African American families. Concepts like the "culture of poverty," Ryan argued (1971), "concentrate on the [supposed] defects of the victim, condemn the vague social and environmental stresses that produced the defect (some time ago), and ignore the continuing effect of victimizing social forces (right now)" (p. 8). To use an education example, we deny people access to equitable educational opportunity, access to preventive health care, even access to air unspoiled by environmental hazards. We do this for generations and then, when some low-income youth don't do well on standardized tests, drop out of school, or seem disengaged in class, we forget about these inequities and blame it on their culture or mindset.

The most obvious problem with the culture or mindset of poverty model, as I mentioned earlier, is its silly presumption that if we know people are from families experiencing poverty, we somehow know all sorts of other things about them: how they learn, how they communicate, their attitudes about education, or their propensity or lack of propensity for violence. It assumes we can somehow erase scores of other factors that inform their values, such as their race, religion, ethnicity, sexual orientation, and nationality, not to mention the many intersections of these identities.

Another problem is the fact that the education world is inundated with culture-obsessed approaches to understanding and responding to almost every phenomenon. We have cultural competence, cultural proficiency, multiculturalism, and intercultural communications, among others. The danger with these approaches or, more specifically, with how they often are implemented in schools, is that they conflate "culture" with race, gender, socioeconomic status, sexual orientation, and other identities, thereby suggesting that disparities or conflicts result from *cultural misunderstandings* rather than *biases and inequities*. Describing this conflation, Gloria Ladson-Billings (2006) explained, "The problem of culture in teaching is not merely one of exclusion. It is also one of overdetermination. What I mean by this is that culture is randomly and regularly used to explain everything" (p. 104).

The intensive and at times exclusive focus on culture masks the bigger reality: People experiencing poverty face innumerable inequities in and out of schools. These inequities have nothing to do with their cultures. We have all sorts of conceptual tools to help us shift this blame from inequities to students and their families, starting with the mindset of poverty notion, but also including increasingly popular notions like *grit* and *growth mindset* discussed in the previous chapter.

This is why a core premise of equity literacy is, *There is no such thing as a culture or mindset of poverty*. In the nearly 60 years since Lewis introduced the culture of poverty concept, social scientists have not been able to replicate his findings, and it's not for a lack of trying. They've attempted to identify the culture of poverty in a variety of contexts, from countries and cities to individual racial groups (see, for example, Billings, 1974; Carmon, 1985; Jones & Luo, 1999), each coming to the same conclusion: People experiencing poverty do not share a predictable, consistent culture (Abell & Lyon, 1979; Rodman, 1977). The fact that we, as a community of educators, have made the most popular framework for understanding poverty and education out of a false idea that was debunked by the mid-1970s should alarm us. It should remind us how important it is to cultivate our equity literacy.

Nor does research support the broader culture or mindset of poverty notion that dysfunctionality abounds in high-poverty communities (Baetan, 2004) any more, at least, than it abounds in every community. Scholars who study poverty have been challenging this dysfunctionality assumption since at least 1972, when Murray Gruber published a study based on interviews with 129 low-income African American male youth. He concluded that the culture of poverty idea persists not because it is real but because it serves as "an ideological insulation for privileged elites" (p. 58) who are grasping at concepts that will hide the ways they benefit from the savage inequalities that bear down on everybody else.

Sure, we can find individuals in high-poverty communities who are, say, inattentive parents or criminals. It might be easy, even with the best intentions, to presume greater instances of these problems in high-poverty communities than in wealthier communities. But the presumption would be wrong, more stereotype than insight. We'll explore evidence of this curious reality in a moment. Suffice it to say for now that if it's equitable schools we want, studying a fictitious culture or mindset of poverty will not get us there.

You might be thinking, *Okay, then, what* will *get us there?* Important question. I promise, we are working toward an answer to that question as we deepen our understandings, exercising our equity literacy muscles.

We must recognize first, though, that even if we reject the culture or mindset of poverty approach, we still live in a society where stereotypes about economically marginalized people abound. They are demonized in the media, demonized by politicians, even demonized in some teacher lounges and school hallways. In fact, the stereotypes that make up the mindset of poverty idea have become, in many ways, part of the "common sense" of achievement gap chatter: how communities experiencing poverty are devoid of positive role models, how they devalue education.

These messages are all around us. But which of these messages is true? How have so many of us bought into the mindset of poverty mythology despite its 5-decade repudiation?

A HINT OF TRUTH?: THE NATURE OF POVERTY STEREOTYPING

A longtime colleague of mine with a penchant for road rage—I'll call him Frederick—is fond of flinging the word "jackass" at drivers whose driving skills offend him. Specifically, he is fond of flinging the word at *male* drivers, or drivers he assumes to be men, and reserves it for them exclusively. When a driver he assumes is a woman neglects to use a turn signal or drives a few miles per hour under the speed limit, his response is different. Rather than calling her a jackass, he shakes his head and exclaims, "Women drivers!"

I have challenged Frederick on what seems a clear case of gender stereotyping. He responds firmly: "That's not a *stereotype*. It's my *experience*. Women are bad drivers." He tends to append to this defense the common refrain, "Plus, there's a hint of truth in stereotypes; otherwise, why would so many people believe them?"

As troubling as his attitude might be, Frederick is not alone in his view or in his tendency to see somebody within his gender group who has offended his sensibilities as an outlier, a *jackass*, while interpreting a woman offender, somebody outside his gender group, as representing all women. A long history of psychosocial research details the human tendency to imagine our own social and identity groups as diverse while we imagine "the other," people belonging to a social or identity group with which we do not identify, as being all the same (e.g., Meiser & Hewstone, 2004).

Cognitively speaking, our stereotyping is connected to a natural and necessary human response in the face of limited context-specific knowledge. A woman's stereotype about men might prove to be an overgeneralization in most instances, but her intuition eventually could protect her from sexual assault. However, the *content* of stereotypes is only partially organic, only partially based upon measured consideration of the totality of our experiences. Stereotypes also grow from how we're socialized (Shier, Jones, & Graham, 2010). They are the result of what we are *taught to think* about people experiencing poverty, for instance, even if we have experienced poverty. We are socialized through celebrations of "meritocracy" or by observing a parent lock the car doors when driving through certain parts of town. They grow, as well, from a desire to find self-meaning by distinguishing between social and identity groups with which we do and do not identify (Hornsey, 2008). That's the heady science of it.

One of the keys to distinguishing between stereotyping as a cognitive process for everyday, nonexploitative decisionmaking (*Where might I find a water fountain in this building?*) and stereotyping as a threat to equity is in determining how much these mechanisms—socialization processes and the drive for group distinction—are in play in any given instance. This is because these mechanisms, in the way they reward selective evidence-gathering, are at the root of group-level biases (Nesdale & Flesser, 2001). In other words, we tend to require less evidence, *and less accurate evidence*, to convince us of the legitimacy of a stereotype about a group to which we do not belong than we require to convince us of a stereotype about a group to which we do belong. Social psychologists have referred to this phenomenon as *in-group bias* because it is based on the tendency to see our social and identity groups more favorably overall than groups with which we do not associate (Greenwald & Pettigrew, 2014).

Certainly Frederick has what he considers good evidence that women are bad drivers. But just as certainly, to extrapolate an experience or two into a generalization about all women, he must suppress considerable counterevidence, such as the number of women drivers he never notices because they do not ignite his road rage or the fact that car insurance is cheaper for women because by virtually every measure women are better drivers than men. This suppression protects him because if he generalizes men the way he generalizes women, he also implicates himself. He becomes the jackass.

We all participate in this sort of faulty generalizing in one way or another, usually unconsciously (Fiarman, 2016). This is not always a bad thing in the sense that stereotypes can help us make decisions when gaps exist in our knowledge and experience, as when we're looking for a water fountain and know to look near a restroom. However, when we apply stereotypes to groups of people and their relative worth rather than to buildings and the consistency of their plumbing infrastructures, we run the risk of bias and inequity. In an interpersonal sense, the socialization behind our stereotypes encourages us to seek evidence to cement our existing biases (Jervis, 2006). We might take an instance of an economically marginalized parent missing a scheduled meeting as evidence supporting our view that *those people* don't value education. Meanwhile, we often fail to note evidence that does not support these biases, perhaps not noticing the number of economically marginalized parents who do make it to meetings *despite* our refusal to schedule those meetings in ways that maximize their accessibility for the lowest-income families.

When I teach a class or deliver a workshop about poverty and schools, I often begin by asking participants to reflect on a question: *Why are people who are in poverty in poverty?* Answers vary. However, even when participants believe that societal inequities are responsible for a portion of or even most poverty, they almost always qualify their responses with a litany of stereotypes: *Poor people are lazy. They don't care about education. They're alcoholics and drug abusers. They don't want to work; instead, they are addicted to the welfare system.* Unfortunately, these are not outlier views.

So what if I told you that many stereotypes commonly associated with people experiencing poverty, such as a propensity for alcohol overuse, are *truer of wealthy people* than they are of people experiencing poverty (Humensky, 2010)? It's a fact. But how often do we apply this stereotype to wealthy people? How often do we hear, "No wonder so many rich kids don't do well at college despite all their advantages; their parents are all alcoholics . . . "?

On the other hand, I might have 5, 10, or 20 students experiencing poverty who do not fit a particular stereotype, but if I have two or three who do fit it, those two or three can become sufficient evidence to confirm my existing stereotype if I don't check myself. As Jervis (2006) explains, "Given the complexity and ambiguity of our world, it is unfortunately true that beliefs for which a good deal of evidence can be mustered often turn out to be mistaken" (p. 643). If a low-income student regularly does not turn in homework, am I quicker to attribute it to her socioeconomic status than I would for a student in my own economic bracket?

Let's consider another example. There are many common stereotypes about people experiencing poverty that brand them inattentive parents. As we've discussed, those who do not make it to school for school engagement opportunities can become targets of stereotyping—or worse, targets of blame—by those educators. So whereas we might be prone to pardon a more well-to-do parent for missing structured opportunities for family engagement—*she's traveling for work*—lower-income parents' lack of school-based engagement might be interpreted as confirming evidence of disinterest in their children's schooling, regardless of whether or not it also is related to work.

In our efforts to become equity-literate educators, one of our first tasks is to understand our own socializations and the ways we have bought into stereotypes that might hinder our abilities to connect with economically marginalized families, or any families, in the most authentic, open way. It's not easy. It takes a lot of humility to acknowledge we harbor stereotypes. The fact that many of us have been trained as teachers and administrators with frameworks like the "mindset of poverty" that *encourage* stereotyping does not help. One important step in this process, though, is to challenge ourselves to rethink some of the most common stereotypes about people experiencing poverty and the extent to which we might have been fooled into believing them.

MISPERCEIVERS ARE WE: QUESTIONING COMMON STEREOTYPES ABOUT FAMILIES EXPERIENCING POVERTY

People experiencing poverty are stereotyped in innumerable ways (Pinto & Cresnik, 2014). Most of these stereotypes are just plain inaccurate. In fact, as I mentioned earlier, some are truer of wealthy people than of people experiencing poverty.

I decided several years ago to compare the most common stereotypes held by my teacher education students about economically marginalized people with social science research evidence (Gorski, 2012). *Is there a hint of truth in every stereotype?* I wondered.

Here's what I found.

Stereotype 1: People Experiencing Poverty Do Not Value Education. Nonsense. The most popular measure of parental attitudes about education among teachers tends to be family involvement (Jeynes, 2011). However, too often our notions of family involvement are limited in scope, focused only on *in-school* involvement—the kind of involvement that requires parents to visit their children's schools. While it is true that parents experiencing poverty are less likely to participate in this brand of involvement (National Center for Education Statistics [NCES], 2005), they engage in home-based involvement strategies, such as encouraging children to read and do homework, *more frequently* than their wealthier peers (Noel et al., 2013).

It might be easy, given the stereotype that families experiencing poverty do not value education, to associate their less consistent engagement in on-site, publicly visible, school engagement, such as volunteering or attending parent–teacher conferences, with an ethic that devalues education. In fact, research has shown that many teachers assume low-income families are completely uninvolved in their children's schooling (Patterson et al., 2008). However, assuming a direct relationship between disparities in on-site involvement and a disregard for the importance of school would require us to omit considerable amounts of contrary evidence.

First, parents experiencing poverty face significant barriers to school involvement, some of which are depicted in Figure 5.1. These include consequences associated with the scarcity of living-wage jobs, such as the inability to afford child care or public transportation, the lack of access to paid leave and inability to miss hours at low-wage jobs, and more (Jarrett & Coba-Rodriguez, 2015). They also include the weight of parents' own school experiences, which in many cases were hostile and unwelcoming, or previous indignities they've experienced when visiting their children's schools (Robinson & Volpé, 2015). These challenges are discussed in more detail in Chapter 7. Although some schools and districts have responded to these challenges by, for example, providing on-site child care or transportation, the fact remains that on average, this type of involvement is considerably less accessible to economically marginalized families than to wealthier ones.

Here is the truth: There is no evidence to support the stereotype that attitudes about the value of education among people experiencing poverty differ in any way from attitudes in wealthier communities. Studies have demonstrated consistently that people experiencing poverty value education

Figure 5.1. Challenges to On-Site School Involvement for Low-Income Families

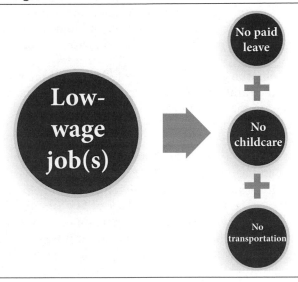

just as much as wealthy people *despite* often experiencing schools as unwelcoming and inequitable.

For example:

- Studying low-income participants of a family literacy program, Esther Prins and Kai Schafft (2009) found that they placed high value on education and pursued education themselves to create a better life for their children.
- In their study on low-income African American parents, Cirecie West-Olatunji and her colleagues (2010) found that they regularly reached out to their children's schools and stressed the importance of education to their children.
- Jennifer Marcella and her colleagues (2014) found high rates of literacy practices in low-income Latinx families' homes and explicitly remarked how their findings challenged common presumptions.
- During an ethnographic study of a racially diverse group of low-income families, Guofang Li (2010) found that parents, including those who were not English-proficient, used a variety of strategies to bolster their children's literacy development.
- African American parents of high school students described in detail the importance of multiple forms of family engagement in a study conducted by Terrinieka Williams and Bernadette Sánchez (2012).

- Robin Jarrett and Sarai Coba-Rodriguez (2015) studied school involvement among low-income African American mothers of students transitioning to kindergarten and found that they were deeply involved despite the strain of numerous hardships and barriers.
- Dwan Robinson and Lauren Volpé (2015), who interviewed low-income rural parents of elementary students, found that they all expressed the importance of involvement in their children's education and lamented the barriers that sometimes made that involvement difficult.
- In their study of 92 Hispanic immigrant mothers, Samantha Berkule Johnson and her colleagues (2016) concluded that participants showed great interest and active involvement in helping their children learn, often despite their lack of English proficiency.
- Using data from the more than 20,000 families that participated in the Early Childhood Longitudinal Study, Carey Cooper and her colleagues (2010) found, quite simply, that "poor parents reported engaging their children in home-learning activities as often as nonpoor parents" (p. 876).

As with any stereotype, the notion—the *lie*—that people experiencing poverty don't value education might have more to do with some of *our* well-intended misinterpretations of social realities than with *their* disinterest in school. For example, some low-income families, and particularly low-income immigrant families, may not be as informed as their wealthier counterparts about how educational systems in the United States work (Lareau & Weininger, 2008), a predictable consequence of the alienation from school systems many have experienced both as students and parents, in part due to educators' stereotypes (Bray & Schommer-Aikins, 2014; Mundy & Leko, 2015). It can be easy to interpret this lack of understanding, which is itself a symptom of educational inequities, as disinterest. Similarly, it can be easy to interpret lower levels of some types of school involvement, including types that are not scheduled or structured to be accessible to economically marginalized families, as evidence that they simply don't care about school. But these interpretations are just plain wrong.

The challenge for us, then, is to do the difficult work of considering what we are apt to misinterpret, not simply as a fluffy attempt at "inclusion," but as a high-stakes matter of student success. After all, research also shows that when teachers perceive that a student's parents value education, they tend to assess that student's work more positively (Hill & Craft, 2003). Shake free from the stereotypes. It matters.

Stereotype 2: People Experiencing Poverty Are Lazy. Another common stereotype about people experiencing poverty, particularly people of color experiencing poverty, is that they are lazy or have weak work ethics (Moses, 2012). Unfortunately, in addition to misinforming individual educators' attitudes about students, this fib-filled stereotype has been used to justify social policy that weakens social supports for our most marginalized students.

The truth is, there is no evidence that people experiencing poverty are lazier or have weaker work ethics than anybody else (Wilson, 1996). To the contrary, all indications are that people experiencing poverty work just as hard as, and perhaps harder than, many people from higher socioeconomic strata. Challenging popular perception, most working-age adults experiencing poverty have jobs. About 45% work *at least* the equivalent of full time (Gould, Davis, & Kimball, 2015), often cobbling together multiple jobs to provide for themselves and their families. Many work more than the equivalent of full time, but their wages are so low that they are still in poverty.

This is an astounding display of resilience. People experiencing poverty are concentrated in the lowest-paying jobs, usually with negligible advancement opportunities. They are in jobs that require the most intense manual labor—that fact alone should dispel the laziness myth—with the most risk of injury, offering the fewest benefits such as paid sick leave (Babic, 2016; Kim, 1999). Mary Babic (2016), reporting for Oxfam America, explains why the realities of low-wage workers make the laziness myth particularly pernicious:

> The US is unique among developed nations in not requiring employers to provide sick days. In fact, the law does not even protect workers from being fired if they miss work due to illness. In a recent Oxfam survey, one in seven low-wage women workers reported having lost a job as a result of taking a sick day. . . . This leaves low-wage workers gingerly walking a tightrope . . . praying no one will catch a cold, contract a flu, break a bone, or get a stomach bug. (¶ 11–12)

People experiencing poverty are most likely to work jobs that have high risks of illness or injury, left unprotected from being fired for missing work due to illness or injury (increasing their chances at unemployment), unlikely to have access to living-wage work, then called "lazy" even if they are working more than the equivalent of full time. If you are thinking, *Well, then, they should find better-paying jobs*, remember from Chapter 3 that for every living-wage job in the United States there are about seven people looking for work (Henry & Fredericksen, 2015). We should ask ourselves, *Whose interests am I really protecting when I buy into these stereotypes?*

I never understood the "lazy" stereotype. My mom's people, as I mentioned, were coal miners—not a career choice most lazy people would make. Whatever job you have in education, you might work *as hard* as they worked, but I doubt you could convince me you work *harder*. Certainly they had issues—lack of basic plumbing infrastructure, lack of health care, exploitation by the coal companies—but laziness was not one of them.

Stereotype 3: People Experiencing Poverty Are Substance Addicts. Alcohol and drug overuse are serious diseases that affect people of every socioeconomic status. They have grabbed ahold of several people in my own family. The fact that these diseases are used as stereotype fodder for any group of people should infuriate us and make us suspicious. The fact that they are more likely to be treated as diseases among wealthy people and criminalized among people experiencing poverty, most harshly in communities of color, should help us see more clearly the troubling double standards of class and race.

Consider the facts. People experiencing poverty have less access than their wealthier peers to addiction cessation treatments, from basic preventive health care with doctors responding to early signs of addiction to inpatient addiction treatment programs. Cigarettes and alcohol are advertised far more visibly and frequently in high-poverty communities than in wealthier ones. So we wouldn't be shocked if research showed that economically marginalized people are more prone to substance overuse than wealthy people, right?

They aren't. They are more likely to be criminalized for alcohol or drug use and less likely to actually use alcohol or drugs.

Although some of the intricacies of the findings vary, research generally shows that rates of alcohol and drug use are proportionate with socioeconomic status: the wealthier you or your family are, the more likely you are to use and become addicted to alcohol or drugs, despite greater access to cessation treatments (Humensky, 2010; Patrick, Wightman, Schoeni, & Schulenberg, 2012). These patterns hold even for young people. For example, using data from the National Longitudinal Survey of Adolescent Health, Jennifer Humensky (2010) found that "Higher parental education is associated with higher rates of binge drinking, marijuana and cocaine use in early adulthood. Higher parental income is associated with higher rates of binge drinking and marijuana use" (p. 1). This is particularly astounding when we consider that alcohol overuse can be a symptom of the stressors caused by discrimination and social deprivation (Lee & Jeon, 2005).

Of course, despite the stereotypes, it is true that alcohol and drug use and overuse can create problems in families experiencing poverty and in high-poverty communities. I certainly am not arguing that we should not attend to drug and alcohol use and how it affects students' opportunities to achieve in school. We should. We must realize that when these problems do exist in low-income families, they have the potential to be particularly devastating because of the aforementioned disparities in access to recovery and treatment opportunities. Nor do they have access to preventive medical attention that might catch and treat emerging dependencies before they become full-fledged addictions. This is one of many reasons to advocate for universal health care as a way to ensure equitable educational opportunity. It's also a good reason to advocate against the criminalization of substance use, a practice that continues to fill prisons disproportionately with low-income People of Color, putting our most economically marginalized students at greater risk of long-term poverty.

What we must try *not* to do is falsely associate drug and alcohol use and addiction with a make-believe "mindset" or "culture" of poverty or attribute addiction to the socioeconomic statuses of families experiencing poverty—something people who haven't experienced poverty are far less likely to do when it comes to wealthy families struggling with addiction.

Stereotype 4: People Experiencing Poverty Are Linguistically Deficient and Poor Communicators. Mirroring attitudes in the broader society, many educators have been led to believe erroneously that people experiencing poverty are linguistically deficient (Pinto & Cresnik, 2014). This is a particularly dangerous stereotype given the extent to which students' identities are associated with their languages or the ways they speak those languages (Grant, Oka, & Baker, 2009; Milner, 2015). Criticizing a person's language means criticizing her deepest self. It can cause students to feel disconnected from school (Christensen, 2008).

Fortunately, there is good reason *not* to criticize. The notion of language "deficiency" in people experiencing poverty is mired in false stereotypes. These stereotypes are built upon two shaky assumptions: (1) due to parental disinterest in their children's literacy, children in poverty do not enter school with the volume or type of vocabulary needed to succeed academically, and (2) the use of particular variations of English reflects inferior language capabilities.

The faulty idea that children from families experiencing poverty enter school linguistically deprived, with smaller or less complex vocabularies than their wealthier peers, and that this condition is a result of family "cultures" that devalue learning, has become part of the "common sense" of school reform. What you might not know is that the much-cited belief that low-income students are linguistically deficient is based largely on a single study of a few dozen economically diverse families around Kansas City (Hart & Risley, 1995). Curt Dudley-Marling and Krista Lucas (2009) discuss this methodological flaw in impressive detail in their essay, "Pathologizing the Language and Culture of Poor Children."

Studies indeed show that children from families experiencing poverty begin school with less developed reading and language skills on average than wealthier classmates (Children's Defense Fund, 2008). Gaps begin to materialize early, even before children's second birthdays (Fernald, Marchman, & Weisleder, 2013). This initial discrepancy can foreshadow lags in reading proficiency that can last throughout students' school lives (Hindman, Wasik, & Snell, 2016). However, there is no evidence that this discrepancy is connected to a language *use* deficiency or that it reflects parental disinterest in education. Similarly, based on their study involving a sample of 1,364 racially diverse public school children, Veronique Dupere and her colleagues (2010) concluded that reading score differences between students experiencing poverty and wealthier students could be explained largely by discrepancies in the sorts of institutions to which they had access throughout early childhood. For example, economically marginalized families, unlike many wealthier families, rarely have access to high-quality early childhood education programs that support children's language learning (Bassok & Galdo, 2016). And families experiencing poverty simply cannot afford to fill their homes with books, computer programs, iPads, and other learning tools that strengthen children's literacy development.

The second shaky notion, that particular variations of English reflect superior or inferior language capabilities, incorrectly assumes the existence of "superior" and "inferior" language varieties (Miller, Cho, & Bracey, 2005). Linguists roundly reject this superior/inferior dichotomy. Some call it "standard language ideology," alluding to the presumptuous and linguistically nonsensical term "standard English" (Lippi-Green, 1994). In fact, since at least the early 1970s (see, for example, Baugh, 1983; Burling, 1973), linguists have bemoaned the ways students are taught to misunderstand the nature of language, including the false dichotomy of "correct/proper" and "incorrect/improper" language varieties.

In linguistic reality, all variations of a language and all dialects, from African American Vernacular English (Pullum, 1999) to the dialect of Appalachian English my grandma speaks (Luhman, 1990), are highly structured, with their own syntaxes and grammatical rules. These variations of English, like so-called "standard" English, are not "errors" of low intelligence or evidence of deficient cultures (Wheeler & Thomas, 2013). Instead, they are indicators of the regional, cultural, and social contexts in which somebody has learned to speak.

Among linguists, this is no revelation. More than 100 years of linguistic research clarifies that all languages and language varieties are communicatively equal because in their contexts they are equally complex and coherent (see, for example, Boas, 1911; Chomsky, 1965; Labov, 1972; Newmeyer, 1985; Terry, Connor, Thomas-Tate, & Love, 2010). As James Collins (1988) explains, "languages are *systems*, of formidable and roughly equal complexity, whether classic 'world languages' or the speech of economically simple societies, whether prestige standards or stigmatized dialects" (p. 301).

Another common misunderstanding is that people experiencing poverty primarily speak with an "informal" register or style, as we might speak with our sibling or close friend, while their middle-class and wealthier peers speak with a "formal" register, as we might speak during a job interview. However, like other forms of code-switching—the ways we modify behavior based on the context in which we find ourselves—*all people* use a broad range of language registers, regardless of the variety of language we speak

(Brizuela, Andersen, & Stallings, 1999). The false association, for instance, of middle-Appalachian English with informal register mistakenly associates "formal" ways of speaking with what we (erroneously) call "standard" English.

I presume we all agree that students, regardless of socioeconomic status, ought to learn the varieties of English that will help them gain access to the fullest range of educational and vocational opportunities. We have a responsibility to help students develop a firm understanding of, and ability to use, that form of English. But if we hope to do so in a spirit of equity, we must do so without denigrating the language varieties spoken in students' homes and communities. We must do so without assuming, when students speak varieties of English that are not rewarded in school, they are speaking improperly, unintelligently.

A related stereotype, featured prominently in the "mindset of poverty" model, paints people experiencing poverty more generally as ineffective communicators. Ruby Payne (2006) has suggested, incorrectly, that people in high-poverty communities often fight with one another because they do not have the necessary verbal communication skills to resolve conflicts: "Words are not seen as being very effective in generational poverty to resolve differences; fists are" (para. 3), she has written.

Despite this stereotype, studies show that people experiencing poverty communicate with the same sophistication as their wealthier peers. For example, Mary Ohmer and her colleagues (2010) studied communication strategies used by members of a high-poverty, predominantly African American community who had assembled to address a variety of neighborhood problems. They documented how people at these gatherings discussed and modeled complex communication techniques that could help them effectively address community challenges with their neighbors. They talked, for instance, about using language to de-escalate conflict, being conscious of their tone of voice, and approaching their neighbors in an inviting, nonhostile manner.

Their study reminded me of the time I spent as a child with my grandma's people in the mountains of western Maryland, where I never heard so much as a raised voice nor saw a single person lay anything other than a friendly hand on anybody else. What I observed was very clear and intentional communication—the kind of communicating you do when resources are scarce and you have to count on your neighbors to survive. This doesn't mean people experiencing poverty never scream at one another; it doesn't mean violence is not a problem in some high-poverty neighborhoods. It does mean we risk the authenticity of our relationships with students and their families when we assume that they must prefer shouting and fighting to peaceful and loving communication because of their socioeconomic situation.

Stereotype 5: People Experiencing Poverty Are Ineffective and Inattentive Parents. In my experience, the bad parent stereotype is based largely on other faulty assumptions, like the ones we've already debunked: *those people* don't value education, *those parents* are substance abusers, and so on. It also is based on decontextualized considerations of other sorts of evidence. For instance, when I hear that children in poverty watch television and participate in other sedentary activities at higher rates than their wealthier peers, my initial reaction might be, *Aha! Further evidence that* those parents *are inattentive to their children's well-being.* Reaching that conclusion, though, would require ignoring the fact that youth in households experiencing poverty have less access to a whole range of after-school and extracurricular activities, as well as to recreational spaces, than their wealthier peers (Lineberg & Ratliff, 2015).

Researchers routinely find that parents experiencing poverty are extremely attentive to their children's needs despite the many barriers they must overcome to provide for their families. This is no less true for single mothers, who often are the most scorned targets of the "bad parent" stereotype. We already established, for instance, that economically marginalized single mothers overwhelmingly claim a sense of responsibility for inspiring their children to pursue higher education. Jonitha Johnson's (2016) study of low-income African American single mothers with college-aged daughters showed that they worked tirelessly to cultivate self-motivation, encourage academic success, and model perseverance, even if they didn't have college degrees. Similarly, following their longitudinal study of low-income families, Annette Lareau and Elliot Weininger (2008) unequivocally denounced the "bad parent" stereotype. They concluded, "Working class and poor parents are no less deeply committed . . . to the well being of their children than are middle class parents" (p. 142).

THE DANGERS OF STEREOTYPES AND STEREOTYPE THREAT

Why, you might be wondering, *are we spending so much time on stereotypes? Why are we focusing on all this negativity rather than how we can strengthen educational opportunities for students?*

I hear you. We are working our way toward three full chapters, Chapters 8 through 10, of practical strategies and initiatives. However, no strategy for creating equitable and welcoming schools is more practical or immediate than this: We *must*, above all else, commit to losing both the stereotypes that paint people experiencing poverty as the problem, and the deficit views that prop up the stereotypes. This is the single most important thing we can do in our commitments to educational equity. It is the foundation of equity literacy. In the end, our understandings of poverty and attitudes toward families experiencing poverty play an enormous role, perhaps the *most* enormous role, in how we see and treat students, not to mention the lengths to which we will or will not go to advocate for them and their educational rights. William Parrett and Kathleen Budge (2012), who spent years studying high-performing, high poverty schools, put it this way:

> Educators who have not challenged their own bias and who do not understand how poverty affects lives and learning are less likely to develop authentic relationships with students and their families who live in poverty. They are also more likely to make harmful assumptions about students' capabilities that lead to low expectations. (p. 103)

No amount of practical strategies can make up for this failing. It is a matter of will. It begins with dislodging our stereotypes and deficit views.

The dangers of not doing so are plentiful. Stereotypes make some educators afraid of or accusatory toward students, including the most marginalized students. They can misguide us into expressing low expectations or blaming families experiencing poverty for the very ways barriers impede their abilities to engage with schools the same way some of us might engage with schools.

Complicating matters, according to Claude Steele (2010), an expert on stereotyping and its dangers, people who are stereotyped are attuned to the ways they are stereotyped. As a result, the *accuracy* of a stereotype about people in poverty might be irrelevant to the *toll* the stereotype exacts on them. He explains:

> whenever we're in a situation where a bad stereotype could be applied to us—such as those about being old, poor, rich, or female—we know it. We know what "people could think." We know that anything we do that fits the stereotype could be taken as confirming it. And we know that, for that reason, we could be judged and treated accordingly. (p. 5)

The weight of this "knowing," of imagining the *possibility* that somebody might target them with a stereotype, can affect students' school performance and emotional well-being, as research on stereotype susceptibility and stereotype threat has demonstrated (e.g., Jaramillo, Mello, & Worrell, 2016; Wasserberg, 2014)—even in young children (Heberle & Carter, 2015). Stereotype threat, according to Bettina Spencer and Emanuele Castano (2007), occurs when people who are marginalized by race, gender, socioeconomic status, or some other identity perform below their potential on an assigned task due to fear that their performance will confirm negative stereotypes about them. The stereotype threat hypothesis might sound farfetched, particularly for those of us who have never been targets of bias. We might wonder how stereotypes can have such an immediate and measureable effect on students. But stereotype threat is real, as evidenced by a robust and constantly growing body of scholarship demonstrating its harm (Steele, 2010).

So our understandings of and attitudes about people experiencing poverty, even if we don't believe we are applying them to individual students, impact students' school engagement and performance. Stereotypes and biases matter. They matter in an extremely practical and immediate way.

CONCLUSION

If we can expunge our negative views, we position ourselves to do a better job recognizing and building on the strengths of students and families. When we let go of the "mindset of poverty" stereotypes, we also position ourselves to see more clearly the barriers families face in their pursuits of educational equity. It's a difficult, critical shift, but one at which educators are especially adept, given our propensities for seeing strengths in every student. If we're willing to do the equity literacy work necessary to make that shift, we can embrace an approach to educational equity that is truly transformative.

In the next chapter we practice that seeing by reviewing the challenges and barriers families experiencing poverty face outside school that inform their school lives.

REFLECTION QUESTIONS AND EXERCISES

1. What stereotypes do you have about people experiencing poverty? Do those stereotypes change as you imagine people experiencing poverty from different racial, ethnic, or religious groups? How will you challenge yourself to let go of those stereotypes?

2. Why do you imagine the "mindset" or "culture" of poverty framework is so popular despite the fact that there is no evidence supporting the idea that people experiencing poverty share a common, predictable culture or mindset? How does this framework lend itself to stereotypes?

3. What are some ways we can challenge stereotypes in our spheres of influence, especially among people who do not see their stereotypes as stereotypes?

Note: Parts of this chapter were adapted from the article "Perceiving the Problem of Poverty and Schooling [Gorski, 2012]," which appeared in *Equity & Excellence in Education, 45*(2), 2012, pp. 302–319.

CHAPTER 6

Class Inequities Beyond School Walls and Why They Matter at School

Principles of equity literacy discussed in this chapter include:

Principle 2: The right to equitable educational opportunity is universal.

Principle 6: We cannot understand the relationship between poverty and education without understanding the barriers and inequities that people experiencing poverty face in and out of schools.

Principle 8: Educational outcome disparities are the result of inequities, of unjust distributions of access and opportunity, not the result of deficiencies in the mindsets, cultures, or grittiness of people experiencing poverty.

I started kindergarten in 1976, a decade before computers began popping up in the homes of families that could afford them, 2 decades before most people had heard of laptops or the Internet. The image of largesse I remember from elementary school is the 64-count box of Crayola crayons—the one with the sharpener in the back. I didn't have precise language for it, but I knew that box symbolized privilege at Guilford Elementary School the same way I knew Air Jordan basketball shoes and Starter jackets signified economic might at Seneca Ridge Middle and Park View High School.

I remember when poster board was a hot commodity, how some classmates trembled when teachers assigned projects requiring its use. I recall the faces of classmates like Melissa and Russell, who were shamed into "outing" themselves as "poor" when the teacher asked, *Who needs help getting poster board?* The teachers I most admired, and this was *most teachers*, were subtler, collecting everybody's crayons at the beginning of the school year and dumping them into community-owned bins or keeping a stash of poster board tucked behind a filing cabinet, distributing it discreetly to students who could not afford it. My own working-class family fell in between. We could afford poster board, a Hong Kong Phooey spiral notebook, or a pack of National Football League pencils, but I settled for the 16-count box of Crayola crayons.

Today I can order 100 sheets of poster board from Amazon.com—10 sheets each in 10 vibrant colors—for $31.03 with shipping and handling. That's 31 cents per sheet. I don't know, all these years later, how much we paid for the poster board in the 1970s. Seventy-nine cents?

My point is, even when the hot commodity was poster board, Melissa and other students who had no say in their families' financial conditions and no control over the affordability of school supplies were at a disadvantage. So too were students who couldn't afford poster board and who, to an even greater degree, couldn't afford the stigma that marks students when teachers ask them to perform their disadvantage by publicly acknowledging their inability to afford poster board. That's when poster board was the hot commodity. Now it's laptop computers. And smartphones.

During a recent visit to a high-poverty middle school, I had an opportunity to hang out with a few dozen 8th-grade students. I had worked with their teachers earlier in the day. I asked the students who among them had a functioning computer and Internet access at home. Only a few raised their hands. Then I asked how many had been assigned homework requiring the use of computers and Internet since the last grading period ended. All of them raised their hands.

Today I can buy a computer from Amazon.com for $639.04, the average cost of the site's five best-selling laptops. These computers do not come with in-home WiFi or Microsoft Office, making them the rough equivalents of one of those boxes of 16 crayons without the sharpener in the back. Despite these limitations, the $639.04 price tag amounts to approximately 2,061 sheets of poster board. And unlike poster board, which our teachers might have required of us a couple of times a year, many students today, including the Melissas and Russells, are expected to have access to computers and WiFi on a regular, if not daily, basis.

As somebody who does have access to these commodities and who has come to take them for granted, it can be difficult to remember that many families experiencing poverty simply cannot afford them. Some families, particularly those who live in the most rural areas, might not even have access to the necessary technological infrastructure for high-speed Internet. Others might own a computer, but cannot afford to repair it when it malfunctions or purchase up-to-date software.

The point is, if we truly want to understand the lives of students experiencing poverty, we must remember that many do not have access to the resources and experiences their wealthier peers enjoy. We must be careful not to interpret the ramifications of this lack of access, like the inability to type assignments, as indications of their attitudes about education, levels of intelligence, or potentials as learners. Rather, these disparities highlight logical, if unjust, outcomes in a society in which access begets access and opportunity begets opportunity, so that advantage and disadvantage compound themselves into ever-widening disparities in access and opportunity (Noguera, 2011).

Many of these disparities fall outside the purview of public schools. As I mentioned earlier, I don't believe that all educators must dedicate their lives to eradicating global poverty; rather, we must recognize and address the effects these disparities have in our classrooms and schools, our spheres of influence. Then, when manageable, we can grow our spheres of influence, perhaps positioning ourselves to chip away at some of the underlying equity issues. However, even modest attempts to quell class disparities are destined to fail if we do not understand their origins. We are destined to fail if we don't acknowledge how, in Worpole's (2000) words, "disadvantaged communities often get penalized twice. Not only do they have to live with fewer economic resources, they . . . almost always live in environments which exact an additional toll on their well-being" (p. 9).

To illustrate this point, below I describe many ways access and opportunity to resources and services that underlie educational engagement are inequitably distributed across the socioeconomic spectrum. I focus here on out-of-school access disparities—the sorts of disparities we might not be able to eliminate, but should take into account in school policy and practice—before turning to in-school access disparities in Chapter 7.

THE UNLEVEL PLAYING FIELD OF POVERTY

Obviously, economically marginalized students do not enjoy the same level of economic support as their wealthier peers. This also means they do not enjoy the same options their wealthier peers enjoy because, as Herbert Gans (1996) explained in *The War Against the Poor*, options are a benefit of wealth. As a result, their access to a wide range of resources and services is limited, not, as the stereotypes go, because they *choose* not to pursue them or are *too lazy* to pursue them, but because they simply cannot *afford* them.

As we strengthen our equity literacy, we begin to see how these disparities are the result of structural disadvantages. These disadvantages, not the cultures or mindsets of the people experiencing them, pose the most significant threats to school engagement and success for students experiencing poverty (Berliner, 2013). Note, again, that none of these barriers are attributable to the cultures, mindsets, or values of families experiencing poverty or to deficiencies in grit.

I have divided them into imperfect overlapping categories, including disparities in access to:

1. living-wage jobs with benefits;
2. health care;

3. adequate and healthy food;
4. stable, affordable, quality housing;
5. healthy living and working environments;
6. recreation and fitness options;
7. community and social services;
8. quality child care;
9. cognitive enrichment resources; and
10. a validating and bias-free society.

Living-Wage Jobs with Benefits

This barrier—the scarcity of living-wage jobs and jobs with benefits—has such a deep and broad impact on families experiencing poverty and their school-age children that we might think of it as the trouble that underlies all troubles. As reported in Chapter 5, most working-age adults experiencing poverty do work. But such a big percentage of newly created jobs pay below a living wage that there aren't enough living-wage jobs for every working-age adult to have one. According to Kids Count (2016), since the economic recession, a majority of newly created jobs pay below a living wage and include few or no benefits.

As long as this is true, many people are going to experience poverty no matter how hard they work. It also means that parents experiencing poverty often have multiple jobs and inconsistent, sometimes chaotic, work schedules, making it harder to spend time with their children or visit their children's schools (Kids Count, 2016). There are other implications, too, like how low wages impact a family's ability to fill their homes with books and other learning materials or how the scarcity of living-wage work forces youth from families experiencing poverty to work so they can support their families' basic needs (Carbis, 2015). To what extent do we take these challenges into account when we schedule opportunities for family engagement or make presumptions about tired students resting their heads on their desks?

Don't overlook the importance of benefits. Consider paid sick, personal, and vacation leave and how important they can be for parents. Then consider this: in the United States, nearly 80% of workers in the highest quintile (upper 20%) of income earners have jobs with paid sick leave, while this is true of only 15% of workers in the lowest quintile of income earners (Glynn, Boushey, & Berg, 2016). Only about 20% of lowest-quintile workers have paid vacation, compared to nearly 80% of workers in the highest-income quintile. Sarah Jane Glynn and her colleagues (2016) offer a pointed bit of equity literacy on the layered implications of this reality:

> Low-wage workers are the least likely to be able to afford to lose a day's wages or to outsource care and household tasks to paid professionals; at the same

time, they are the most likely to take unpaid leave or risk losing their income completely if illness strikes them or a family member or if they experience some other conflict between family caregiving and paid employment. (p. 5)

Health Care

Obviously, access to health care and opportunities to interact with physicians greatly influence families' health (Cutler & Lleras-Muney, 2010). Unfortunately, families experiencing poverty are less likely than their wealthier peers to be able to afford consistent access to health care professionals and less likely to receive care when they need it. But they also have less access to regular checkups and preventive screenings (Centers for Disease Control, 2017), putting them at higher risk of developing more serious ailments from undiagnosed health problems.

Gaps in access to health insurance are beginning to close, which might be a good sign. Unfortunately, although closing or eliminating the gap in access to health insurance alleviates health care discrepancies to some extent, other complexities are in play. For example, having health insurance does not guarantee one's ability to afford a co-pay or secure transportation to a clinic. Nor does it make up for lost wages if somebody without paid leave must take time off work to visit, or take children to visit, a doctor. Imagine, if you haven't experienced it, having to choose between keeping the heat turned on or visiting the doctor because you cannot afford to do both.

The implications of health care disparities are plenty, and they take hold even before children experiencing poverty are born. For example, economically marginalized children are more likely to have been born prematurely and with lower than normal birth weights (Temple, Reynolds, & Arteaga, 2010), largely due to gaps in prenatal care access. As a result, they are born with increased respiratory health risks, a condition exacerbated by their disproportionate exposure to environmental hazards and poor-quality housing (Davis, Gordon, & Burns, 2011), then further exacerbated by inconsistent health care access throughout childhood.

The unfortunate outcomes include high rates of obesity, asthma, diabetes, and neurodevelopmental disorders in students experiencing poverty (Klebanov, Evans, & Brooks-Gunn, 2014; Lineburg & Ratliff, 2015). These conditions can cut into school attendance and focus. When we embrace equity literacy, we learn to see these sorts of implications of poverty, like missing school or coming to school late due to health issues, not as punishable misbehaviors, but instead as barriers to mitigate. That way we can respond to the inequities and barriers rather than blaming families for ways they are already marginalized.

Lack of access to health care also affects economically marginalized families' mental and emotional health (Perrin et al., 2016). As Kimberly

Fulda and her colleagues (2009) found based on their analysis of data from 40,000 participants, youth experiencing poverty are significantly more likely than their peers to have unmet mental health challenges such as depression or anxiety, also putting them at risk of missing school or struggling to concentrate at school. Their finding is especially troubling in light of research demonstrating causal links between stress related to the stigma commonly experienced by economically marginalized students and a wide range of other health concerns (Perrin et al., 2016).

Adequate and Healthy Food

Families experiencing poverty disproportionately face both food insecurity (when a family lacks resources to attain adequate food) and reduced access to healthy food options. Both conditions have been tied to school readiness and performance in early education (Meisenheimer, 2015). For example, food insecurity is associated with iron deficiency, which affects pre-school-aged children's cognitive development (Skalicky et al., 2006).

Lauri Andress and Cindy Fitch (2016) remind us to drop the deficit view of families experiencing poverty and their diets by considering the availability, accessibility, and affordability of healthy food in high-poverty communities. Both food insecurity and insufficient access to healthy food options are tied to societal factors, including the scarcity of living-wage jobs. More directly, eating healthily, consuming organic foods and fresh vegetables, is cost-prohibitive for many families (Cutler & Lleras-Muney, 2010). Big grocery stores are scarce in high-poverty communities (Ghosh-Dastidar et al., 2014), which often forces families to purchase groceries at convenience stores, which, in turn, means they pay more for their groceries than those of us who have access to supermarkets. These conditions disproportionately hurt high-poverty communities, and particularly high-poverty communities of color (Morrissey, Oellerich, Meade, Simms, & Stock, 2016).

DeNeen Brown (2009), who studied this problem in the D.C. metro area, explained,

> You don't have a car to get to a supermarket, much less to Costco or Trader Joe's, where the middle class goes to save money. You don't have three hours to take the bus. So you buy groceries at the corner store, where a gallon of milk costs an extra dollar . . . A loaf of bread there costs you $2.99 for white. For wheat, it's $3.79. The clerk behind the counter tells you the gallon of leaking milk in the bottom of the back cooler is $4.99 . . . The milk is beneath the shelf that holds beef bologna for $3.79. A pound of butter sells for $4.49. In the back of the store are fruits and vegetables. The green peppers are shriveled, the bananas are more brown than yellow, the oranges are picked over. (pp. 7, 8)

In their study of food shopping habits among families experiencing poverty, Andress and Fitch (2016) found that they were on average health-conscious, but they also were forced to be resource-conscious. Unfortunately, despite healthy intentions, the families often had "to concede their food preferences due to personal household determinants related to money and their monthly budget" (p. 154). There, again, are those gaps in access and opportunity.

Meanwhile, fast food restaurants and liquor stores are located disproportionately in high-poverty neighborhoods, where grocery stores are scarce (Ghosh-Dastidar et al., 2014; Pampel, Krueger, Denney, 2010). Economically marginalized communities also are subject to a disproportionate amount of advertisements for fast food (Boggs, 2007). We might think of this as predatory advertising, given the inequitable circumstances.

Stable, Affordable, Quality Housing

Another out-of-school barrier that disrupts economically marginalized students' educational experiences is the scarcity of stable, affordable, quality housing for their families. They move nearly twice as often as wealthier families (Cohen & Wardrip, 2011). Despite the stereotype that families experiencing poverty tend to move due to evictions from unpaid rent, they most often move to follow job opportunities, seek better neighborhoods for raising their children, or escape housing with issues like mold, lack of heat, and vermin infestation (Coulton, Theodos, & Turner, 2012)—common conditions in low-cost housing.

Unfortunately, affordable housing is slim pickings in many areas. According to the National Low-Income Housing Coalition (2016), for every 100 extremely low-income (income 30% of regional median family income) families looking to rent a home, only 31 affordable housing units are available. Creating even more housing instability among families experiencing poverty, during the recent tidal wave of much-reported but underprosecuted predatory lending practices by financial companies, low-income families, especially those of color, were targeted most adamantly (Rugh, Albright, & Massey, 2015).

Unsurprisingly, these barriers create other barriers. Housing instability and the resulting stress have negative impacts on cognitive and social development (Ziol-Guest & McKenna, 2014). Based on their study of 14,000 students in the Cleveland area, Claudia Coulton and her colleagues (2016) concluded that kindergarten readiness was hampered in students experiencing poverty by "cumulative exposure to low-quality housing" (p. 69). Other studies connect residential mobility—having to move—with stalled academic achievement (Schmitt & Lipscomb, 2016).

Notice here, again, that parents want stability for their children. When we find ourselves thinking, *Why don't they just move?*, it's time to tap into our structural view and compassion and ask a different set of questions. For example, *Why, in a society that can afford to provide every family with quality, stable housing, do we choose not to do so?* Remember, as well, that some families do not have housing at all, presenting additional challenges and stressors.

Healthy Living and Working Environments

Disparities in health care and quality housing are exacerbated by other health risks that people experiencing poverty disproportionately face. For example, they experience greater exposure to lead poisoning (Rosner & Markowitz, 2016) and are more likely to live near environmentally hazardous sites, largely because toxic waste dumps and storage facilities for hazardous materials are disproportionately located near high-poverty neighborhoods (Mohai & Saha, 2015), increasing their exposure to toxic levels of radon and carbon monoxide. Overall air and water quality in high-poverty neighborhoods is lower than in wealthier areas (e.g., Clark, Millett, & Marshall, 2014).

Making matters worse, people experiencing poverty are more likely than wealthier people to have jobs exposing them to hazardous materials (Pampel et al., 2010), making health care disparities even more alarming. I remember my coal-miner kin, how every day they, like many low-income laborers, risked work-related injuries. Milbourne (2010) found that these conditions, despite the ways they *target* economically marginalized people, can embolden stereotypes *against* them. This is the backward thinking of deficit ideology.

Intensifying these wellness threats, families experiencing poverty are exposed disproportionately to advertisements promoting unhealthy habits such as smoking (Hillier et al., 2015). However, thanks to their difficulties accessing preventive health care, they experience significantly *less* exposure to warnings about the effects of smoking, unhealthy eating, and a lack of exercise (Siapush, McNeil, Hammond, & Fong, 2006). Devastatingly, even when they are aware of these risks, they are more likely than wealthier people to struggle to afford, say, tobacco cessation aids or memberships in weight-loss programs (Cutler & Lleras-Muney, 2010).

We build our equity literacy when we analyze how we make sense of the symptoms of these inequities. The overweight child from a family experiencing poverty: Would you tend to interpret his weight as irresponsible parenting, or would you first consider that it might be an unfortunate outcome of limited options? It is important to remember that what somebody with more economic stability might interpret as unhealthy choices among healthier options—*Why do they stay in that unhealthy neighborhood? Why do they send potato chips rather than fruit as a snack?*—rarely are markers of bad decisionmaking and usually are the results of limited access to healthier options.

Recreation and Fitness Options

Exacerbating health risks associated with poverty, families experiencing poverty have less access than wealthier families to physically enriching activities and exercise equipment (Brann-Barrett, 2010; Lineburg & Gearheart, 2013). They often cannot afford to participate in organized sports leagues or other formal opportunities for exercise. Youth might struggle to find time for recreational activities, given their greater likelihood of needing to work to help support their families or having to care for younger siblings while parents work. Meanwhile, they are less likely to live near playgrounds or other recreational areas (Evans, Wells, & Schamberg, 2010). Unfortunately, parks and recreation centers located in high-poverty communities are more likely to be in disrepair than those in wealthier areas (Macpherson, Jones, Rothman, Macarthur, & Howard, 2010), putting children using them at risk of injury.

Reflecting on her study of low-income youths' responses to these sorts of neighborhood conditions, Tanya Brann-Barrett (2010), explains,

> What was painful for many was that they remembered when the parks and playground in their neighborhoods were cared for and functioned as places to play and have fun. The now neglected basketball courts with no nets and defunct playgrounds with rusted remnants of equipment are perceived as a visual reminder of how it used to be. These physical illustrations are read by participants as an indication that their communities are forgotten. (p. 11)

Consider the ramifications of these conditions on top of economically marginalized children's decreasing access to physical education in school. (More on this in the next chapter.)

Community and Social Services

Families experiencing poverty disproportionately live in neighborhoods with fewer and lower-quality social services than wealthier families (Meade, 2014). Even the most basic services—water, electricity, or roads—are less attentively maintained in high-poverty communities, as demonstrated by the ongoing water fiasco in Flint, Michigan. Local and state governments tend to invest significantly less in the infrastructure of high-poverty communities than they do in wealthier areas.

Although these disparities are well-documented across many sorts of services, one in which we, as educators, should be particularly interested is the class-tinged disparity in access to libraries. Literacy scholars long have bemoaned the fact that children experiencing poverty have access to fewer books than their wealthier peers, whether at home or elsewhere in their communities (McGill-Franzen & Allington, 2014). After all, access to books is directly related to reading proficiency (Krashen, 2013).

The good news is, in a multinational study, Stephen Krashen and his colleagues (2010) found that public libraries mitigate this disparity, offering children access to a wide variety of media as well as computers and the Internet. Unfortunately, families experiencing poverty have less access than wealthier families to libraries, which are unlikely to be located in high-poverty neighborhoods. When libraries are located nearby, they tend to have shorter hours and fewer resources than libraries in wealthier communities.

Quality Child Care

Child care programs vary widely. Some offer engaging educational experiences, while others are little more than group babysitting services. Programs prioritizing learning and staffed by certified preschool or early childhood educators often are called "high-quality" programs. These programs, usually thriving in wealthier communities, are scarce in high-poverty communities (Hillemeier, Morgan, Farkas, & Maczuga, 2013). Even when high-quality child care programs exist in close enough proximity to high-poverty communities (where people are less likely to own a functioning automobile) to be *physically* accessible to economically marginalized families, they generally are *financially* inaccessible, even to most working-class families and, increasingly, to middle-class families (Children First for Oregon, 2016). CFFO determined that many low-income families in Oregon would have to spend two-thirds of their incomes to afford child care.

Based on their study of 1,364 racially and economically diverse families, Veronique Dupere (2010) and her colleagues concluded that

> children raised in advantaged neighborhoods appear to receive higher quality child care . . . even when family characteristics, such as the quality of the home environment, are held constant. In turn, access to advantaged institutions may explain why children in comparatively advantaged neighborhoods tended to have higher vocabulary and reading scores than their peers in less advantaged neighborhoods. (p. 1241)

Notice, again, that this disparity cannot be understood as a measure of educational commitment or parenting effectiveness. It only can be understood as a reflection of access and opportunity. Unfortunately, conversations about school readiness rarely account for structural conditions like the quality of child care programs to which families have access.

Cognitive Enrichment Resources

I struggled with what to call this kind of access because the common perception about young people's access to "cognitive enrichment" resources sometimes lacks nuance. People in all socioeconomic conditions have access to opportunities for cognitive enrichment. For example, from a young age I developed an ear for the poetic beauty of language listening to my grandma's middle-Appalachian English; today I am a creative writer. I had early opportunities to practice deconstructing complex social conditions while hearing about her decision to pursue a nursing degree the year she turned 50, an experience that continues to inspire my equity work. Of course, these forms of enrichment do not necessarily align with the types of enrichment valued in school settings.

People experiencing poverty have less access than their wealthier peers to cognitive enrichment opportunities that mirror notions of intelligence most rewarded at school. This is especially true for experiences that require financial resources (Lineburg & Ratliff, 2015). After all, some families cannot afford to participate in out-of-school academic training or tutoring, music lessons, athletics, or other extracurricular activities. What makes this disparity in access especially frustrating is that participation in all these activities has been correlated with higher levels of academic achievement and stronger school engagement.

As discussed earlier, youth experiencing poverty also are less exposed to reading than their wealthier peers for similarly complex reasons. According to a report from the Children's Defense Fund (2008), children in poverty are three times as likely as their wealthier peers to not have a parent who regularly reads to them. Additionally, they are less likely to be able to identify the letters of the alphabet or spell their names.

Given these conditions, we might assume that parents in families experiencing poverty do not care as much about their children's literacy development as their wealthier peers. You might be thinking, *Why not make time to read to your child*? But again, if we want to understand these conditions, we have to consider *why* they exist.

For example, one privilege associated with wealth is *time*. The term *time poverty* helps us think of time as a currency to which people experiencing poverty have little access (Williams, Masuda, & Tallis, 2016). As discussed earlier, adults in economically marginalized families often work multiple jobs with chaotic hours. Obviously, they are less likely to be able to afford "help" with housekeeping, lawn maintenance, and home repairs, which could give them more leisure time to read with their children.

Exacerbating time poverty, people experiencing poverty are less likely than wealthier people to have been surrounded with books when they were kids. They are more likely to have experienced challenges with their own literacy. A growing percentage of people experiencing poverty in the United States are immigrants for whom English is a second, third, or fourth language; they likely are learning English—research shows that immigrants to the United States are learning English faster today than any previous generation of immigrants—but may not have the fluency needed to read to their children in English.

In addition to having less access to reading materials, children experiencing poverty have less access to computers and the Internet at home and in their communities (Holmes, Fox, Wieder, & Zubak-Skees, 2016). And when they do have computers and Internet access at home, they tend to use them in less sophisticated ways (Evans, 2004)—this, again, is not a symptom of lower cognitive potential but rather of less access. Not having grown up immersed in the digital world like many of their wealthier peers, low-income youth may not have the skills, familiarity, and confidence to construct and interact with digital platforms. It doesn't help that families experiencing poverty generally cannot afford the growing variety of children's technology camps and other programs that could mitigate these gaps. These conditions limit many young people's access to a slew of learning resources, such as online or computer-based educational games and other interactive media.

A Validating and Bias-Free Society

If bearing the brunt of these opportunity deprivations is not enough, many youth experiencing poverty also weather a storm of bias from the media, peers, and even teachers (Comber, 2016). Unfortunately, perhaps because teachers do not recognize it as readily as some other kinds of bias, when this bullying happens in school it rarely is addressed adequately.

Additionally, people experiencing poverty see few positive reflections of themselves in mainstream media—a situation that is even worse for people of color experiencing poverty (van Doorn, 2015). Most often they are portrayed as intellectually deficient or morally deviant (Kendall, 2011). Even when some characters display resilience and strength, they almost always are balanced by characters that embody the stereotypes discussed in Chapter 5. Think *Shameless* or *Justified*. Maura Kelly (2010), studying television news portrayals of women in poverty, found the exact same thing.

Alarmingly, negative portrayals of people experiencing poverty also infest educational materials, including children's books (Kelley & Darragh, 2011). Even if we cannot control the larger media, we can decide right now to do whatever we can to bolster our equity literacy so we can spot and address these negative depictions. Silence looks to students like complicity.

WHY THE "ACHIEVEMENT GAP" IS REALLY AN *OPPORTUNITY* GAP

Health care, safe recreational facilities, supermarkets, WiFi access: Which of these resources do you take for granted? How might your life be different without them? How might their absence have affected your ability to meet your full potential at school?

I think of these disparities in terms of a metaphorical toolbox. All people, regardless of their families' economic conditions, begin gathering tools literally from the moment of conception. Some are material, such as access to financial support or WiFi. Some are service-oriented, like access to prenatal care or a speech pathologist. Others are experiential, like access to the arts, or educational, like access to tutors. Still others, such as a feeling of interconnectedness, are dispositional.

Those dispositional tools are important. They equip us with the attitudes and understandings that help us thrive. The trouble is, even if a student experiencing poverty has all the "right" dispositions, the impact of the other disparities is still there. As discussed earlier, grit or growth mindset is no threat to inequities in access to health care, quality child care, or healthy food options. This is why the condition we call an "achievement gap" is more rightly understood as an *opportunity* gap. After all, these disparities have nothing to do with student effort or intelligence or with families' attitudes about school. They only reflect students' disparate levels of access to the resources and opportunities other students, no smarter or more dedicated to school, enjoy. We have decided as a society to put more access in some students' toolboxes than others', often based on identities like socioeconomic status, race, gender identity or expression, and immigrant status. We pretend to offer *equal opportunity*, then blame people whose toolboxes we've least filled for not doing as well as those whose toolboxes we filled to the brim. If we care about educational equity, we must grapple with why these conditions exist at all. We then need to grapple with how we might re-create them, even if unintentionally, in our own spheres of influence. (Chapter 7, coming up next, will get us started.)

The best way to strengthen our equity literacy around these barriers is to consider their effects both as individual and as accumulative sets of conditions. Any one of these access disparities can have a substantial impact on students, but when we look at them together we begin to understand why neurological research has become an important part of the poverty and education conversation. The accumulation of access disparities creates tremendous stress for many families experiencing poverty. This stress, along with disparities in access to healthy food, health care, and the sorts of cognitive enrichment rewarded in schools, have measurable effects on children's brains. The effects can begin as early as pregnancy (Lefmann & Combs-Orme, 2014).

Researchers have called the result of persistent adversity based on the accumulation of these inequities and of coping with other forms of discrimination *toxic stress*. They have found that eventually this accumulation impacts neuroanatomy and brain functioning (Perrin et al., 2016). It literally changes people's brains.

It can be tempting to wiggle ourselves out of considering what these out-of-school disparities and the toxic stress they create for many students mean for us as educators. With all the talk about grit and growth mindset, we might take any one of these barriers and think that with a little perseverance students experiencing poverty can overcome the mess of inequity. We might, in our search for an easy solution, soak up all the brain research and think we can institute a couple pedagogical shifts or a grit initiative and fix students' "ailing" brains. Certainly, some pedagogical shifts can help. However, harkening back to our discussion of deficit ideology, the allure of these notions can tug us away from seeing the big picture, from considering how we might change what we're doing to be responsive to these barriers before putting the pressure back on our most marginalized students to power through barriers they should never have had to experience.

CONCLUSION

Remember, we chip away at the opportunity gap first and foremost by redistributing access and opportunity in our spheres of influence. We protect inequity when we leave the current access and opportunity distribution unchanged, then help students learn how to cope with inequity. This is why the trendy focus on brain research is both important and inadequate. It, too, should be filtered through an equity view, or it threatens to obscure the inequities that ought to be the central focus of our equity attention.

Next, in Chapter 7, we examine how inequities described in this chapter are reproduced within school walls. Equipped with that knowledge, we move, in Chapters 8, 9, and 10, into strategy mode, responding to and redressing these inequities.

REFLECTION QUESTIONS AND EXERCISES

1. This chapter covered 10 examples of barriers and inequities families experiencing poverty face outside school that have measurable effects on their engagement and performance in school. Identify at least two additional barriers and inequities pressing upon families experiencing poverty not addressed in this chapter. How might they impact educational engagement and performance?

2. The barriers discussed in this chapter might appear outside the spheres of influence of most educators. For each of the 10 barriers, identify at least one way educators and schools could be *responsive to* these barriers even if educators and schools cannot completely *eliminate* any of them. What sorts of policies and practices might we employ to ensure that we are not replicating the effects of these barriers in our classrooms and schools?

3. How might discussing what traditionally has been called the *achievement gap* as the *opportunity gap* change the way we understand the problem of disparate educational outcomes across socioeconomic status?

CHAPTER 7

The Achievement—
er, *Opportunity*—Gap in School

Principles of Equity Literacy discussed in this chapter include:

Principle 2: The right to equitable educational opportunity is universal.

Principle 6: We cannot understand the relationship between poverty and education without understanding the barriers and inequities that people experiencing poverty face in and out of schools.

Principle 7: Test scores are inadequate measures of equity.

Principle 8: Educational outcome disparities are the result of inequities, of unjust distributions of access and opportunity, not the result of deficiencies in the mindsets, cultures, or grittiness of people experiencing poverty.

Here is how the Scholastic Aptitude Test (SAT) and the American College Testing (ACT) test work. Imagine one student, Evelyn, born in a high-poverty neighborhood to an economically marginalized family—perhaps to a single mother. She has no say in her socioeconomic status. She learns in school that the United States is a meritocracy, but she grows up with little access to preventive health care, stable housing, or green spaces where she can run and play. Her mother works hard. She has two jobs. Between those jobs, cooking, and cleaning, she has little time to read to Evelyn or help her with homework, and little money to buy her a roomful of books and a computer. Evelyn and her friends spend 13 years, from kindergarten to 12th grade, attending their neighborhood schools, which receive some Title funds as high-poverty schools. Still, compared with students at district schools in the wealthier part of town, Evelyn's schools have fewer advanced courses, more rote pedagogies, larger class sizes, and less access to the arts. She struggles in math. Her teachers are willing to help, but Evelyn takes the bus to school, so coming early or staying after school for help aren't options. Unfortunately, her mother can't afford to hire a math tutor, which is especially unfortunate because in a few weeks she is scheduled to take the SAT test.

Imagine another student, Allison, born in an upper-middle class neighborhood to an economically privileged family—perhaps to a single mom. She has no say in her socioeconomic status. She learns in school that the United States is a meritocracy, and all evidence points to this being true. Her mother works hard. She has one full-time job with benefits including health care and paid leave. Allison grows up seeing a doctor whenever she needs to and at least once a year just for a checkup. She lives in a community with a lot of green space in a house full of books. She's never known life without her own computer and tablet. Allison and her friends spend 13 years in well-resourced schools with fully equipped science labs, manicured athletic fields, and wide ranges of advanced courses and extracurricular activities. She struggles in math. Throughout high school her mother has paid $60 per hour once a week for a private tutor. With the SAT test around the corner, her mother has added a second day of math tutoring each week as well as an SAT prep class.

In the name of equality, in about 1 month Evelyn and Allison will receive the same SAT test. The test will determine their levels of access to higher education. What is the single variable that best predicts how well people do on the SAT test? Family income. Does that sound like meritocracy to you? Does it sound like equity?

As this story illustrates, one reason standardized tests don't work well for assessing students' aptitudes, besides the fact that it makes little sense to assess people the way we assess widgets, is that the tests don't measure what we might think they measure (Toch, 2011). More than ability, aptitude, or learning potential, they measure the opportunity and access test-takers have enjoyed up to test time. A considerable portion of this opportunity and access is linked to resources and services described in Chapter 6. How many academic enrichment camps could their families afford? How many books? Did their parents have ample leisure time to read to them or help with their homework, or were they working evening hours at a second or third job, a result of the scarcity of living-wage work?

Another portion of the opportunity gap relates more directly to educational access disparities, or differences between school and school-related experiences available to families in different economic situations. As Pedro Noguera and Antwi Akom (2000) explained, "An analysis of test scores . . . reveals a close correspondence between the scores children obtain and broader patterns of social inequality. With few exceptions, children of the affluent outperform children of the poor" (p. 29). In my experience, we do a decent job acknowledging their second sentence. It's consideration of their first sentence that so often is omitted from conversations about poverty and education.

Complicating attempts to understand access disparities are the popular beliefs briefly mentioned in Chapter 1, that education is the "great equalizer" and public schooling is meritocracy in its purest form. Access to public schooling, this line of thinking goes, counteracts the many disadvantages with which people experiencing poverty contend, assuming they work their buns off to achieve "academic success." The trouble with the "great equalizer" notion is that it presumes a level playing field, where economically marginalized students have access to the same educational opportunities as their wealthier peers. It seems we're desperate to grasp onto the idea that education itself is a panacea for poverty.

Wouldn't it be great if that were true? It's not (Katz, 2015). The inequities many families in poverty face outside school are reproduced with great precision inside schools. Schools, since the birth of public education, have been sites of social *reproduction* rather than leveling (Bourdieu, 1982). If we continue the way we're going, schools will continue reproducing, rather than mitigating, existing patterns of poverty and inequity, as Peter Cookson (2013) explains:

> When the birth lottery and educational stratification meet, the result is a social class sorting and selection machine that consistently reproduces class differences. . . . Advantage is a cumulative process, as is disadvantage; the process of rewarding and punishing children based on their parents' wealth and social status begins at birth. . . . . [S]chools . . . accelerate advantage and disadvantage by channeling, legitimating, and credentializing as objective successes the cultural achievements of the advantaged and discarding and delegitimizing the cultural achievements of the disadvantaged. (p. 15)

Luckily, in our own spheres of influence we can decide whether to comply with or challenge these conditions. First, we need to understand how they operate.

Start with what we know. Researchers for decades have documented the relationship between socioeconomic status and a variety of measures of academic achievement and educational attainment, including standardized test scores and graduation rates (Reardon, 2013)—what we commonly, and as I have argued, mistakenly, call the "achievement gap." Reading, writing, math, graduation rates: If we know anything about poverty and education, we know that on average students experiencing poverty do not do as well as wealthier students in any of these areas. As we learned in the previous chapter, these conditions can be traced in large part to inequities in families' access to a wide variety of resources and services outside school, such as preventive health care, housing stability, and living-wage work.

In this chapter we turn to the educational opportunity gap: the troubling ways youth experiencing poverty are denied the educational opportunities more likely granted to more affluent youth. These are the kinds of disparities against which many students must struggle to succeed academically once they enter our classroom, school, office, or other sphere of influence. This is our last bad news chapter.

But hold tight, because later, in Chapters 8 through 11, we explore research-driven strategies for eliminating, or at least mitigating, the atrocities described in this chapter.

THE GREAT UN-EQUALIZER?

By 2013, 52% of students in U.S. public schools were eligible for free or reduced-price lunch (Suitts, 2016), up from 32% in 1989 (Suitts, 2013). We know, again, that on average these students miss more school, fare worse on standardized tests and in classes, experience lower rates of validation and affirmation and higher rates of bias and bullying, and leave school without graduating at significantly higher rates than their wealthier peers. While it's true that a select few schools and districts are finding ways to close or, very occasionally, eliminate these disparities at least temporarily—we will explore some of the strategies they've used in the next few chapters—the bigger picture is clear: Students experiencing poverty do not perform as well in school on average as wealthier students.

We looked at some bigger structural reasons for these disparities in Chapter 6—conditions we can mitigate through policy and practice, but not necessarily eliminate, as they primarily exist outside our spheres of influence. How do we, as educators and policymakers, reproduce these barriers and inequities within classrooms and schools? In this chapter we account for this reproduction in an equity literacy quest to become reproduction disrupters.

First, it's important to acknowledge here, again, that there will be dimensions of the educational opportunity gap that some readers might consider outside their spheres of influence. For example, maybe you do not decide which schools individual students attend or how those schools are resourced. However, as with all those out-of-school challenges described in Chapter 6, one important way to understand and forge meaningful relationships with students and families experiencing poverty is to understand as completely as possible how they experience schools, including how they experience school conditions we do not control. Unfortunately, there is no way to do this without considering some harsh realities. *There is no path to equity that does not include a direct confrontation with inequity.* Fortunately, by equipping ourselves with these understandings, we're also equipping ourselves to respond to and redress these harsh realities in informed and effective ways.

For example, examining elements of the educational opportunity gap can help us better understand the relationship between poverty and school performance. We might imagine the relationship as a simple cause-and-effect sort of thing: Poverty causes low levels of reading proficiency. However, this view is too simplistic; it fails to consider important contextual factors related to poverty that affect students' performance. Instead, as we consider educational access disparities, we might work to recognize the relationship between poverty and school performance as a chain of conditions, as Joseph Flessa (2007) invites us to do. He explains:

> One might link poverty to lack of employment opportunities that pay a living wage, in turn to a family's need to move frequently, in turn to inconsistent school attendance, in turn to low reading scores; or one might link poverty to economically segregated neighbourhoods to low school quality to novice teachers to low reading scores. (p. 10)

With these complexities in mind, we now turn to the many dimensions of the educational opportunity gap, including disparities in access to:

1. preschool;
2. well-funded schools;
3. adequately resourced schools;
4. shadow education;
5. school support services;
6. affirming school environments;
7. high academic expectations;
8. well-paid, certified, and experienced teachers;
9. student-centered, higher-order curricula and pedagogies;
10. opportunities for family involvement; and
11. instructional technologies.

Preschool

Brain development during children's earliest years is critical. It influences their rates of cognitive development throughout their lives (Hair, Hanson, Wolfe, & Pollack, 2015). This does not mean that children who have been denied early access to, say, opportunities to build literacy skills lack the *potential* to excel academically. It only means that they will begin that pursuit at a disadvantage, and through no fault of their own. And because disadvantage begets more disadvantage when not interrupted by an opportunity intervention, early intervention is essential to eliminating the educational opportunity gap (Duncan, Magnuson, Kalil, & Ziol-Guest, 2012).

Unfortunately, in the same way families experiencing poverty lack access to quality child care, they lack access to quality preschool, if they can afford any preschool at all (Waldfogel & Putnam, 2016). Recent studies show that about 72% of preschool-age children living in homes with family incomes at least twice the federal poverty line attend preschool, compared with only 46% of children whose family incomes fall below the poverty line (Child Trends, 2014). In another example of intersectionality, immigrant children in low-income families have even less access to quality early childhood education than their nonimmigrant peers (Karoly & Gonzalez, 2011). Moreover, when economically marginalized families do have access to formal preschool programs, the programs to which they have access tend to be of lower quality than the programs attended by wealthier children.

It might be easy to cite these conditions, like so many of the societal conditions discussed earlier, as further evidence that people experiencing poverty don't value education. *Why don't parents enroll their kids in better preschools?* you might wonder. *Why don't they make preschool a priority?*

Like high-quality child care, high-quality preschool with certified teachers, well-equipped learning centers, and advanced pedagogical methods, is cost-prohibitive for most families experiencing poverty (and even most working-class families) when not provided free by local school districts. Because many preschools do not offer busing service, the simple act of transporting children to and from a preschool is a challenge for many families experiencing poverty, particularly if the school is beyond walking distance of their homes (Karoly & Gonzalez, 2011).

Other barriers exist as well. For some immigrant families experiencing poverty, language is a barrier to enrolling children in preschool (Gelatt, Adams, & Huerta, 2014). Sometimes they also contend with bias among early childhood education staff, part of a larger pattern of alienation experienced disproportionately not only by many people experiencing poverty, but also People of Color, people with (dis)abilities and learning differences, transgender people, and LGBQ people, among others (Gilliam, Maupin, Reyes, Accavitti, & Shic, 2016).

Well-Funded Schools

In *Savage Inequalities: Children in America's Schools*, former teacher Jonathan Kozol (2012) detailed the many ways schools attended predominantly by children from families experiencing poverty are grossly underfunded, even when compared with wealthier schools a few miles away. Even today, high-poverty schools, generally identified as those in which a majority of students are eligible for free or reduced-price lunch, receive significantly less funding on average than schools with wealthier student bodies. Based on their analysis for the Education Trust, Natasha Ushomirsky and David Williams (2015) found that, on average, districts in the United States with the highest poverty rates receive $1,200 less in funding per student per academic year than districts with the lowest poverty rates. Demonstrating the race/class intersection, they also found that districts serving the highest percentage of Students of Color received on average $2,000 less per pupil than those serving the highest percentages of White students.

In part these disparities result from the inequitable practice of funding schools with property taxes, all but ensuring an opportunity gap. In fact, the United States is unique among industrialized countries in its failure to centralize school funding and to primarily rely, instead, on state and local funding. So even when we look at the investments different states make in public school students, inequities abound (U.S. Census Bureau, 2015), as shown in Figure 7.1.

For many of us, the term *high-poverty schools* evokes images of urban students—perhaps, more specifically, urban Students of Color. But the savage inequalities of underfunding, like all aspects of the opportunity gap, wreak similar havoc on rural schools. Rural communities, like their inner-city and predominantly of-color counterparts, often do not enjoy educational funding levels comparable with nonrural districts, even within their own states (Strange, 2011). Consider the case of Lake View, Arkansas, a rural district comprised almost entirely of families experiencing poverty. In 2001, 18 years after the state claimed to have changed its school funding policy when the old policy was ruled unconstitutional by the state Supreme Court, the community was forced to take the state, under Governor Mike Huckabee, back to court for continuing to cheat economically marginalized rural families out of the levels of funding it granted wealthier districts. The case, *Lake View v. Huckabee,* ascended back to the Supreme Court, which found in the district's favor. Testimony showed that the Lake View schools could afford only one mathematics teacher. The teacher was unlicensed and paid as a long-term substitute while doubling as a school bus driver,

Figure 7.1. Top and Bottom Five Average Per-Pupil Spending in Public Schools by State, 2013

Geographic Area	Per-pupil spending
United States	$10,700
Top Five	
New York	19,818
Alaska	18,175
Washington, D.C.	17,953
New Jersey	17,572
Connecticut	16,631
Bottom Five	
Mississippi	8,130
Oklahoma	7,672
Arizona	7,208
Idaho	6,791
Utah	6,555

Based on data from the U.S. Census Bureau (2015), *Public Education Finances: 2013.*

earning roughly $15,000 per year. Unfortunately, Arkansas responded, not by equalizing funding, but by shuttering the district, merging it with other nearby districts (Strange, 2011).

You might be thinking, *What about Title I (of the Elementary and Secondary Education Act)?* Title I, like some other programs, provides supplemental funding to schools and districts serving large numbers of economically vulnerable families. However, on average these funds only provide a boost of about $500 per pupil (Dynarski & Kainz, 2015), hardly offsetting the many other inequitable conditions with which high-poverty schools contend, such as lower levels of overall funding or the need to commit more resources to basic building maintenance. Also, as Goodwin Liu (2008) demonstrated in his analysis of allocations of Title I funds, there are serious inequities even in how these funds are dispersed. He explained, "In particular, small or mid-sized districts that serve half or more of all poor children in areas of high poverty receive less aid than larger districts with comparable poverty" (p. 973).

Adequately Resourced Schools

It stands to reason that lower-funded schools will be less adequately resourced than well-funded schools disproportionately situated in wealthy neighborhoods. It comes as no big surprise, then, that students in high-poverty schools are more likely than peers attending low-poverty schools to be taught using insufficient or outdated classroom materials in inadequate learning facilities, such as science labs (Kids Count, 2016). Kozol (2012) mentions these sorts of disparities as well among the "savage inequalities" of public schooling.

It might be hard to imagine how such glaring inequities persist in public education even as we call it the great equalizer. The explanations are many and varied. For example, schools in higher-income neighborhoods tend to be newer than those in low-income neighborhoods, requiring fewer resources for general upkeep. Parents in wealthier districts are more likely to have the resources and time to raise money for everything from state-of-the-art learning materials to additional teachers. They also have more power to lobby and pressure school boards and other decisionmaking bodies. Additionally, because affluent parents are more likely to have time, resources, and paid leave to volunteer in their children's schools, they can help create time for teachers to work on grant-writing and other activities that could increase students' access to learning resources and opportunities.

The resource disparities affect students experiencing poverty in other ways as well. For example, as we learned in Chapter 6, libraries can play a mitigating role, shrinking the portion of the opportunity gap created by the fact that economically marginalized students have less access to books than their wealthier peers. They *can*. Unfortunately, they usually *don't*. Libraries in high-poverty schools have fewer books on average than libraries in wealthier schools (Allington & McGill-Franzen, 2015). Sadly, in a study conducted in the Los Angeles metro area, Rebecca Constantino (2005) found that in some communities wealthy families had access to more books at home than families in poverty had access to at home and school combined.

Certainly, some students experiencing poverty do not attend dilapidated schools with Mini-Me libraries and no microscope in sight. In fact, as increasing numbers of economically marginalized families move to the suburbs, a trend we explored in Chapter 3, a growing population of students experiencing poverty attend schools that, until recently, might have been considered bastions of economic privilege. However, despite shifting demographics in some districts, research shows that an overall *re*-segregation of public schools along class lines has been in full effect for the last 25 years (Owens, Reardon, & Jencks, 2016), mirroring simultaneous trends toward racial re-segregation (Rothstein, 2013). Starting in preschool (Wright, 2011), students in many parts of the country attend schools that are more class- and race-segregated than local schools were *before Brown v. Board of Education.*

Shadow Education

Shadow education refers to informal educational programs designed either to remediate or support formal schooling (Buchmann, Condron, & Roscigno, 2010). The SAT or ACT test prep course you and Allison took, if your family could afford to sign you up for one, is shadow education. Academic camps for children at the local college or university are examples of shadow education, too. Another example, the most common form of shadow education, is the private tutoring industry (Bray, 2013), with its colorful brochures and exorbitant fees.

Even as it flourishes into an expansive industry, I rarely hear references to shadow education in conversations about educational outcome disparities. This is partially why it's called *shadow* education: It takes place in the shadow of formal schooling, out of public sight lines. We may not always know which of our students are participating in shadow programs. Systemically speaking, nobody is weighing schools' test scores or schools' yearly progress based on who can afford summer academic camps and private tutoring. Perhaps we should, though, because these programs make a considerable difference in academic performance.

The trouble from an equity perspective is that some families, by virtue of their wealth, have greater access to shadow education than others. Considering the cost of some of these programs—summer technology camps, for instance—some students, like Evelyn, have considerably less access to shadow education, not because they don't want to bolster their learning with a math camp or calculus tutor, but because their families are priced out of the shadow education marketplace. This discrepancy begins early with camps, tutors, music lessons, and other experiences. It accumulates throughout students' educational careers, particularly as they approach high school graduation. Wealthy families literally can purchase higher achievement for their children.

Good for them if they choose to do so, but we should be careful about how we interpret outcome disparities when "achievement" is attached to affordability. As with many dimensions of the opportunity gap, we have little control over whether students' families can afford shadow education programs. However, we do have control over whether we consider this and other access discrepancies as we form perceptions of students and initiatives for erasing the opportunity gap.

School Support Services

All students ought to have access to basic support services at school, like those provided by school counselors and nurses. As we know, students experiencing poverty are more likely than wealthier students to need these services, and to need them more often, not because they are inherently "deficient," but because their families are less likely to be able to afford physical or mental health care, counseling, and other types of services that many wealthier families take for granted. Unfortunately and astoundingly, students experiencing poverty also have less access to these services at school than their wealthier peers.

For example, high-poverty schools commit fewer resources on average to college counseling than wealthier schools (DeLuca et al., 2016). *Obviously,* you might be thinking. *Students from families experiencing poverty attend college at lower rates than wealthier students.* True. There is a discrepancy in college attendance rates across socioeconomic status. The question is, *Why?*

Cost, or perceived cost, is one barrier. Even if they want to attend college, economically marginalized students are less likely to see it as a realistic possibility, financially speaking (Radford, 2013). In this sense, their lack of access to college counseling, a service that could mitigate these concerns by helping them explore financial aid options, is an equally formidable barrier. Ellen Amatea and Cirecie West-Olatunji (2007) extend the conversation beyond college counseling by urging school counselors to imagine a wide variety of ways they can support students experiencing poverty, from challenging deficit views to helping foster a family-friendly school culture. Unfortunately, school counselors are not immune from funding cuts, so they are becoming scarcer and scarcer in schools.

Students attending high-poverty schools also have less access to school nurses than their peers at wealthier schools. High-poverty schools are more likely than wealthier schools not to have a nurse on staff, and if they do, they tend to have greater pupil-to-nurse ratios (Berliner, 2009). This disparity has important implications. School nurses play a key role in addressing student health concerns that affect learning and school performance, especially for students experiencing poverty (Maughan, 2016). Studies have shown that access to school nurses improves school attendance rates by minimizing lost time due to illness (DeSocio & Hootman, 2004). Similarly, a study of more than 16,000 elementary school students (Baisch, Lundeen, & Murphy, 2011) showed that access to school nurses has a positive effect on students' immunization rates.

Recognizing the importance of student access to school nurses, several health care associations, including the American Academy of Pediatrics, the American School Health Association, and the National Association of School Nurses, have advocated placing a nurse in every school (Baisch et al., 2011). Unfortunately, like counselors, school nurses often are budget cut casualties, a trend disproportionately affecting the highest-poverty schools and districts.

Affirming School Environments

Safety and inclusivity are popular themes in conversations about diversity and education. Educators are responsible, at the very least, for ensuring students have access to learning environments free from bias, harassment, and bullying. Do students experiencing poverty in your sphere of influence have access to such an environment?

Perhaps some do. On average, though, there are many reasons students experiencing poverty might feel less connected and affirmed at school than their wealthier peers. Part of the challenge we face responding to and redressing this disparity is that even if we are trying to provide safe, equitable learning environments, we are not always privy to the ways students experience bias and invalidation. We aren't always in earshot of students' interactions with other students or with adults in our schools.

For example, as we learned in Chapter 6, economically marginalized students are more likely than wealthier students to be bullied. Most of this bullying happens beyond the earshot of adults. In an ethnographic study of economically marginalized youth, Tanya Brann-Barrett (2010) learned that many struggled to fit in at school because they couldn't afford what their peers considered fashionable clothes, an experience about which they would be unlikely to talk with teachers. This is one among many reasons I discourage educators from complimenting students on material possessions like name-brand clothes. We don't need to encourage the bullying students experiencing poverty already face for their clothes or other material possessions (Carbis, 2015).

On the other hand, low-income students experience other forms of bias to which we *are* privy, sometimes of our own doing. Consider, for example, class bias in learning materials (Kelley & Darragh, 2011). This brand of bias begins in the earliest grades, according to Stephanie Jones (2008), who synthesized research on picture books and found consistently biased portrayals of economically marginalized families. She pointed out an example of what some people call the *null* or *omitted* curriculum, explaining that there is a "great void in children's literature," a lack of "everyday stories of working-class and poor families' lives that validate and value daily living experiences including the happy, sad, ecstatic, tragic, and the mundane" (p. 46). Illustrating another example of intersectionality, literature written for English language learners contains a particularly egregious amount of class bias (Sano, 2009).

If bias in learning materials isn't enough to make economically marginalized students feel disconnected, the conditions of the schools some of them attend could do so. For example, students experiencing poverty are more likely than their wealthier peers to attend schools with cockroach and rat infestations or with dirty or inoperative student bathrooms. They are more likely to have bigger class sizes, less experienced teachers, and fewer extracurricular activities (Jackson, Johnson, & Persico, 2015; Phillips & Putnam, 2016).

Finally, studies continue to show significant levels of class bias and deficit ideology in teachers, counselors, and other authority figures with whom students interact (Bray & Schommer-Aikins, 2014; Mundy & Leko, 2015). Most troubling about the persistence of these attitudes is that they are not reserved for raging bigots. Many of us presumably well-intended educators have them, too, even if we see ourselves as equity champions. Make no mistake: Students see our biases, which is why thinking we can change this or that practice without confronting our attitudes and ideologies does not— *cannot*—work. If we aren't vigilant, we might be doing damage we never wanted to do by subtly shaming or humiliating students in ways we never intended to shame or humiliate them, sometimes through actions we thought were helpful.

As Melanie Cloutier-Bordeleau (2015) explains, based on her school life as a child in an economically marginalized family, "When teachers would say things along the lines of 'if you don't have the money for whatever reason, or you are unable to afford it . . .' it only deterred me even more from engaging in conversation, because in statements like these lie undertones of pity and the simultaneous projection of shame" (p. 98). In Chapter 9 we examine this and the other repressive practices that humiliate students by forcing them to perform their poverty publicly.

High Academic Expectations

In my experience, people who choose an education career overwhelmingly are committed to helping each student thrive in school. Why work in schools otherwise? Unfortunately, as over a decade of research shows, despite this commitment, educators in a variety of roles regularly show lower academic expectations for students experiencing poverty than for economically privileged students. Sometimes low expectations are a matter of bias about who is capable of what kinds of learning. These sorts of low expectations might reflect our attitudes about why people are in poverty to begin with. Sometimes, though, low expectations can emanate from good intentions, such as when we desire not to put too much pressure on students who we worry are overburdened in other areas of their lives.

Whatever our intentions, low teacher expectations are bad for students, and high expectations breed stronger student performance (Boser, Wilhelm & Hanna, 2014) regardless of socioeconomic status. Patterns of low expectations help explain some of the behaviors popularly associated with economically marginalized families. For example, students experiencing poverty are less likely than their wealthier peers to experience positive reinforcement from teachers (Parrett & Budge, 2012). They regularly are steered away from advanced and honors classes and toward less rigorous classes, even when their grades do not warrant it (Latz & Adams, 2011). They disproportionately are labeled learning-disabled (Loughan & Perna, 2012) as well. And, illustrating another intersection of race and class inequity, in their study of teacher expectations for low-income Mexican American students, Rebecca and Encarnacion Garza (Garza & Garza, 2010) found that teachers regularly expressed high expectations for them in the short term, mostly around standardized test performance. However, teachers tended to display low long-term expectations for them regarding their abilities to succeed in college or secure anything other than minimum-wage work. These sorts of long-term low expectations, they shared, help explain why the most economically marginalized students are subject on average to the most lower-order pedagogies.

You might be thinking, *Well, yes, they disproportionately do not perform as well as wealthier students, so it makes sense that they are more likely to be placed in remedial classes with less rigorous curricula.* As an exercise in equity literacy, consider how the cycle works. First, consider that this sort of ability grouping, whether formal or informal, is tinged with bias (Latz & Adams, 2011). The U.S. Department of Education (2003) reported that 10% of teachers make about 80% of special education referrals. It might be easy, even commonsensical, to interpret the disproportionate number of students experiencing poverty in special education or remedial tracks as evidence of lower academic ability, lower levels of motivation, or other "weaknesses" attributed to high-poverty communities. But what if it's something else? For example, what if our processes for determining who is grouped where are based largely on measures that approximate students' levels of access and opportunity and not their potential or intelligence?

Well-Paid, Certified, and Experienced Teachers

Like most of their colleagues in wealthier schools, teachers who work in high-poverty schools are determined to help students succeed. In fact, it would be easy to argue that teachers who choose to work in high-poverty schools even when they have opportunities to work in wealthier schools demonstrate a unique sort of commitment to educational equity. Sadly, most teachers with an opportunity to move from high-poverty schools to low-poverty schools do just that. This often leaves schools in the most economically repressed communities struggling to hire and retain fully certified, experienced teachers. One result is a disproportionately high proportion of new teachers working in high-poverty schools (Gagnon & Mattingly, 2012). Another is a disproportionately high teacher turnover rate in high-poverty schools (Goldring, Taie, & Riddles, 2014).

High-poverty schools also have greater percentages of uncertified teachers teaching core subject courses (Glazerman & Max, 2011). To be sure, pay, experience, and even certification are not always good predictors of effective teaching. I would never make presumptions about a teacher's effectiveness based on these factors alone. However, if we consider the accumulative pattern of disparities in the distribution of teachers, students experiencing poverty are considerably more likely than their wealthier peers to have a steady stream of teachers teaching outside their certification areas and with little formal training.

It might be tempting to see disparities as implicating teachers. However, these conditions often reflect the impact of *disaffected* teachers who share students' frustrations about being in underresourced schools. Let's be careful not to mistakenly redirect the deficit lens off families and onto one another.

Student-Centered, Higher-Order Curricula and Pedagogies

Students experiencing poverty have less access than their wealthier peers to the student-centered, higher-order curricula and pedagogies that encourage deep learning and foster student engagement (Battey, 2013; Dudley-Marling, 2015). They are assigned disproportionately to schools offering few, if any, college preparatory or honors classes (Gándara, 2010), the types of classes in which higher-order, constructivist, provocative pedagogies are most commonly used. Meanwhile, economically marginalized students are more likely to be subject to rote-like or "skill-and-drill" instruction, the kinds of teaching students themselves report as unengaging and ineffective (Cookson, 2013; Shields, 2014). These disparities exist not only *between* high-poverty and low-poverty schools, but also *within* mixed-income schools, where students experiencing poverty are disproportionately assigned to or "grouped" in lower academic tracks. Figure 7.2 compares higher-order and lower-order learning activities.

Figure 7.2. Higher- and Lower-Order Thinking Activities

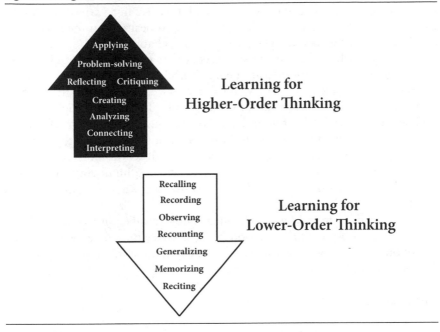

The overemphasis on direct instruction in high-poverty schools and classrooms is only one example of this phenomenon, but it's a particularly pertinent example. We know, based on 15 years of research on the effectiveness of various pedagogical models, that *some* direct instruction and even some amount of the dreaded skill-and-drill approach can help students acquire basic skills or knowledge, especially if that instruction is followed by opportunities to *apply* what they learn in relevant, engaging ways. However, we also know that an overemphasis on direct instruction robs students of opportunities to learn deeply and comprehensively. For example, according to Stephen Krashen and his colleagues (2010), direct instruction can, at least in the short term, improve the mechanics of student reading, but it does not improve reading comprehension or scores on assessments that "require children to understand what they read" (p. 28).

It's worth mentioning again: These pedagogical disparities are not, as one might suspect, purely an indication of the abilities or commitments of teachers. For example, teachers in high-poverty schools often feel intensified pressures to teach to the test or rely heavily on direct instruction, sometimes based on administrators' orders. Teachers who teach predominantly low-income students also contend with larger class sizes than their colleagues at higher-income schools (Kids Count, 2016), which could make them more uneasy about implementing higher-order pedagogies than, say, colleagues who teach 12 students at a time at the wealthiest independent schools. In other words, in my experience working with teachers in a variety of schools, this is less an indication of teacher capacity and desire than the result of a combination of the inequities described in this chapter.

Of course, the impact is the same regardless of the cause. Students experiencing poverty know they are being shortchanged, denied access to the instructional engagement their wealthier peers enjoy. In fact, in a recent focus group study of economically marginalized students, Michelle Fine and her colleagues (2016) found that students considered the hyperfocus on high-stakes testing at their schools "a betrayal of teaching as a relationship built on" (p. 506) rich, engaging practices. We all work under constraints. But even those of us who work in schools where administrator-instituted constraints are stringent can find ways—*must* find ways—to subvert these conditions whenever possible.

It's a hard balance, I know. The idea is not for all equity-minded educators to create hostile work situations for ourselves or, worse, to be pushed out of our jobs. But we can find ways in our spheres of influence to win back the trust of students who feel betrayed.

Opportunities for Family Involvement

Family involvement: Is anything more vigorously pitched as the panacea for educational woes? I rarely participate in a conversation about poverty and education without hearing impassioned attempts to blame everything imaginable on "disinterested" or "lazy" parents who refuse to participate in their children's education. There is ample evidence that family involvement can play a considerable role in student performance. But we should be careful not to use this evidence to mask everything else that needs fixing.

We might consider asking ourselves a couple of important questions. First, are opportunities for on-site family involvement accessible to parents experiencing poverty the way they're accessible to wealthier parents? What kinds of obstacles might exist for low-income parents who want to be involved in on-site family involvement opportunities like classroom volunteering, parent–teacher conferences, or back-to-school nights? What sorts of time constraints might they face, given the time poverty discussed in Chapter 6?

Imagine, if you haven't experienced it, that you are an economically marginalized parent of two elementary school children. You *want* to attend events at your children's school, but you work the evening shift at your second job. And because you're a wage employee, you don't have paid leave, so missing work means losing wages, which, by extension, could result in another late electricity payment: bad news with winter approaching.

Remember, now, that your poverty—or, more specifically, the economic injustice that propels poverty—means that you are more likely than wealthier people to work multiple jobs, including evening jobs. In fact, because, like Evelyn's mom, you likely work multiple jobs, you have less free time and time flexibility than more economically privileged parents (Robinson & Volpé, 2015). Regrettably, this is one of many obstacles you face in attempting to engage with your children's school. You might not be able to afford child care or transportation (Jarrett & Coba-Rodriguez, 2015). *Have the people scheduling these events ever had to rely on public transportation?*, you wonder, trying to calculate the least expensive and most time-efficient bus route from your first job to the school, then to your second job.

Still, you're committed to being involved in every possible way, so you hope that finally this year the school will be more flexible when scheduling family engagement events. Usually, as you've learned the hard and humiliating way, schools schedule these events at times that don't make sense for people like you. You clearly are not the school's priority.

Making matters worse, a couple of decades ago you attended school as a student in poverty, and often experienced it as an unwelcoming or even hostile place. So on top of worries about the financial cost of attending, you feel trepidation about the possible emotional or psychological toll visiting the school might take on you (Graham, 2009). You worry, based on previous experiences at the school, that you will be perceived as uneducated or inarticulate by teachers, maybe because you don't understand some of the terms or acronyms they're using (Robinson & Volpé, 2015). With all these concerns, in some ways you still feel like one of the lucky parents. You worry even more for the parents who are learning English, concerned with the stress they might feel about whether the school has underinvested in interpreters again.

With all these worries, you also know what your children's teachers will assume about you if you fail to attend. You know those assumptions might trickle down to your children.

What will you do?

Instructional Technologies

Equity advocates use the term "digital divide" to describe inequities in physical access to computers and the Internet among various groups of people. For example, students experiencing poverty have lower rates of access to computers and the Internet at home than their wealthier peers (File & Ryan, 2014). Despite 15 years of considerable progress toward eliminating the digital divide at school, gaps persist there, too. Even as gaps in physical access to computer technologies in schools have narrowed, more insidious disparities have emerged, not in physical access to the technologies, but in ways teachers use technologies in the classroom depending on student demographics. The term often used for the accumulation of these disparities is the *digital use divide* (U.S. Department of Education, 2017).

This is an important place to exercise our equity literacy abilities. The easy way to conceptualize access to technology is to think only in terms of *physical* access: Any student can walk up to a computer at home, in a library, or in a school classroom, sit down, and start typing. But there are social, cultural, and other dimensions of access, too. When we consider the digital use divide, adopting a more complete notion of "access," we find that computer and Internet use in high-poverty schools tends to mirror the pedagogical trends detailed earlier. For example, teachers in low-poverty schools, especially predominantly White low-poverty schools, most often use these technologies to support the development of critical or creative thinking. On average, students in these schools are encouraged to engage with computer and Internet technologies in constructivist and creative ways: doing research, constructing multimedia projects, practicing critical thinking skills, solving problems. On the other hand, as both localized and national studies have shown, in high-poverty schools computer and Internet technologies tend to be used to support rote, skill-and-drill learning (Gorski, 2009). As a middle school teacher at a high-poverty school once told me, "We're encouraged to use these machines as if they are big digital flash cards."

Many schools and districts have implemented plans and spent significant resources trying to mitigate computer technology access disparities. Some provide laptops or tablets for each student or partner with local Internet service providers to offer low-cost Internet access to economically marginalized families. Unfortunately, schools that provide computers for students to take home often find that they had failed to anticipate the costs of repairs, software updates, and other upkeep. They also often realize that, absent intensive teacher and student training on how to use them as learning devices, they are not the magic achievement bullet they often are presumed to be (Barshay, 2014). However, if schools provide intensive training and modeling by teachers on how computers can be used for higher-order tasks rather than just word processing and rote learning, this is a barrier that can be demolished through equity-literate policy and practice.

OPPORTUNITY GAPS AND NEOLIBERAL SCHOOL REFORM

In some ways it's hard to figure: Even as we are sold the virtues of data-driven decisionmaking, many common responses to educational outcome disparities reflect the inverse of what data suggest we ought to do, thus widening opportunity gaps. This is a clear indication that what we're often sold is the illusion of concern for the interests of the most marginalized students—that somebody else's interests are being prioritized.

I say it's hard to figure only in *some* ways because in other ways it's sadly predictable. Like most complex organizations, schools are slow to change; whole school systems, even slower. Add to this slowness the economic and other interests powerful people and organizations have in leading our equity efforts astray, and we have a recipe for inequity.

Consider, for example, the hyperfocus on standardized testing. It can be instructive, first, just to question who believes the outrageous volume of testing many students endure is a good idea. Students generally don't like it. Parents don't like it. Many teachers lament the stress the testing causes in their lives and how the testing obsession has come to influence the pedagogical expectations their supervisors have of them. I'm certain Pearson and the other corporations profiting from the testing craze are enjoying the destruction. But who else?

The pitch for the testing avalanche is that it holds schools accountable for boosting the achievement of groups of students who had not previously fared well in school. But where has it taken us? A few years ago, while attending a conference on educational equity, I listened to a U.S. Department of Education official deliver a presentation ostensibly about strategies for creating more equitable schools for Latinx youth. During a 75-minute presentation, he never talked about eliminating racism or xenophobia as a strategy; never talked about racist and inconsistent-with-decades-of-research anti-bilingual-education policies. Oddly, despite delivering his keynote in Arizona, he never even acknowledged Arizona politicians' quest to eliminate ethnic studies programs in Tucson schools—a program that data indisputably proved was having tremendous impacts on Latinx and other students' learning and graduation rates.

Instead, he talked for 75 minutes about *raising test scores*. He recommended doing so in part by adding instructional time in reading, writing, and math, even if it meant sacrificing "non-core" subjects like art, music, and physical education. Of course, according to mounds of data, this would be nonsensical. As we know, students perform better and feel more engaged in school when physical education and the arts are integral parts of their educational experiences (Landsman & Gorski, 2007). To be fair, this speaker wasn't alone. Endless schools and districts are responding similarly to test score pressures. Many high-poverty schools and districts have drastically cut their budgets for art and music. Many mixed-class schools and districts cheat the students who are not performing well on tests out of these opportunities, disproportionately impacting students of color, English language learners, and, of course, students experiencing poverty. Now a political appointee representing the body that creates federal education policy offered his official endorsement of data-ignorant decisionmaking.

Why, given what we know, would anybody with the interests of economically marginalized students at heart think it's a good idea to eliminate arts education as a strategy for bolstering academic achievement? Why do schools and school systems ostensibly committed to data-driven decisionmaking do all sorts of things in the name of "equity" that, according to the data, are doing more harm than good?

Many factors are at play, including our own grappling with bias and deficit views. More insidious, though, are societal factors that misguide equity efforts and mask the very existence of opportunity gaps. Most damaging among these is the growing influence of neoliberal thought on education policy and practice, an influence easy to spot in school reform initiatives once you know where to look. What makes neoliberal school reform dangerous is how it is marketed, with language like *school choice* and *merit pay*, as a pathway toward more equitable educational opportunity, even as it has by almost every measure intensified existing inequities. We will return to this point in a moment.

In the most general sense, neoliberalism is a political movement and ideology that imposes supposedly "free market" ideals on every aspect of social and political life. Especially vulnerable in this process today are community resources once considered the domain of government, part of the common social good, not to be soiled by profiteers. (Think "public education.") In an essay detailing neoliberalism's growing hold on public schools, Pauline Lipman (2011) describes it as "the commodification of all realms of existence" (p. 116). The telltale signs of neoliberalism include efforts to privatize public goods and services, to turn public roads, the prison system, schools, even parks into profit-driven commodities, rather than public-service-driven community goods. They also include the application of corporate-style reforms in the public sphere. The very language we use to talk about school reform brims over with the influence of neoliberalism: *standardization, annual yearly progress, accountability, data-driven decisionmaking.* Often it begins with efforts to defund or underfund public services and to redirect once-public funding to private enterprise, as with school voucher initiatives and privately run charter schools. Does any of this sound familiar?

The language of neoliberal school reform has become so pervasive that it often seems to drive conversations about education today, including conversations about educational equity. Think of the way so many of us, knowing how the obsession with standardized testing—an obsession so out of whack even kindergartners are given standardized tests in some states—deteriorates our agency as educators and students' access to fulfilling learning experiences, still somehow join the chorus of voices talking about student success in terms of test scores. Today I hear much, much more about raising economically marginalized students' test scores than about eliminating inequities and creating equitable schools. Worse, I often hear school officials using the goal of raising test scores as a proxy for creating equitable educational opportunity. It is a detour, not a proxy.

I know why this happens. I understand that all this talk about test scores is a set-up for teachers and administrators. I recognize that livelihoods are at risk, especially for people who work in high-poverty schools.

In Chapter 4 we learned about deficit ideology, the view that families experiencing poverty are intellectually, morally, or spiritually deficient, that they are "the problem." I believe that educators, particularly when we work in high-poverty schools, are targets of a kind of deficit ideology, too. The media, informed mostly by people who have never experienced the challenge and delight of teaching 30-some young people with all manner of gifts and needs and curiosities, love to target teachers and ignore shrinking budgets and the pressures of high-stakes testing. Political commentators and policy wonks love to compare test scores between schools resourced at vastly different levels while remaining remarkably silent on the inequitable distribution of pristine science labs, Advanced Placement programs, athletic fields, and school nurses. Do we hear about the studies showing how devastating the high-stakes testing craze has been on the morale of teachers committed enough to economically marginalized youth to teach in high-poverty schools (Byrd-Blake et al., 2010), where they, too, are denied resources and opportunities provided their colleagues at wealthier schools? Do we hear about the anxiety these testing regimens cause educators (Croft, Roberts, & Stenhouse, 2016), who often are compelled to teach and lead in ways they know are not ideal because of the narrow goal of raising test scores? When newspapers compare school or district test scores, how often do they account for disparities in school funding, preschool and shadow education access, or access to preventive health care?

Given this media scorn, I worry that some of us might buy in as a matter of survival. One friend, an elementary principal at a high-poverty school, recently explained to me, "If we don't raise those scores, we risk the state taking over our school, firing our teachers, and stealing from us whatever integrity we have left." Test scores, test scores, test scores.

Obviously, most of us want students from every background to succeed. Who would dedicate their lives to teaching if they weren't committed to so basic a goal? There are plenty of better paid and better respected careers for people who decide they just aren't invested sufficiently in the well-being of marginalized youth to stay in the profession. Those folks don't tend to stick around very long—at least not at high-poverty schools.

However, after spending the past several years studying families' experiences in public schools, I am concerned with what we are and are not doing when it comes to realizing the goal of equitable schools for students experiencing poverty. The problem, as I mentioned several chapters ago, is not that we don't *want* to create more equitable classrooms and schools, but that we spend tremendous resources pursuing initiatives that either do not work or, like neoliberal school reforms, widen gaps we desperately want to eliminate. If we want to avoid being swept up by the neoliberal wave, we must learn to recognize the ways many school reform initiatives pitched as efforts to equalize educational opportunity have had the opposite effect, growing the inequities detailed in this chapter.

Back to the standardized testing regimens. We've long known that the tests themselves are class-biased as well as race- and language-biased.

Imagine, for example, being a student in urban Minneapolis, from a family experiencing poverty, required to answer a series of word problems about camping and boating in the rural Minnesota Northwoods: word problems full of words like "portage," words you've never heard describing activities your family can't afford to do. Not long ago a graduate student of mine, a Minneapolis teacher, showed me a chunk of a standardized math test with an entire section of word problems along these lines. Based on whose lives were these questions written? It's bad enough—isn't it?—that students have to endure these tests. Even worse, youth in high-poverty schools are more likely than wealthier peers to have to sit through hours of test-taking lessons during instructional time. On top of all of this, they must manage tests designed with somebody else's life in mind.

Again, cross-group, cross-school, and cross-district score comparisons rarely account for the inequities informing students' performance on high-stakes tests. As we've acknowledged, many of these inequities (access to equitable health care, for example) are mostly beyond schools' control. As a result, the most vulnerable schools are often punished repeatedly for the implications of the very inequities that hamper them and their students (Darling-Hammond, 2013). In essence, these testing regimens place an additional burden on schools with high percentages of students experiencing poverty, rather than alleviating or mitigating the inequities that undermine student engagement and achievement.

Similarly, despite how vouchers and other school choice initiatives are sold as solutions to racial and economic inequities, for the most part they provide families who already have the widest-reaching access with even greater access while not significantly changing bigger access patterns (Orfield & Frankenberg, 2013). For example, a district might provide transportation for students experiencing poverty who choose to attend a charter school outside their neighborhoods, but they almost universally do not provide transportation for students who want to get to school early for extra help or stay at school late to use the computer lab or participate in an extracurricular activity. For students who have parents who own a car, have paid leave, or have flexible work schedules, these might not be dealbreakers. For families experiencing poverty who might not have these resources, it could make the choice prohibitive or less helpful. As you might imagine, the disparities are elevated in rural areas (Zhang & Cowen, 2009), where many youth already travel considerable distances to attend their "neighborhood" schools.

Step back for a wider view and the picture grows bleaker. Because choice programs generally do not guarantee the option to "choose" schools outside a student's home district, many economically marginalized families, especially if they live in rural or urban districts, are free to "choose" only among a sample of segregated high-poverty schools (Holme & Wells, 2008). So again, when interdistrict choice options exist, they generally provide greater choice to those who already have the most choice, exacerbating racial and class segregation and stratification.

Perhaps individually we do not have the power to calm the tide of these troubling initiatives, although there are powerful teacher collectives and movements pushing back, including those highlighted in Figure 7.3. When we are ready to expand our spheres of influence, they can provide excellent points of departure. In the meantime, we can attune ourselves to the impact these initiatives have on students and communities. We can get curious about what their popularity suggests about whose interests drive educational policy. We can choose to think critically about any school reform initiative before buying in, even if it is pitched on an illusion of equity.

Figure 7.3. Teacher Activist Collectives and Organizations

Association of Raza Educators: razaeducators.org

Caucus of Rank and File Educators: coreteachers.org

Chicago Grassroots Curriculum: grassrootscurriculum.org

Creating Balance in an Unjust World (Math Education and Social Justice): creatingbalanceconference.org

D.C. Area Social Justice Teachers: teachingforchange.org/teacher-resources/dc-teachers-for-change

Education for Liberation Network: edliberation.org

Educators' Network for Social Justice–Milwaukee: ensj.weebly.com

EduColor: educolor.org

Free Minds, Free People: fmfp.org

Montessori for Social Justice: montessoriforsocialjustice.org/about/our-mission

New York Collective of Radical Educators: nycore.org

North Dakota Study Group: ndsg.org

Northwest Teachers for Social Justice: nwtsj.org

The People's Education Movement: peoplesed.weebly.com

Rethinking Schools: rethinkingschools.org

Science Educators for Equity, Diversity, and Social Justice: seedsweb.org

Science Teachers for Social Change: facebook.com/groups/scienceteachers4socialchange

Social Equality Educators: Seattle: socialequalityeducators.org

Teacher Action Group: Philadelphia: tagphilly.org

Teacher Activist Group: Boston: tagboston.org

Teachers 4 Social Justice: San Francisco: t4sj.org

Teachers for Social Justice: Chicago: teachersforjustice.org

Teachers' Democracy Project: Baltimore: tdpbaltimore.org

Teaching for Change: teachingforchange.org

CONCLUSION

The education system as presently constituted is not the great equalizer it is advertised to be. In many ways it's just the opposite, bestowing on the most privileged families additional privilege and denying the least privileged families access to what they and their children deserve. The great *un-equalizer*, we might call it.

We can become overwhelmed trying to consider all these conditions simultaneously, especially those of us who don't feel much control over high-level education policy or individual families' access to preschool. The idea, remember, is not to feel guilty or centrally responsible for these inequities, but instead to ask ourselves what they mean for us and our students within our spheres of influence. At the very least, they should help us to better understand why some students experiencing poverty might feel disengaged from school or why others might appear so far behind some of their wealthier peers academically. Our critical initial task is to ditch the deficit view and acknowledge that it's not their fault. The odds are stacked against economically marginalized students. Our critical second task is to ask ourselves what we're willing to do to make sure we're not reproducing these disadvantages in our classrooms and schools.

Next, in Chapter 8, we begin our exploration of inequity-alleviating strategies. We start with instructional strategies before moving to relational and leadership strategies in later chapters.

Reflection Questions and Exercises

1. Do any of the in-school opportunity gaps discussed in this chapter stand out to you as especially egregious? If so, which ones? How does this in-school opportunity gap combine with the out-of-school disparities discussed in the previous chapter to reproduce existing socioeconomic disparities in access and opportunity?

2. A basic principle of equity work described in this chapter is, *There is no path to equity that does not include a direct confrontation with inequity.* What are examples of ways schools have attempted to respond to the socioeconomic opportunity gap without addressing inequity? How has this avoidance of directly confronting inequity informed popular school reform initiatives?

3. What are some of the policies and practices in schools you have attended (or in which you have worked) that reflect these opportunity gaps? How would you change them through a structural equity literacy lens?

CHAPTER 8

Teaching Students Experiencing Poverty in Effective, Equitable, and Even *Data-Informed* Ways

Curricular and Pedagogical Strategies

Principles of equity literacy discussed in this chapter include:

Principle 10: Strategies for creating and sustaining equitable classrooms and schools must be based on evidence for what works.

Principle 11: Simplistic instructional strategies, absent a commitment to more intensive institutional change, are no threat to inequities.

Principle 12: There is no path to educational equity that does not involve a redistribution of access and opportunity.

Despite the disheartening realities of poverty and the inequities harming youth and families experiencing it, I have hope. During my 20 years working with public school educators, I have found an almost universal vigilance when it comes to advocating for economically marginalized students. Plus, while it is sadly true that the literature spilleth over with evidence of persistent bias and inequity in schools, it also spilleth over with evidence that we can do something about it. We can do many somethings, actually.

I describe in this chapter several such somethings, focusing on instructional and curricular strategies before I turn, in Chapters 9, 10, and 11, to relational strategies, leadership strategies, and then bigger school- and district-level initiatives. These are strategies that have proven effective at bolstering the learning and engagement of low-income students and families by redistributing curricular and pedagogical opportunity and access.

A COUPLE CAVEATS

Before delving into the strategies, I want to reemphasize a troubling but important reality. We never will realize educational equity in any complete sense until we address bigger economic justice concerns. The symptoms of economic injustice infest schools in myriad ways. Those of us who have worked in or with high-poverty communities or their schools tend to be deeply attuned to this because, in addition to incredible resiliency, we see in people experiencing poverty the effects of food insecurity, living-wage–work scarcities, housing instability, unequal access to preventive health care, and class bias. In a society that prides itself on being a meritocracy, we haven't even managed to guarantee equitable access to education. This is a notable failure, especially when it happens in wealthy countries like the United States.

As I have said, educators are no more culpable for the effects of these injustices than anyone else; obviously, the change needed to shrink wealth and income inequality and to reconstruct systems built to support existing patterns of access and opportunity requires a series of long-term policy and ideological projects. But it is also true that we can't afford to wait, and that families experiencing poverty can't afford to wait, for an economic revolution. We must commit *now* to doing what we can do *today* to address what economically marginalized families are experiencing in this moment, right before us. Once we strengthen our equity literacy and construct change at that level—a classroom, perhaps, or a school—we can work on expanding our spheres of influence to work on that bigger change.

Even at the classroom level, we must remember that there is no simple solution; in Eric Freeman's (2010) words, "there is no one-shot inoculation for neutralizing the consequences of disadvantage" (p. 693). Low-income students and communities are infinitely diverse. You know your students better than I know them and better than any researcher or educator cited in this book knows them. No matter what anybody says and no matter how prettily packaged it might be, no set of scripted strategies will work for *all* economically marginalized students *everywhere*, as Robert Balfanz and Vaughan Byrnes (2006) found in their study about strategies for raising mathematics achievement in high-poverty schools. There is no magic bullet, no cookie-cutter approach to improving anything when it comes to poverty and inequality (Thurston & Berkeley, 2010).

Neither can we hope to create any significant change by embracing one or two instructional strategies while we fail to embrace a bigger vision for equity literacy that is responsive to the barriers impeding students experiencing poverty. In fact, aside from advocating any way we can for the social change necessary to alleviate the very existence of poverty, the most important thing we can do for educational equity is to draw on the expertise of economically marginalized people to identify and implement community-specific strategies for educational equity (Cookson, 2013).

INSTRUCTIONAL STRATEGIES THAT WORK

Given those caveats, the strategies I describe here should not be interpreted as a prescribed blueprint for eliminating class inequity. Instead, they are strategies I accumulated during a two-tiered, decade-long process. The first tier involved synthesizing mountainous mounds of research about what has been generally effective at strengthening the engagement and, as a result, the academic performance of students experiencing poverty. The second has been a considerably longer process, observing and talking with students, teachers, and other people in high-poverty schools and districts who were trying to find a better path to equity. With context-specific adaptations, these strategies can be important components of a holistic plan for making classrooms and schools more equitable, engaging, and validating for economically marginalized students and families. The equity educator has the knowledge, skills, and will to:

1. consider data humbly, responsibly, and collaboratively;
2. prioritize literacy instruction across the curriculum;
3. promote literacy enjoyment;
4. have and communicate high expectations;
5. adopt higher-order, student-centered, rigorous pedagogies;
6. teach critical literacy;
7. teach about poverty, economic injustice, and class bias;
8. analyze learning materials for class (and other) bias;
9. make curricula relevant to students experiencing poverty;
10. incorporate music, art, and theater across the curriculum; and
11. incorporate movement and exercise into learning.

Reading this list, you might think to yourself, *These strategies just sound like good teaching.* You're right. And because you're right, we should be alarmed that in most schools and districts these strategies are not distributed equitably, as discussed in Chapter 7.

As a final caveat, the strategies I describe in the next few chapters will be more or less relevant based on your job description and sphere of influence. I encourage you to focus first on the strategies you can adopt, adapt, and implement immediately through an equity literacy lens in that sphere and then build toward incorporating the other strategies. Work in teams, across subject areas, whenever possible.

Strategy One: Consider Data Humbly, Responsibly, and Collaboratively. I cringe a little when I hear the phrase "data-driven decisionmaking." I know that students experiencing poverty, like Students of Color, English language learners, and students with (dis)abilities, bear a disproportionate toll from the data-gathering, especially in unfortunate cases when school and district leaders become so obsessed over test scores they all but demand what teachers know to be ineffective teaching. (More on that later in this chapter.) I struggle to find a student, parent, or teacher who sings the virtues of voluminous standardized testing. As I mentioned earlier, I'm certain that Pearson and other corporations profiting from the testing craze are enthusiastic about these trends. But who else thinks it is a good idea?

Some amount of testing is sensible if results are used in meaningful ways to identify patterns of instructional strengths and weaknesses. One data-informed practice that several researchers studying high-poverty, high-performing schools have observed is teams of teachers gathering to collaboratively examine assessment data to identify individual and group strengths and areas for improvement. Imagine that we are 4th-grade teachers at the same school. Your students performed better on some measure of literacy than mine. We can sit as part of a grade-level team and talk about why that discrepancy happened. If I have the humility and will to strengthen my equity literacy, I can learn from your curricular sequencing and pedagogical choices. We also can identify patterns of struggle across all our classes to pinpoint common instructional challenges and discuss how we might collaborate toward more effective teaching in those areas (Chenoweth, 2009; Reed, 2015).

Of course, for this to work, we need some process agreements. It cannot be a judge-and-shame game—no boasting or finger-wagging allowed. After all, at our next meeting we'll be looking at math scores. It is quite possible that my students performed better than your students on some aspect of that test. We are accountable for one another's instructional success. This is a process; it doesn't come easy. The trust we need to make ourselves vulnerable develops over time. But if we can develop it, we win the benefits of a whole team's instructional expertise and strategies—a tremendous collective gift to ourselves.

(I know some of you are thinking, *Somebody needs to tell my principal to create time for this practice and an institutional culture that values collaboration over competition for my colleagues and me to do this successfully.* Worry not. I demand this of your principal in Chapter 10.)

Strategy Two: Prioritize Literacy Instruction Across the Curriculum. Learning begins with and is supported by literacy. There are few agreements in educational research as solid as this. In nearly every case study of a high-poverty school with outcomes rivaling those of wealthier schools, researchers have found that everybody prioritizes literacy, not just in language arts, but also in math, science, and even physical education (Parrett & Budge, 2012; Reed, 2015). Every teacher in these schools is a literacy teacher.

Even if your school does not embrace this approach, you can embrace it. Use every opportunity to strengthen students' literacy (Milner, 2015). Incorporate reading and writing into your daily teaching (Reed, 2015), whatever you are teaching. If you teach math, ask students to write about how they solved a problem, what mathematical principles or problem-solving techniques they used. Every little bit helps.

First, though, as we learn how to cultivate in students experiencing poverty—in all students—the literacy that will help them in school, help them secure a job, help them do whatever they want to do, we must check ourselves on deficit ideology. Remember, linguists reject the presumption of a "proper" or "correct" English. When we scold or mock students who speak a variety of English not presently rewarded in most educational or vocational contexts, when we use words like "improper" or "incorrect" to describe the way everybody in their families or communities might speak, we cast a deficit light, not just on their ways of speaking, but also on their families or communities. Instead, we can teach the way of speaking we previously and mistakenly might have called "proper English" as a tool or skill without demeaning the students who are learning it. As Rich Milner (2015) explains in *Rac(e)ing to Class*, "the goal of vocabulary and pronunciation development is to add to—not take away from—students' ability to navigate and participate in multiple worlds" (pp. 87–88). We can say, "In this space, for this particular lesson, we are going to practice the variety of English that will help you do well in school. It is a tool for your literacy tool belt."

Strategy Three: Promote Literacy Enjoyment. According to Mary Kellett (2009), "If we . . . acknowledge that literacy proficiency can be a route out of poverty . . . the most powerful strategy is to create cultures that promote reading enjoyment. This is likely to make the biggest impact on literacy proficiency" (p. 399). Literacy instruction should not focus solely on reading or writing mechanics or rote skill-building. We must find ways to foster excitement about reading and writing even when students respond reluctantly at first.

Creative people that we tend to be, educators have used an exciting range of strategies to do just that. For example, Debbie Vera (2011) tracked low-income prekindergarten students whose teacher took advantage of their adoration of television characters like Dora the Explorer to engage them in literacy education activities. Compared with a control group, students engaged in this manner showed larger gains in their knowledge of the alphabet and a variety of written language concepts. Vera concluded, "Incorporating the media interests of children within the emergent literacy curriculum can assist high-poverty [students] with early reading skills" (p. 328). In another recent study, teachers sent kindergartners in 31 Title I schools home with a DVD of fairy tales designed to teach vocabulary words. Their use of the DVD led to a mean 20% improvement on a standardized vocabulary test (Evans et al., 2016). Of course, before using any popular media source we should examine it carefully for bias or other problematic power dynamics, not only related to class, but also to race, gender, sexual orientation, and other identities. The last thing we want to do is elevate inequity through mindless adoption of a strategy for creating more equity.

Other creative and effective strategies abound. For example, in order to promote literacy enjoyment in high-poverty schools, teachers have:

- instituted literature circles in which small groups of students read and discussed books they chose collaboratively (Whittaker, 2012);
- provided reading material options that aligned with students' stated interests (Reis & Fogarty, 2006);
- used learning tools, such as multimedia software programs and blogs, that engaged students actively and interactively (Karemaker, Pitchford, & O'Malley, 2010; Yollis, 2012); and
- incorporated drama into literacy instruction (Baldwin, 2007).

Strategy Four: Have and Communicate High Expectations. The constant stream of low expectations experienced by many economically marginalized students can have palpable psychological effects on low-income families. Cecilia Rouse and Lisa Barrow (2006) explain,

> If teachers have lower expectations for children from disadvantaged families, regardless of their ability, and if their perceptions about which children are disadvantaged are on average correct, then the lower expectations for disadvantaged children may raise the psychological costs of education relative to their more privileged peers and thus help explain why children of disadvantaged parents attain less education. (p. 99)

In other words, low expectations become an additional weight on the shoulders of students experiencing poverty, helping create the very outcome inequalities for which their families are blamed.

Despite these realities, some people dismiss high expectations talk as self-esteem fluffiness. The reality is, expressing high expectations is fluff only when it is all talk, when we fail to demonstrate our high expectations in real ways during daily interactions with students. When high expectations are expressed in our instruction—more on what this looks like in a moment—those expectations can have a significant positive effect on students' intellectual development (Figlio, 2005; Jessim & Harber, 2005). Students learn more, and more deeply, when we demonstrate that we believe in their abilities to do so (Papageorge, Gershenson, & Kang, 2016).

This is an important reminder of why ideological shifts matter. We cannot settle for little actions that suggest high expectations; it is about actually *believing* all students can succeed (Chenoweth & Theokas, 2013). If we believe students and families experiencing poverty are incapable; if we ever think, *These students can't do that*; if we apply that deficit label our expectations will be clear even if we fake high expectations (Prins &

Schafft, 2009). Without those beliefs, the other strategies described here are ineffective. Students know the difference between high expectations and pity (Milner, 2015).

Strategy Five: Adopt Higher-Order, Learner-Centered, Rigorous Pedagogies.
Incongruence often reigns. I hear a lot of talk about having high expectations, but the unfortunate reality is that students experiencing poverty are disproportionately subject to the most rote, least engaging, lowest-expectation teaching. In fact, when Eithne Kennedy (2010) reviewed the findings of a broad range of studies on what makes for effective literacy teachers in high-poverty schools, she found, among other things, that they "emphasize higher-order thinking skills" and "teach basic skills in *meaningful* contexts" (p. 384; emphasis added). She concluded, though, that despite consistent evidence of the effectiveness of these instructional commitments, "this kind of approach to instruction is not the norm and is less likely to be encountered by students who . . . attend high-poverty schools" (p. 384). What sorts of expectations are we communicating when economically marginalized students are disproportionately subject to the least effective pedagogies?

We can choose a different path. We can demonstrate high expectations by teaching in student-centered ways that support higher-order learning, offering what Carolyn Shields (2014) calls "enrichment instead of low-level remediation" (p. 131) and what Curt Dudley-Marling (2015) calls a "high-expectations curriculum" (p. 7). The research is on our side. For example, based on their study of more than 3,800 students, Valerie Lee and David Burkam (2003) found that students labeled "at-risk" who attended schools that combined rigorous curricula with learner-centered pedagogies achieved at higher levels and were less likely to be early school-leavers than their peers who were subject to less engaging instruction. Similarly, in a study of working-class elementary school students, those exposed to math instruction built around cognitive questioning and high student participation in class discussions outperformed peers on a variety of learning measures (Schuchart, Buch, & Piel, 2015). In fact, a decade and a half of scholarship is nearly unanimous on this point: Low-income students, like *all* students, learn best when we teach in student-centered ways that emphasize deep engagement and higher-order learning.

Let's start with higher-order learning. Generally, students experiencing poverty, like all students, learn best when instruction is driven by high expectations, when standards aren't lowered based on socioeconomic status or other factors (Milner, 2015; Ramalho, Garza, & Merchant, 2010). The job begins with preschool teachers in programs that foster social and cognitive growth with intellectually stimulating curricula (Judge, 2005). Unfortunately, pedagogical segregation begins in preschool, so even at the earliest ages, if they have access to any formal educational experiences at all, children experiencing poverty are disproportionately subject to those that lack the intellectual stimulation to which children in wealthier communities have access. But each of us, regardless of what subject or grade level we teach, can choose to bolster the learning and engagement of students by adopting cognitively challenging pedagogies like problem-solving over memorization-and-regurgitation methods that cultivate only lower-order thinking (Battey, 2013; Reed, 2015).

In fact, although I hate to encourage pedagogical decisions based on their potential to improve test scores, which in and of themselves do not guarantee deeper learning improvements, research has shown that higher-order pedagogies based on high academic expectations are associated positively with test score increases in both reading and math. For example, according to Stanley Pogrow (2006), instituting a higher-order pedagogical approach "yields substantially higher test score gains than remedial or test-prep approaches—approximately three times the growth in reading comprehension—even as it produces gains in overall intellectual and social development" (p. 227). Similarly, after examining data on 13,000 low-income kindergartners, Annie Georges (2009) discovered that students whose math instruction focused on reasoning and analytic skills rather than on worksheets and other skill-and-drill pedagogies scored higher on standardized math tests than their peers. She concluded, "Students in poverty would benefit to be in classrooms that emphasize problem-solving and reasoning skills with greater frequency" (p. 2148).

Recognizing the vagueness of terms like "higher-order pedagogies," I scoured two decades of scholarship on the relationship between teaching and poverty in hopes of identifying specific higher-order instructional strategies that commonly bolster learning and engagement among economically marginalized students. Based on this process, I concluded, not surprisingly, that a good general rule is to teach students experiencing poverty the same ways their wealthier peers are taught. More particularly, though, two themes appeared repeatedly: (1) the power of cooperative and collaborative instruction, and (2) the effectiveness of interactive or "dialogic" teaching.

It turns out that cooperative pedagogies, in which students work in pairs or small groups to support one another's learning, are virtually universally effective for increasing engagement and learning, regardless of socioeconomic status (LaGue & Wilson, 2010; Slavin, Lake, & Groff, 2009). One especially effective form of cooperative learning for students experiencing poverty is peer tutoring, which has been shown to improve learning for the tutor and the tutee (Maheady, Mallette, & Harper, 2006). Notably, students who participate in peer tutoring become more engaged in school overall (Greenwood & Delquari, 1995), and even the tutors emerge with a better grasp of the tutored content (Galbraith & Winterbottom, 2011).

Although it can be difficult to pinpoint why these and other cooperative learning strategies work especially well for students in poverty, experience tells me it has something to do with conditions in many high-poverty communities that encourage cooperative tendencies. In many such communities, like the one from which my mom's people hail, where affordable child care, means for transportation, health care access, and other basic services are scarce, people cooperate as a matter of survival. In my Grandma's community, nobody could afford child care. Only one person owned a car in the entire town when she was a child. There was no option but to work together. Given these sorts of similar life circumstances, it could be that some students experiencing poverty have an easier time than teachers connecting what they are learning to the lives of their economic peers. Whatever the reason for its effectiveness, try to incorporate cooperative learning whenever appropriate, especially in mixed-ability groups.

Similarly, like their wealthier peers, students experiencing poverty tend to respond favorably to interactive or "dialogic" pedagogies and to pretty much any instructional strategy that recognizes them as inquirers rather than mere receptacles. According to Robin Alexander (2006), dialogic teaching is characterized by five principles. Dialogic methods are

1. *collective*, so that learning happens interactively among teachers and students;
2. *reciprocal*, so that learning is based on teachers and learners listening to and learning from one another and considering a broad range of viewpoints;
3. *supportive*, so that students feel that they can participate and share their ideas without fear that they will be shamed, and with the goal of striving for shared understandings;
4. *cumulative*, so that students and teachers build on their own and one anothers' thinking over time; and
5. *purposeful*, so that teachers employ dialogic methods in the service of specific learning goals.

All students, including low-income students, learn better and score higher on those pesky tests when their teachers adopt dialogic methods. This is true across the curriculum. Several studies have demonstrated a link between dialogic teaching and literacy achievement (Barr & Parrett, 2007; Howard, 2007), even for the youngest learners. For instance, following their evaluation of dialogic teaching in early childhood classrooms in Miami, Judith Bernhard and her colleagues (2008) concluded that literacy interventions based on "increasing children's participation in meaningful literacy activities, and that do not overemphasize direct teaching of literacy skills and subcomponents, are effective in increasing the language skills of diverse, urban young children in poverty" (p. 100).

Similarly, according to a great deal of research, participatory, inquiry-driven, problem-solving math instruction is far more effective than lecture, direct instruction, and other lower-order pedagogies (Battey, 2013; Van de

Walle, 2006). The National Council of Teachers of Mathematics (NCTM, 2000) took its stand on this point almost 20 years ago. It's time for the rest of us to catch up.

I doubt any of us are surprised that students experiencing poverty, like their wealthier peers, prefer engaging pedagogies that validate them as thinkers. Unfortunately, higher-order pedagogies remain uncommon in classrooms comprised predominantly of economically marginalized youth (Cookson, 2013; Dudley-Marling, 2015; Parrett & Budge, 2012). Commit today to doing better.

Strategy Six: Teach Critical Literacy. We can begin the shift to higher-order engagement by teaching critical literacy (Milner, 2015). In and out of school, economically marginalized students are inundated with media that render them invisible or morally and vocationally deficient. TV shows that caricature urban poverty have been plentiful for decades. More recently, following the commercial success of shows like *Justified,* a growing number of programs mock and romanticize rural poverty. Some, like *Duck Dynasty,* depict economically privileged men growing more economically privileged by offensively "performing" backwoods poverty. Youth also are inundated with enthusiastic messages about meritocracy, about education being the great equalizer—messages that implicitly demean them and their families by suggesting that there must be something inherently wrong with them if they are experiencing poverty. Making matters worse, they sit through history and literature lessons with bits of class (or race or gender or . . .) bias and the erasure of narratives of solidarity and activism in poor and working-class communities.

Critical literacy cultivates in students the ability and confidence to challenge deficit narratives, to critique the omission of narratives, and to question the troubling conditions upheld in part through these narratives. Students and teachers with critical literacy develop skills that help them, according to Stephanie Jones (2012), "reposition themselves as readers" (p. 218). Rather than internalizing deficit-laden messages about themselves and their communities in, say, children's books, students can "better imagine challenging, changing and critiquing practices and structures" (p. 218) depicted in them.

Wealthier students, especially wealthier White students, are socialized with a sense of entitlement and confidence to engage critically with texts in school. Jones (2012) challenges us to cultivate in economically marginalized students, who are more likely than their wealthier peers to have been labeled as disruptive or disrespectful for posing critical questions about what they are consuming in school, the same sense of entitlement. It is their right to critically analyze the world around them, including what we are feeding them in school.

We should begin early in students' school lives. Imagine being a 2nd-grade student from a family experiencing poverty. How likely are you to find books that accurately and positively reflect your life experience in your school's library? (Hint: not very.) One solution is to assemble a more equitable and inclusive collection of books. In the meantime, Jones (2012) describes an early lesson in critical literacy wherein, rather than asking students to manufacture connections between themselves and characters or storylines that reflect nothing about their own lives, the teacher engaged them in a critical conversation about how the story could be rewritten to reflect their experiences.

Research has revealed more generally that students experiencing poverty are hungry for critical literacy. Based on their exploration of these issues in high-poverty schools, for example, Fine et al. (2016) concluded that students were

> thirsty for an education that helps them analyze critically their current circumstances, values their critique and feeds their desire, introduces them to histories of struggle and possibility, equips them with skills to build a different tomorrow . . . (p. 510)

In an age of standardization and high-stakes testing, the kind of education that can quench this thirst is growing scarcer, especially in high-poverty schools and lower-track classes in mixed-class schools. The question for me as an educator is, do I have the knowledge, skills, and will to do what I can in my sphere of influence to water what needs watering?

Strategy Seven: Teach About Poverty, Economic Injustice, and Class Bias. On an August day in 1967, 4 years after his "I Have a Dream" speech, The Reverend Dr. Martin Luther King Jr. delivered a presidential address at the Southern Christian Leadership Conference titled "Where Do We Go from Here?" "In elementary schools," Dr. King lamented, "Negroes lag one to three years behind whites, and their segregated schools receive substantially less money per student than the white schools." Although recast as a civil rights activist who advocated only for equal rights for African Americans, Dr. King's most important contribution, illustrated by this short quote, might have been his insistence that race and class are linked. Read the speeches he delivered the last few years of his life. You'll see he bemoaned poverty as he bemoaned racism (as he also bemoaned the Vietnam War because of how poverty and race largely predicted who was sent to the front lines). He was about intersectionality before intersectionality was cool.

Later in this speech Dr. King said, "And one day we must ask the question, 'Why are there forty million poor people in America?' And when you begin to ask that question, you are raising questions about the economic system, about a broader distribution of wealth. When you ask that question, you begin to question the capitalistic economy." When we teach about Martin Luther King Jr., how often do we discuss how he championed the rights of economically marginalized people? How often do we teach that he organized marches against poverty or that when he was assassinated he had traveled to Memphis to help organize African American sanitation workers striking due to unsafe working conditions and unfair pay?

It can be difficult introducing these intense issues in class, unsure how students, parents, or administrators will respond. But it's important to remember that despite adults' impulse to protect students from controversial topics or difficult issues, youth are more cognizant than we know about economic and other forms of inequity (Labadie, Pole, & Rogers, 2013). In fact, Jessi Streib (2011) has documented ways even preschool-age children understand and act out class distinctions and stereotypes, often resulting in the reproduction of inequity. Summarizing her findings for the *Classism Exposed* blog, Streib (2012) wrote, "The ways that four year olds interacted with each other and with teachers . . . created disadvantages for the already disadvantaged and privileges for those born into privilege. Well meaning people and organizations can produce unintended outcomes" (¶ 6).

One well-researched way to bolster engagement for students experiencing poverty is to teach explicitly about issues associated with poverty and economic justice (Comber, 2016; Kelley & Darragh, 2011; Mistry, Brown, Chow, & Collins, 2012). Martin Luther King Jr. gives us an in, as do several other historical figures about whom many of us teach: Helen Keller, César Chávez, Eleanor Roosevelt, Maya Angelou, the Black Panthers, and even Albert Einstein. Each spoke, wrote, or acted for economic justice and denounced local and federal government agencies—the same agencies that continue to fall short in their support of low-income families—for failing to respond adequately to poverty or to intersections of poverty and racism. Toni Morrison and others continue to do so today, providing important opportunities to introduce conversations about poverty in the present rather than the past tense.

Of course, we should not wait until famous people come up in class to teach about poverty and class. A math teacher might ask students to calculate a living wage for people in their communities. Judith Chafel and her colleagues (2007) suggest a more direct approach, asking students to draw images of people experiencing poverty to begin a conversation about biases and class issues. An elementary school teacher might include picture books that introduce concepts related to poverty in a classroom library. My personal favorite is Doreen Cronin and Betsy Lewin's (2000) *Click, Clack, Moo,* in which farm animals organize to demand better working conditions from Farmer Brown.

We should be mindful to select books that depict people experiencing poverty standing up to bias and injustice and engaging with social causes without sugar-coating or romanticizing the realities of poverty. Especially avoid (or critically analyze with students) books meant to elicit pity or portray economically marginalized people solely as victims (Kelley & Darragh, 2011). I asked Stephanie Jones, who has studied portrayals of working-class characters in picture books, which were her favorites. She responded enthusiastically, sharing fabulous options. Her top recommendations included:

- *Amber Was Brave, Essie Was Smart* by Vera B. Williams (2001, Greenwillow Books, ages 8 and up)
- *Bud, Not Buddy* by Christopher Paul Curtis (2004, Laurel Leaf, ages 8 and up)
- *In My Family/En Mi Familia* by Carmen Lomas Garza (1996, Children's Book Press, ages 6 and up)
- *A Kid's Guide to Hunger & Homelessness* by Cathryn Berger Kaye (2007, Free Spirit Publishing, ages 11 and up)
- *Night Shift* by Jessie Hartland (2007, Bloomsbury Children's Books, ages 4 and up)
- *Pop's Bridge* by Eve Bunting and C. F. Payne (2006, HMH Books, preschool to 3)
- *¡Sí, Se Puede!/Yes, We Can!: Janitor Strike in L.A.* by Diana Cohn and Francisco Delgado (2005, Cinco Puntos Press, ages 5 and up)
- *Somebody's New Pajamas* by Isaac Jackson and David Soman (1996, Dial, ages 3 and up)
- *The Streets Are Free* by Monika Doppert Kurusa (1995, Annick Press, ages 7 and up)
- *Those Shoes* by Maribeth Boetls and Noah Z. Jones (2009, Candlewick, ages 5 and up)
- *Voices in the Park* by Anthony Browne (2001, DK Children, ages 7 and up)

Beyond teaching about poverty, we bolster the engagement of students experiencing poverty when we encourage critical analysis of the social conditions repressing them and provide opportunities for them to use what they are learning in school to respond to those conditions (Comber, 2016). The possibilities are vast. Students can use math and science to critically analyze forms of environmental injustice in high-poverty communities (Haine, 2010), use social studies and language arts knowledge to critically analyze portrayals of working-class people in their history textbooks or the local news (Latz & Adams, 2011), or use interdisciplinary knowledge not just to run a canned food drive but to learn about conditions that make the canned food drive necessary (Cloutier-Bordeleau, 2015).

And again, we can start young. Preschool and kindergarten students are interested in and capable of developing sophisticated understandings about issues like race and class, and learning how to challenge bias and inequality if we have the will to facilitate this kind of learning (Gorski & Swalwell, 2015; Labadie, Pole, & Rogers, 2013). Those who teach in mixed-class or wealthier schools can do their parts, too, by educating economically and otherwise privileged students about issues like poverty, racism, sexism, and heterosexism. Katy Swalwell (2015) has written extensively about engaging privileged youth in critical civic education. She reminds us when we do so to move beyond notions of service and volunteerism and toward "deepening justice, democracy, or equality" (p. 506). Here, again, is a reminder of why we must begin by nurturing our own equity literacy. What does it say about me if I allow my own lack of confidence or misperceptions to keep me from adopting every possible proven strategy for strengthening the engagement of my most marginalized students?

When we develop the knowledge, skills, and will to teach sophisticatedly about poverty and economic injustice, we prepare ourselves to serve several purposes. We uncover the biased and all-too-popular deficit narratives of students experiencing poverty and build their learning around opportunities to offer counternarratives. We acknowledge the barriers with which students experiencing poverty contend and build part of their learning around analyzing and responding to those barriers. We provide opportunities for economically marginalized youth to talk back at biases and stereotypes their wealthier peers might have about them (Dutro, 2009). And we do not necessarily have to add more content to our curriculum to do this. Instead, we can find ways to weave these opportunities into existing learning activities just by being a little more determined to find appropriate ways to do so.

Several well-respected organizations host resource-rich websites chockfull of free ideas, activities, and strategies for teaching about poverty, class, economic justice, and a wide range of other social issues. Figure 8.1 highlights some of my favorites.

Figure 8.1. Online Resources for Teaching about Poverty and Class

Amnesty International Human Rights Education: amnestyusa.org/resources/educators

Class Action: classism.org

Make Poverty History: makepovertyhistory.org/takeaction/

New York Collective of Radical Educators: nycore.org

Teachers Against Poverty (Facebook Group): facebook.com/teachersagainstpoverty/

Teaching Economics as if People Mattered: teachingeconomics.org/

Teaching Social Justice Resource Exchange (Facebook Group): facebook.com/groups/teachaboutjustice/

Teaching Tolerance: tolerance.org/

TeachUNICEF's Poverty Curriculum Materials: teachunicef.org/explore/topic/poverty

United for a Fair Economy: faireconomy.org/

Strategy Eight: Analyze Learning Materials for Class (and Other) Bias.
In her analysis of picture books with working-class themes, Jones (2008)
found that working-class families regularly were depicted in stereotypical
ways. For example, books tended to understate the proportion of White
people in poverty while overstating poverty in Communities of Color.
Often these sorts of biases are implicit and difficult to spot if we are not
looking for them. Luckily, a variety of tools can help us uncover class biases,
including the National Association for the Teaching of English Working
Party on Social Class and English Teaching's (1982) checklist for class bias.
Despite being more than 35 years old, the checklist is comprised of still-
relevant questions for determining the extent of bias in children's literature.
Some of the questions we might consider when choosing literature and other
resources include:

- How are [people experiencing poverty or] the working class portrayed? As
  subservient? Brutal? Stupid? Crude? Sexist? . . .
- Are [people experiencing poverty or] working class people portrayed as
  being in control of their lives?
- Are the middle class or upper class characters shown as being the saviors of
  the working class? (p. 34)

Better, we should incorporate the critical literacy strategy discussed earlier
and collaborate with students to identify and discuss biases in their learning
materials. Remember, if students are finding bias in learning materials
that we as teachers fail to acknowledge, they could interpret our lack of
acknowledgment as agreement. Needless to say, this will hamper our efforts
to create equitable learning environments. As equity-literate educators, we
must learn how to spot even the subtlest biases and deficit narratives and
have the will to challenge them.

Remember, class bias pops up not just in language arts materials, but
also in social studies textbooks, math workbooks, children's magazines, educational films and websites, and even learning materials made especially
for English language learners. Joelle Sano (2009), who analyzed 50 children's books popularly read aloud to English language learners in public
schools, found alarming rates of class and race bias. I worry when I imagine
what percentage of the teachers using those books did not have the equity
literacy to respond to or even recognize the bias. Noting the considerable
overlap of English language learners, Students of Color, and students experiencing poverty, I shudder wondering how many students sit through flurries
of curricular indignities, not because their teachers intended to participate
in their marginalization, but because we lacked the ability or will to extract
ourselves from their marginalization.

Here is a start: Examine learning materials for bias. Keep in mind that
bias can be subtle. Consider, for instance, how students experiencing poverty

are depicted with regard to their dispositions toward school and reading, their attitudes about possessions, and their morals (Sano, 2009). If you find bias in mandated learning materials, use those critical literacy skills. Tear them apart. Acknowledge the problem. If you have the will to make them, these simple moves are vehicles for little bits of advocacy—something experienced too infrequently by economically marginalized students.

Strategy Nine: Make Curricula Relevant to Students Experiencing Poverty. Would you recognize "portage" if you saw it? I shared the story earlier about how several years ago one of the Minnesota state standardized math tests contained an entire section of word problems on boating, hiking, and camping in the Northwoods, a rural resort area a couple hours' drive north of the Minneapolis-St. Paul area, where I was living at the time. On the face of it, these questions put students from Minneapolis and St. Paul who were experiencing poverty at a considerable disadvantage. Their families could not afford vacations in the Northwoods, much less equipment for camping, ice fishing, snowmobiling, and other common Northwoods activities. In fact, I spent time in high-poverty schools in St. Paul in which most students had spent little time at all outside the Twin Cities metro area. Yet they, like their wealthier peers, were expected to relate to word problems full of words like "portage," which, by the way, is the act of carrying a canoe overland between navigable waterways. Portage is not the kind of thing urban youth experiencing poverty do in their spare time.

All students learn better when the curriculum is relevant to their lives (Gorski, 2013; Lee, 1995). In his essay "The Pedagogy of Poverty Versus Good Teaching" (1991), Martin Haberman urges us to find ways to connect what students learn to their daily lives and to the lives of people in their communities. Better yet, he says, put students to work applying what they learn to solve community problems. He explains, "In good schools, problems are not viewed as occasions to impose more rules and tighter management from above. Far from being viewed as obstacles to the 'normal' school routine, difficult events and issues are transformed into the very stuff of the curriculum" (p. 293).

Lenny Sánchez (2014), during an ethnographic study of a high-poverty 3rd-grade class, captured a fantastic example of how this approach can work to engage even elementary-age students and deepen their learning. Their teacher crafted an interdisciplinary project in which they combined math, literacy, and other skills to explore and respond to issues they deemed relevant to their own lives. One small group of students, calling themselves the "Park Fixers," chose to focus on an issue that had frustrated them and their classmates for months: safety concerns due to the deterioration of the school's playground, which also served as a community park after school. Sánchez, also a product of a low-income upbringing, marveled at the students' determination to collaborate with one another and to invite community members into their problem-solving processes. Because they were dealing with issues that were very real to them, they engaged vigorously, always a good sign for learning.

Barbara Comber and her colleagues (2006) described similar projects led by teachers in a low-income Australian neighborhood suffering disintegration, literally and figuratively, because of a government "urban renewal" initiative. The teachers constructed curricula around the many challenges this disintegration posed to students, integrating complex architectural and design concepts as well as spatial and visual literacy. The authors explained,

> children were able to become producers of space, re-imagining, redesigning, and remaking part of their school grounds within a neighborhood almost overtaken by urban renewal. Teachers worked with children to build a critically inflected curriculum and pedagogy around the redesign of a barren outdoor space. (p. 229)

Even if we aren't developing big new multidisciplinary projects, we can be more mindful about our everyday classroom practices. We can:

1. use examples and illustrations relevant and compelling to students experiencing poverty;
2. avoid creating quiz and test items around experiences students experiencing poverty are unlikely to have had, like golfing, skiing, or vacationing in the Northwoods; and
3. commit to learning about the lives of students experiencing poverty so that we can do #1 and #2 effectively.

Strategy Ten: Incorporate Music, Art, and Theater Across the Curriculum. In-school access to music, art, and theater education fortifies learning, engagement, and retention for all students, but can be particularly important for students experiencing poverty (Gorski, 2013; Pogrow, 2006). Economically marginalized families are less likely than wealthier families to have the money to provide these experiences outside school (Bracey, 2006). In-school access to the arts has an especially motivating effect on students who generally feel alienated at school. It can make them more likely to show up and stay engaged (Tranter & Palin, 2004).

Regrettably, as we discussed earlier, art and music programs are being slashed from public schools, and the fiercest slashing usually happens at the highest-poverty schools, sometimes because of insufficient funding, often to carve out additional time for reading, writing, and math instruction. Notably, according to Stacey Joyner and Concepcion Molina (2012), who synthesized a broad range of research on how extending instructional time affects student learning, there is scant evidence that simply lengthening instructional time for math or writing increases student achievement. More important than instructional *time*, they found, was instructional *quality*. Doing a better job teaching literacy is far more important and far less damaging than eliminating the arts to spend more time on literacy.

Given the potential of the arts to bolster learning and engagement for students experiencing poverty, a worthwhile strategy is to find ways in our own classrooms to integrate the arts into whatever we teach, especially at schools that have scaled back or cut art, music, and theater programs (Landsman & Gorski, 2007). Whether pointing to Picasso's use of geometric shapes in his paintings as part of an elementary mathematics lesson (Holtzman & Susholtz, 2011) or using Augusto Boal's Theatre of the Oppressed techniques with high school students to teach about community-based environmental science (Sullivan & Lloyd, 2006), the possibilities are endless.

As a place to begin, I provide in Figure 8.2 resources and guidebooks full of ideas for incorporating the arts into teaching.

Strategy Eleven: Incorporate Movement and Exercise into Learning. In too many high-poverty schools, recess and physical education are disappearing as quickly as art and music programs. Obviously, physically fit students fare better in school on average than their less fit peers, as Charles Basch (2011) found in his synthesis of 2 decades of research. Moreover, childhood physical fitness is a good predictor of lifelong health trajectories (Fahlman,

---

Figure 8.2. Resources for Incorporating Arts Across the Curriculum

Beginner's Guide to Community-Based Arts by Mat Schwarzman and Keith Knight (2005, New Village Press)

Engaging Films and Music Videos in Critical Thinking by Charlene Tan (2007, McGraw-Hill)

Handbook for K–8 Arts Integration: Purposeful Planning Across the Curriculum by Nan L. McDonald (2012, Pearson)

The Hip-Hop Education Guidebook by Marcella Runnell and Martha Diaz (2007, Hip-Hop Association)

Integrating the Arts across the Elementary School Curriculum by R. Phyllis Gelineau (2011, Wadsworth Publishing)

Music and Movement in the Classroom by Greg and Steven Trough (2004, Creative Teaching Press)

Schooling Hip-Hop: Expanding Hip-Hop Based Education Across the Curriculum by Marc Lamont Hill and Emery Petchauer (2013, Teachers College Press)

Teaching Music across the Curriculum by Valereai Luppens and Greg Formena (2011, Alfred Publishing)

Theatre of the Oppressed by Augusto Boal (1993, Theatre Communications Group)

Hall, & Lock, 2006); in other words, physically fit youth tend to become physically fit adults.

Unfortunately, due to the relative dearth of well-maintained recreational facilities like ball courts, sports fields, playgrounds, and recreation centers in high-poverty communities (Brann-Barrett, 2010; MacLeod, Gee, Crawford, & Wang, 2008), coupled with growing costs of recreational sports leagues, youth experiencing poverty may rely on recess or physical education as their only opportunities for organized exercise. This is especially true after middle school, when economically marginalized youth often care for younger siblings or work to help support their families (Fahlman et al., 2006). Making matters worse, students who are least likely to have access to out-of-school exercise opportunities also have the least access to school-based exercise opportunities, including physical education classes (Basch, 2011).

The good news is that there are several easy, applicable ways to incorporate physical movement into classroom instruction, and the list of available resources on how to do so in specific subject areas, or across subject areas, is growing longer every day. Take math, for example. Greg Hatch and Darla Smith (2004) have proposed powerful interdisciplinary ways to integrate physical education into math and physics classes to study, among other things, projectile motion. In her article "Students Hop, Skip, and Jump Their Way to Understanding," Andrea Elkin (2012) shares strategies for using movement to bolster young students' mastery of math competencies. When we follow these educators' leads and incorporate movement into our instruction, we take advantage of links among physical activity, brain power, and learning while also providing youth who, on average, have fewer chances to exercise than their wealthier counterparts with valuable opportunities that improve their health and bolster school engagement.

CONCLUSION

Perhaps the most outstanding feature of these strategies is that many are used as a matter of course in schools and classrooms full of middle-class and wealthier students. In those schools and classrooms, we might call these strategies "good teaching."

Perhaps we do not have the power to ensure that all students have access to preventive health care or shadow education or academic summer camps. But we all have the power to ensure that we are doing all we can so students experiencing poverty receive the best possible education when they are in our spheres of influence.

Whereas in this chapter I described research-supported instructional strategies, I set aside a separate chapter, Chapter 9, to share relational strategies. *How*, I ask in Chapter 9, *can we build authentic, equitable, respectful relationships with students and families experiencing poverty?*

REFLECTION QUESTIONS AND EXERCISES

1. Were you surprised by any of the data-informed instructional strategies discussed in this chapter? If so, which one? Why did it surprise you?

2. Develop or revise a curricular unit incorporating at least three of these strategies. Try incorporating one strategy you initially thought you would have a difficult time incorporating into your teaching.

3. Develop an idea for a project in which students use what they are learning in school to study class issues and poverty in their communities. Use the resources in Figure 8.1 to get started.

4. Are there other strategies you have used with students experiencing poverty that have proven successful? If so, what were they? How might you combine those strategies with the strategies described in this chapter?

CHAPTER 9

The Mother of All Strategies

Nurturing Equity-Informed Relationships with Students and Families

> Principles of Equity Literacy discussed in this chapter include:
>
> **Principle 1:** People experiencing poverty are the experts on their own experiences.
>
> **Principle 5:** What we believe about people experiencing poverty informs how we teach, interact with, and advocate (or fail to advocate) for them.
>
> **Principle 6:** We cannot understand the relationship between poverty and education without understanding the barriers and inequities that people experiencing poverty face in and out of schools.
>
> **Principle 9:** Equitable educators adopt a structural view rather than a deficit view of families experiencing poverty.

Instructional strategies are important, but they mean nary a whit if we are not equally vigilant about building equity-informed relationships with students and families (Battey, 2013). Students are smart and intuitive; it's hard to get one over on them. So every practical strategy in the world is mostly meaningless if we relate to economically marginalized youth or their families as though they are some lesser "other." Remember, as we learned earlier, who or what we choose to blame for poverty guides the policies and practices we are willing to implement (Lampert et al., 2016; Williams, 2009). What we believe about students experiencing poverty and how we relate to them is just as important as the mechanics of how we teach them; in fact, it plays a considerable role in determining both how we teach them (Comber, 2016; Robinson, 2007) and how we engage with their families (Parrett & Budge, 2012).

It is not always easy. When sincerely pursued and equity-informed, relationship-building is far more difficult than incorporating music or co-operative learning into our teaching. It requires, first, tremendous humility and a willingness to ask ourselves uncomfortable equity-literacy–type questions: *What stereotypes do I have about people experiencing poverty? What assumptions do I have about how relationships between teachers and families ought to look? Do I see youth experiencing poverty as broken or their families as morally deficient even if I try not to show it? Do I pity them or see myself as their fixer? How do my stereotypes, presumptions, and equity literacy weak spots show up in my interactions with students and families?* These sorts of questions help us take stock of our relational commitments to economically marginalized students because they force us to reveal to ourselves the biases and presumptions we carry into interactions with them. They nudge us to reflect on *our* attitudes, *our* behaviors, and *our* roles in improving the educational lives of youth experiencing poverty when it might be easier to shift blame or rest on the laurels of our good intentions.

Here's the equity-informed reality: Good intentions are of little mitigating consequence against bias (including unintended bias) and a lack of will to learn how to see and respond to the inequities explored in Chapters 6 and 7. As a result, sometimes we might create or broaden gulfs between ourselves and the most marginalized students, not because we want to harm them but because we fail to see the ways we are harming them. For example, one marker of economic privilege in schools is the ability to afford the newest fashions and name-brand clothes. The expectation to dress fashionably at school can create considerable stress for students whose families can't afford trendy clothes, as Tanya Brann-Barrett (2010) found in the ethnographic study of working-class youth mentioned earlier. Obviously, aside from enforcing a general dress code, I cannot control what students wear unless my school institutes a uniform policy. But I can control what I wear, which is something I never considered relevant before reading Brann-Barrett's study. I can think twice before donning a sweater or carrying a bag with an expensive brand name or logo plastered across it. I can choose never to compliment students on material possessions like fashionable clothing or pricey schoolbags. I can do the work to identify other ways I unintentionally highlight the economic gap between groups of students or between some students and me. I can become intentional about never doing those things again. This is equity literacy in action in my immediate sphere of influence. No amount of practical strategies gets me there if I do not have the knowledge to recognize the need to adjust the ways I relate to students and the will to make those adjustments.

EQUITY-INFORMED RELATIONAL COMMITMENTS

As I reflected on my experiences in schools, recalled conversations with educators, and pored over decades' worth of research on poverty and education looking for equity-informed relational commitments associated with high levels of engagement and success for students experiencing poverty, eight themes kept reappearing. We strengthen relationships with students experiencing poverty when we

1. embrace a structural view rather than a deficit view of families experiencing poverty;
2. demonstrate respect and compassion in relationships with families;
3. cultivate trusting relationships with students grounded in ethics of equity and humility;
4. broaden our notions of family engagement;
5. ensure that at-school opportunities for family engagement are accessible;
6. avoid making students or parents "perform" their poverty at school;
7. become inequity-responsive by finding ways to mitigate barriers they experience; and
8. elicit input from families experiencing poverty, but only if we have the will to follow it.

Commitment One: Embrace a Structural View Rather than a Deficit View of Families Experiencing Poverty. As we explored in earlier chapters, when we adopt a deficit view of students experiencing poverty, we begin with an assumption, however implicit, that they are somehow broken, needing to be fixed or rescued from a deficit-laden culture or "mindset of poverty." As we fixate on their "deficiencies," we risk failing to acknowledge the opportunity gaps they experience inside and outside schools—gaps that constitute the bulk of educational outcome disparities. As a result, we weaken our abilities to be responsive to the inequities and barriers bearing down on them, sometimes in our own classrooms. So our first relational commitment is to root out of ourselves any remnant of the deficit view and to embrace a structural view of families experiencing poverty.

Rejecting the deficit view, like having high academic expectations, is not self-esteem fluffiness. It is research- and equity-informed commitment-making. And it might just be the most essential ingredient in the effective relationship recipe between us and our most marginalized students.

Remember, again, that economically marginalized youth constantly see deficit reflections of themselves and their communities in the media as well as educational materials. Making matters worse, the dominant perception of people experiencing poverty is drenched in deficit views. Even if they are unwilling to say so in polite company, many people believe that poverty itself is a symptom of deficiencies in people experiencing it (Carreiro & Kapitulik, 2010), that "the poor" are undeserving of a more equitable or humane lot in life. We are flooded with rags-to-riches stories and celebrations of meritocracy even as upward mobility is rare and becoming rarer (Chetty et al.,

2016). When common misperceptions are nourished, a deficit view can feel natural and justified, especially among people who have never experienced homelessness, prolonged hunger, or the steady grind of class bias. Making matters worse, studies (see, for example, Smiley & Helfenbein, 2011) are revealing how some of the most popular teacher professional development programs ostensibly meant to help us better understand students experiencing poverty perpetuate the deficit stereotypes and perceptions they ought to dispel. (Oops!)

When we adopt a deficit view, seeing students' poverty as evidence of intellectual or moral inferiority, their academic performance and school engagement recede. We make ourselves incapable of seeing the biases and inequities students and families experience, which means we also make ourselves incapable of responding to or redressing those biases and inequities. The opposite happens when we adopt a structural view. We learn to see the biases and inequities clearly. We become curious about them. We eliminate the ones we can eliminate and mitigate those residing outside our spheres of influence. We make ourselves trustworthy to students and families who often have good reason not to trust authority figures.

Kathleen Cooter (2006), who reviewed research on best practices for partnering with low-income, illiterate mothers to strengthen youth literacy skills, urges us to focus not just on student strengths, but on parent and community strengths, to celebrate what they bring to the table in spite of the barriers they face. "Build on what the mother can do," Cooter advises. "Value what she knows, how she lives, and the uniqueness of her family." By adopting this approach, she explains, "we can respect the mother who can't read as her child's first and best teacher" (p. 701). And we can do so without alienating students or their families. Harkening back to Chapter 4, notice that this may require an ideological shift and the will to make that shift.

If it helps to think in selfish terms, J. Gregg Robinson (2007) found in his study of more than 400 teachers in high-poverty urban schools that those who rejected a deficit view were happier with their jobs than colleagues who retained a deficit view. Plus, teachers who adopted a structural view, who understood the barriers and inequities bearing down on families experiencing poverty, were more effective educators for students from low-income families. Why? They were more equity-responsive, better able to respond to the challenges with which students experiencing poverty contended. Robinson calls this phenomenon a "structurally mitigated sense of occupational competence" because it helped teachers understand their work in a larger context of inequities and economic injustice, even if they were not positioned to eliminate structural-level inequities and injustices. So being intentional about letting go of deficit views and focusing, instead, on understanding and responding to the challenges and barriers experienced by the most marginalized students is good for teaching, but it's also good for teacher morale: a win-win.

It begins with the will of equity literacy. We must cleanse ourselves of stale notions. Then we must cleanse ourselves of the temptation to grasp at well-marketed and shiny but misleading concepts that yank us out of a structural view and toward a deficit view. Consider all the frameworks thrown our way. Grit. Mindset of poverty. Growth mindset. Learn to notice how, when applied to school success for students experiencing poverty, these frameworks so often replace structural mindfulness with narrow deficit explanations and strategies. As equity-literate educators, we know (and research shows) that educational outcome disparities are almost entirely the result of inequitable distributions of access and opportunity in and out of schools, not deficient mindsets or shortages of grit.

If you struggle to understand or embrace a structural view despite the mounds of evidence, your first relational task is to examine why you hold so stubbornly to deficit notions—which notably are also *inaccurate* notions—and to find a way to cast them out of yourself. After all, our belief systems drive everything: how we interpret student behavior, which sorts of policy we adopt in our classrooms or schools, and even how we assess student work. Our beliefs drive how we interpret what we observe. How we interpret what we observe determines the solutions we are capable of imagining in response to what we observe. There is no path toward equity that incorporates a deficit view or that does not incorporate a structural view. We must position ourselves ideologically to see and eliminate biases and inequities (Gorski, 2016a).

Here's a hard reality: *Pretending* to have a structural view is not sufficient. Nor is having a deficit view but believing we can hide it from students and families. We can't. The crux of the matter is what we *believe*, the ideologies we embrace (Lampert et al., 2016; Prins & Schafft, 2009). This is where humility helps. Again, if we have spent our lives quietly believing that poverty exists because some people are too lazy or criminally minded to take advantage of their equal opportunity, and if we believe the most common stereotypes about people experiencing poverty (see Chapter 5) despite contrary evidence, our task is not to hide these views, but to rid ourselves of them. There are a variety of ways to do this, but good places to start include studying the history of economic injustice and reading about the societal and educational inequities that continue to plague communities and schools.

I was raised, as I mentioned, by a father from an urban working-class family and a mother from an economically impoverished Appalachian coal-mining family. Despite this heritage, I have to work vigilantly to shake myself free from the stereotypes I hear from the media, school, and peers *about my own family*. I spent a lot of time with my mother's Appalachian family growing up and always appreciated the determination and goodwill I saw around me. Nobody in that small mountain town needed any lessons on grit, I assure you. Still, it wasn't until I read Jonathan Kozol's *Savage Inequalities* (2012) and Herbert Gans's *The War Against the Poor* (1996) that I could appreciate these attributes in their proper context—a context of structural disadvantage. It wasn't until I read *Where We Stand: Class Matters* by bell hooks (2000), who grew up experiencing poverty, that I began to understand how remarkable my grandmother was. (I list other books that deepened my understanding of poverty and strengthened my equity literacy in Figure 9.1.) But I had to seek out this knowledge; nobody handed it to me. Mainstream media remain largely silent on it. In most ways, the structural view rubbed against every other message I consumed growing up about poverty and class.

I was conditioned for the deficit view and *chose* to remake my understanding, a process that continues today, not without its challenges.

Commitment Two: Demonstrate Respect and Compassion in Relationships with Families. For many economically marginalized families, schools and other public systems have been hostile environments for generations (Gorski, 2012). Families of Color and immigrant families experiencing poverty often face intensified levels and forms of hostility. If we sense hesitance as we reach out to some families experiencing poverty or families marginalized in other ways, it could reflect a justified response to a history of mistreatment, to generational injustice, a reasonable distrust for an education system that historically has not validated or welcomed those families. On the other hand, what we interpret as hesitance could be the result of long work hours or inadequate time to reload pay-as-you-go cellphones. Or it could be us—something we did or said perhaps unintentionally that cued a parent that we don't have their interests at heart. Do we have the will to consider this possibility?

Figure 9.1. Books about Poverty That Grew My Equity Literacy

The Corporation: The Pathological Pursuit of Profit and Power by Joel Bakan (2005, Free Press)

Just Mercy: A Story of Justice and Redemption by Bryan Stevenson (2015, Spiegel & Grau)

The New Jim Crow: Mass Incarceration in the Age of Colorblindness by Michelle Alexander (2012, The New Press)

Savage Inequalities by Jonathan Kozol (2012, Harper)

The Story of Stuff by Annie Leonard (2011, Free Press)

The Travels of a T-Shirt in the Global Economy by Pietra Rivoli (2009, Wiley)

The United States of Appalachia by Jeff Biggers (2007, Counterpoint)

The War Against the Poor by Herbert Gans (1996, Basic Books)

Where We Stand: Class Matters by bell hooks (2000, Routledge)

Women, Race, and Class by Angela Davis (1983, Vintage Books)

Respect, compassion, and vigilant nonjudgment are crucial. We must establish and sustain our trustworthiness and, perhaps more importantly, demonstrate *our* trust in families experiencing poverty (Hoy, Tarter, & Hoy, 2006). We do this first by eliminating lingering deficit attitudes and deepening our structural understandings of the barriers with which they are contending (Parrett & Budge, 2012). Enter the relationship with the respect and compassion that grow out of that understanding.

How might we nurture these trusting relationships? Consistent two-way communication (Barr & Parrett, 2007) is key, rather than only reaching out with negative news, which sadly is what many families have come to expect (Milner, 2015). But equally important as how often we reach out is *how* we relate to families when we do. Susan B. Neuman (2009), who has studied poverty and literacy for a couple of decades, urges us to recognize parents as partners and gear our outreach with that sort of relationship in mind. By doing so, and by being persistent and compassionate even during stretches when parents might appear unresponsive, we increase the likelihood that they will feel comfortable sharing information about their children's home lives that might be relevant to our teaching (Howard, 2007).

Researchers have found a direct, on-the-ground relationship between meaningful parental relationship-building and student achievement. For example, in a longitudinal study of 71 high-poverty elementary schools, student achievement grew faster in both reading and math when teachers engaged more actively in parent outreach (U.S. Department of Education, 2001). In fact, "Growth in [reading] test scores between third and fifth grade was 50 percent higher for those students whose teachers and schools reported high levels of parental outreach . . . than students whose teachers and schools reported low levels of parent outreach activities for the third grade" (p. 1).

Of course, as I've stressed, test scores are inadequate measures of equity. Coming at the issue of family relationship-building from a different angle, Derek Messacar and Philip Oreopoulos (2012) explain, "When . . . educators communicate more regularly with parents regarding their children's performance, they provide a means for parents to take a more active role" (p. 14), increasing the chances their children will stay in school. Similarly, Katherine Curry and her colleagues (2016) emphasize the importance of reciprocal relationships. Provide meaningful opportunities for engagement, they implore. Build relationships with families that prioritize their needs and barriers, enhancing "the agency . . . of parents . . . in influencing their children's education" (p. 867).

Lose the deficit view, respect what families bring, have compassion for the inequities and biases they face, and be willing to fight those inequities and biases in your sphere of influence. This is the recipe for productive relationships with families experiencing poverty.

Commitment Three: Cultivate Trusting Relationships with Students Grounded in Ethics of Equity and Humility. Meditate for a moment on this question: Is there a place you've been where you didn't feel safe or accepted? We all have attended social gatherings where we felt out of place. But try to recall somewhere you *had* to be for sustained periods of time, somewhere from which you could not just walk away when discomfort set in. If you struggle to recall such a place, you are experiencing the protection of privilege. Unfortunately, for many students experiencing poverty, one of those places is school. If you share that experience, you know how difficult it can be.

I don't believe that this sad reality is mostly the fault of rabidly class-biased teachers and administrators doing purposefully class-biased things. Sure, there are some unapologetic and purposeful bigots in education, as in every field. But most of the inequities experienced by economically marginalized students at school are the result of a web of implicit, often unintentional, policy and practice humiliations.

This, then, is our challenge. Like their parents, many youth from families experiencing poverty, who are more likely than their wealthier peers to have experienced these inequities and humiliations, have no particular reason to trust institutions like schools. As discussed earlier, economically marginalized Students of Color or English language learners or Muslim students or transgender students or others who might have experienced multiple layers of inequities and humiliations could—*should*, really—be cautious with their trust. Nor, like their parents, do some economically marginalized students have much reason to trust institutional authority figures, whom they might see as representatives of institutions in which they have experienced these inequities and humiliations. One of the most troubling components of the popular "mindset of poverty" view for understanding poverty is the way its proponents often identify this sort of distrust of authority as a deficiency in the characters of economically marginalized youth. This, of course, is a classic case of the deficit view: People experiencing poverty must cope with bias and other indignities and then are deemed deficient or troublemakers for responding in perfectly reasonable ways to these experiences. It's the double whammy of injustice and bias.

My point is that, as educators, we cannot and should not rely on our positional authority when it comes to gaining the trust of students experiencing poverty (Hughes, Newkirk, & Stenhjem, 2010). We need deeper ways to build that trust because it relates directly to student achievement (Kannapel & Clements, 2005; Ramalho et al., 2010). This can take time because it might require us to undo damage done previously by teachers or counselors who have expressed low expectations of them, assigned books with stereotypical portrayals of people like them, or treated their parents condescendingly.

Some important ways to build trusting relationships with students experiencing poverty are described in the previous chapter: pedagogically demonstrating high academic expectations, responding to bias in educational materials, and making the curriculum relevant to their lives. But there are other things we can do, or do better, to nurture strong, trusting relationships. Lois Weiner (2003) encourages us to pay serious attention to the full range of equity concerns in our classrooms, because it is difficult for students to trust us when we allow any sort of bias or inequity to go unchecked. Our best shot at doing so requires us to cultivate our equity literacy, not just related to class and poverty, but also related to gender identity and expression, race, sexual orientation, religion, (dis)ability, and other issues. If we hope to thrust these inequities out of our classrooms, we need to learn how to see them, even in their most insidious, implicit forms. It's not just about interrupting racist or heterosexist name-calling. It's also about recognizing ways in which Whiteness and heterosexuality are presented as "normal," which can be difficult to spot, especially if I haven't been the target of racism or heterosexism.

Based on her study of how the most effective teachers teach children from low-income families, Lizette Howard (2007) argues that we build trusting relationships with them when see them as *whole* students, when we take the time to get to know their hopes, fears, and interests. Like all these relational commitments, this means resisting the temptation to think that all students experiencing poverty are alike or share a singular culture or mindset. It means getting to know students individually.

The most efficient way to lose trust of low-income students is to invalidate concerns they raise about the biases and inequities they're experiencing (Hamovitch, 1996). It's important, at all costs, to avoid telling a student who is attempting to self-advocate that she is overreacting or seeing things all wrong. This, too, is where humility is important. Are we willing to listen to students' concerns and be responsive to those concerns even if we don't see the bias they see? Do we have the humility to consider the possibility that our not seeing what they see is a call to strengthen our equity literacy and not a call for us to question their experience?

Commitment Four: Broaden Our Notions of Family Engagement. As we learned in Chapter 5, study after study of families experiencing poverty, urban or rural, of Color or White, has reached the same conclusion: They care as deeply as any other family about their children's education (Jarrett & Coba-Rodriguez, 2015; Lucio et al., 2016; Marcella et al., 2014; Robinson & Volpé, 2015). Study after study after study. Still, the most pernicious and *inaccurate* stereotype I hear from teachers is, *Those parents don't care about their children's education.*

Remember, sometimes what we interpret as disinterest is evidence, instead, of educators' collective struggle to imagine family engagement through an equity literacy lens, in ways that consider the barriers economically marginalized parents face. When we hold onto old notions of family engagement that were conceived through middle-class norms, we implicitly communicate to families experiencing poverty that their needs are unimportant, that we will not be responsive to the inequities they bear. This can only deteriorate our relationships with them—something none of us wants.

What if we rethink our approaches to family engagement, building them around the realities of economically marginalized families? What if we learn as much as we can about the challenges individual parents face—working multiple jobs, working evening shifts, being denied access to paid leave—and broaden our notions of family engagement around those challenges? This can be an informative equity literacy exercise. We start by wiping away everything we thought we knew about family engagement. Then we list all the barriers families experiencing poverty in our communities face. Finally, we reshape our notions of family engagement around those challenges. We prioritize the interests of the families with the least access and opportunity in our family engagement practice. This is what equity looks like.

For example, many parents experiencing poverty simply cannot come to school often. This is not because they are irresponsible—there's the troubling deficit view again. Perhaps they are working multiple jobs into the evening, lack transportation, cannot afford child care. If somebody cannot attend school events or volunteer during the school day because they are working or taking care of younger children, we need to drop the deficit view and recognize that they *are* being responsible. In the case of ELL parents, some might worry that they do not have language skills to communicate effectively, especially if we have failed to provide adequate interpreters. Whatever might be keeping them from coming to the school as often as their wealthier peers, they remain our partners. They can still be engaged. Even parents who are not fluent in English can play crucial roles in their children's literacy. They can help to strengthen their children's literacy in their home languages, which is crucial to their acquisition of English.

Others can encourage their children to read, encourage them to do their homework. They can model a joy for learning or set aside even a small space for children to do schoolwork. In fact, some studies show that parents experiencing poverty already are *more likely* than their wealthier peers to be involved in these ways (Noel et al., 2013). We must recognize and encourage this kind of engagement rather than wag our deficit fingers at those whose life circumstances, a product of inequity and not deficiency, limit their abilities to be engaged in other ways.

We also can commit to a true partnership approach. In a partnership, we do not dictate the terms of engagement. We do not offer lists of demands. Instead, we begin by soliciting from our partners their ideas or descriptions of what they're already doing. We celebrate what they're doing. We ask what they need from us in addition to sharing what we need from them. If they do come in to volunteer, we collaborate toward identifying meaningful opportunities for engagement. Whatever partnership emerges, it must be driven on our end by humility, compassion, and equity literacy.

Commitment Five: Ensure That At-School Opportunities for Family Involvement Are Accessible. Are the opportunities we provide for school-based family involvement as accessible to families experiencing poverty as to wealthier families? Think a moment about standard approaches for scheduling back-to-school events, parent–teacher conferences, and other school functions. What obstacles might they present for parents?

Time constraints pose one challenge. In her study comparing the lives of low-income and middle-class 1st-graders, Annette Lareau (1994) found that low-income families experienced considerably less time flexibility, making some forms of school involvement, like volunteering during the school day, nearly impossible. As we schedule opportunities for family involvement, we must consider time poverty—the way time as a resource is not distributed equally (Williams et al., 2016). For example, events often are scheduled at times inaccessible for people who work late shifts or work multiple jobs, disproportionately affecting economically marginalized parents (Van Galen, 2007).

Affordability is another concern. Family involvement might appear free, but it comes at a cost for many families. Adults in families experiencing poverty usually work wage jobs and do not have access to paid leave, which is another currency often taken for granted by those who have it. Economically marginalized families also are more likely than their wealthier peers to rely on public transportation, which is another cost, of both money and time. Then there's the cost of child care if parents are unable to bring their children with them.

When we fall short of responding to, or even acknowledging, these challenges, we send the kinds of messages that most of us never want to send. We say, however implicitly, that we do not value the involvement of low-income parents or, worse, that we do not *expect* them to want to be involved. When we fail to respond to or acknowledge these challenges and then, against the clearest contrary evidence, blame educational outcome disparities on the supposed disinterest of parents experiencing poverty, we brew a perfect recipe for inimical parent relationships.

Among our most important relational commitments is to make family involvement as accessible to families experiencing poverty as possible (Cooper, 2010). Schools increasingly are finding ways to mitigate the time and financial challenges associated with on-site school involvement, providing child care and transportation or hosting events at community centers in high-poverty neighborhoods (Kiyama et al., 2015). Teachers might offer the option of phone conferences when parents cannot leave work to attend an event at the school. The same strategy can defray child care and transportation costs.

Another important strategy is scheduling events or individual parent–teacher conferences more flexibly. Some parents will have more availability early in the morning, on Saturday, or during late evenings than during late-afternoon or early-evening blocks (Howard, Dresser, & Dunklee, 2009; Robinson & Volpé, 2015). For those of us who feel we have little influence over how our schools schedule events or whether other challenges are addressed adequately in school event planning, we can at the very least apply the spirit of these principles to our individual communications and relationship-building practices whenever possible.

Imagine the mental calculus. I am the parent of a child experiencing poverty. I work two wage jobs to make ends meet. I receive an announcement about an event at school that I want to attend. I know what you are going to think of me if I don't attend because several of my child's previous teachers have directed some subtle finger-wagging my way when I missed school events. But as a wage worker, I sacrifice pay when I miss work—if I'm lucky enough to have permission to miss work—and that threatens my ability to pay the heating bill and feed my child. The event is only an hour, but I need to take the bus, which means additional time and additional cost. I'm working my buns off trying to make ends meet, but I know there are people in that school building thinking, if not actually saying, that I don't care enough to show up. I want to go, but economically I cannot afford to go. What do I do?

Finally, try to remember that on top of time and financial constraints, school has been a hostile place for many economically marginalized people, both as students and as adults (Graham, 2009). Making family involvement accessible also means making it socially, culturally, and emotionally accessible for people who have negative associations with schools. This includes people who are worried based on previous experiences that they will be perceived as uneducated or inarticulate (Robinson & Volpé, 2015)—a concern that could be elevated for parents whose home languages are not English. It means that everybody in the building must learn how to treat each parent with respect and without presumption or bias.

There is only one way to do this: Ditch the deficit views and push the prejudices out of our thinking. Treat all parents respectfully, as collaborators and as the primary experts about their children and communities. Start by eliminating from our spheres of influence the old thinking about "uncaring parents." We can look at our individual and institutional family involvement practices through an equity literacy lens instead and flip the conversation: Do we care enough about the involvement of families experiencing poverty to prioritize their experiences and interests in the way we schedule involvement opportunities?

Commitment Six: Avoid Making Students or Parents "Perform" Their Poverty at School. Working with schools and school districts around the world, I'm almost always impressed by the compassion educators show students experiencing poverty. I have seen in classroom after classroom boxes full of coats and sweatshirts, cabinets full of snacks, and stockpiles of poster board, pencils, and paper. Several schools host food pantries and other services. I have watched teachers allocate these resources to students who need them, often spending their own money to help students whose families struggle to afford various necessities. This is all good.

Even in these classrooms and schools, and despite the compassion, I also have witnessed policies and practices that force students and parents to "perform" their poverty—to interact or behave in ways that spotlight their economic marginalization, reminding them and everyone within eye-shot they do not belong. In most cases it is a subtle forcing, like the promise of a needed resource dangling in reach if only they are willing to "out" themselves once again as poor and ask for it. Single cases of this performing can be humiliating to economically marginalized people, who often also are required to perform their poverty outside of schools, whether purchasing food using government assistance programs or interviewing for jobs without being able to afford a fashionable outfit. But the bigger potential harm comes into view when we consider the accumulation of these single humiliations.

Sometimes it is a matter of good intentions short on equity literacy. For example, in many—perhaps *most*—of the high-poverty and mixed-class schools I've visited, somebody controls a fund students or families can tap to cover expenses they cannot afford, such as a fee for an extracurricular activity or field trip. They can tap it, that is, if they ask around to learn who controls the fund and approach that person to request help. This week they might need help to pay the fee for the robotics club. Next month it might be for the forensics team trip or a band instrument: each one a performance, students or their parents having to mentally prepare for a series of grinding humiliations. We could wipe these forced performances of poverty out immediately (Shields, 2014) by refusing to charge families money for any educational experience. As a general rule, we re-create inequity when students' access to educational opportunities is determined by their wealth. We exacerbate this inequity when we then force families who ought to have equitable access to keep asking for that access.

There are subtler but equally damaging examples. We ask students on the first day of school to describe what they did on summer vacation, high-lighting the socioeconomic differences between those whose families could afford to travel and send their children to camps and those who spent the summer working and taking care of younger siblings. We send packets of class photos home, requiring families to return the ones they do not wish (or cannot afford) to purchase. We celebrate dress-up days or weeks (where each day is a different theme), inconsiderate of what this means for families who cannot afford closets full of play clothes. We host a fundraiser, auction-ing student art to the highest bidder. In some schools we inexplicably and indefensibly still send students using free or reduced-price lunch through separate lunch lines. We subtly associate school spirit with the ability to afford school swag such as t-shirts and hoodies with school logos. We fail to interrupt the social pressure students feel to purchase yearbooks or dress up for homecoming or prom. We can end all of this now if we have the will to do so. Start by reconstructing policy and practice around the experiences and interests of our most marginalized students. Sure, we all have practices or procedures we've used for years, decades, generations. A clear sign we are off the equity path is when we defend them or continue using them because we've always used them when we have the option to be more compassionate and equitable.

Figure 9.2 lists some of the ways students and parents are forced to "perform" their poverty in school. Notice that even when participation appears optional, nonparticipation is in and of itself a sort of forced performance. Maybe you or your school do not do anything described in this list. But chances are you do something akin to items on this list. A commitment to equity requires us to identify and eliminate these somethings.

Commitment Seven: Be Inequity-Responsive by Finding Ways to Mitigate Barriers Economically Marginalized Students Experience. It might be beyond our spheres of influence to completely erase disparities in students' access to computers, adequate food, and warm clothes. However, we can find ways to mitigate those disparities even in our own classrooms. We also can use our equity literacy to ensure that we are not unintentionally recreating those disparities.

Figure 9.2. Practices and Procedures that Force People Experiencing Poverty to "Perform" Their Poverty

1. Charging extra fees for school activities, then offering financial help if students or their parents ask for it.
2. Requiring students who cannot afford a fee to participate in an activity to raise money for it by selling things.
3. Running more general fundraisers in which students compete to sell items like chocolate or candles.
4. Offering educational opportunities such as field trips only for families that can afford them.
5. Withholding diplomas or altogether refusing to allow students to graduate or participate in end-of-year ceremonies due to unpaid fees.
6. Instituting bring-your-own-technology policies.
7. Hosting dress-up days.
8. Having holiday events such as Valentine exchanges.
9. Instituting a rotating process for parents to provide snacks for the class.
10. Asking students to bring donations to school to pay for special activities or projects.

This commitment begins with curiosity about students' lives. As mentioned way back in Chapter 6, it can be easy to assume that access and opportunity disparities students experience outside school are irrelevant in school. Unfortunately, that assumption is dead wrong. When families see our willingness to respond to the challenges they face, trust comes a little easier.

Most of us have individual and institutional head starts on this commitment, keeping general supplies around for students who need them (Guinan & Hansell, 2014). We keep snacks in our classrooms for students who are hungry and coats for students who might need them on blustery days. We hide poster board behind the bookcase for students who need it. We pour students' school supplies into community bins so that all students have access to a wealth of resources and not only those their parents could afford.

Institutionally, as I mentioned earlier, many schools have food or clothing pantries. Others provide packs of take-home school supplies to students who need them. Some offer free access to washers and dryers, responding to research showing that some students are hesitant to come to school because of the bullying they experience due to unwashed clothes (Lineburg & Ratliff, 2015). In Chapter 10 we explore the value of wraparound services, in which we can collaborate with local service providers to offer services like health screenings.

As we consider ways we can mitigate inequitable access to resources, we must keep Commitment Six in mind and make sure we find quiet ways to distribute whatever mitigating access we can provide. We do not want to redistribute access and opportunity in ways that require families to perform their poverty. In that spirit, as we seek ways to mitigate disparate access to resources, we also can assess our policies and practices to avoid unintentionally exacerbating disparities. For example, if we have students who do not have access to computers and the Internet, do we assign homework that requires use of these resources? Are there any educational opportunities at our schools that are disparately accessible to students based on their families' abilities to afford the fees?

Commitment Eight: Elicit Input from Families Experiencing Poverty, but Only If We Have the Will to Follow It. Families experiencing poverty are the experts on their own lives and experiences. If those of us who have never experienced poverty cannot acknowledge this reality and treat them as the experts they are, we have little chance of building positive collaborative relationships with them. We should invest energy and time getting to know them and nurture our compassion about and responsiveness to the barriers they face, becoming co-conspirators in the struggle for equity in and perhaps even out of schools.

Still, by a large margin, the most important resources in our movement toward educational equity, whether we are battling racism, heterosexism, transphobia, economic injustice, or any other structural inequity, are the communities of people struggling for their own liberation on these fronts. Our way forward should be determined in large part by their expertise and desires. No matter how committed to equity we imagine ourselves to be, if we have not experienced poverty, there will always be gaps in our understandings and reach. This is not a criticism. It is not about shame. It is an embraceable value, a strategic relational insight.

What does input-eliciting look like in practice? We should work with economically marginalized communities to identify the most salient challenges and strategize toward eliminating or mitigating them (Cookson, 2013; Gorski, 2016b). Classroom teachers can work directly with parents. Whatever our role in schools, we can invite community leaders into conversations, building lasting strategic collaborations. Some schools host focus groups to elicit feedback from parents and other community members. Focus groups can be a good starting point, but only after we do the work to cultivate strong relationships. Of course, we also should elicit feedback from and strategize with students about what we could do better to create equitable educational lives for them.

Unfortunately, too often teachers or schools elicit this input, creating the illusion of partnership, then refuse to adjust policy or practice in response to it. Do not pretend to partner if you do not have the will to be responsive to what you hear, if you are not willing to make concrete changes based on the community's expertise. Seeking collaboration and then ignoring what we hear is exploitative and can elevate distrust. But seeking collaborations and then being responsive to what we hear will almost surely elevate trust.

CONCLUSION

Relational commitments are just as important as practical strategies. They might be *more* important, because they determine our abilities to cultivate trust and collaborative connections with students and their families. They also can be harder to implement than practical strategies because they require honest examinations of our biases and presumptions about poverty and people experiencing it.

In my teacher education classes I usually have students keep daily journals in which they record the moments their biases crop up. They are always surprised at how often it happens. There's no shame in the biases, I insist to these teachers-in-training, unless we choose not to work through them when we identify them. It helps to have a community of colleagues to support us in the process. And it helps to remember, in the end, that owning our biases and the harmful aspects of our ideologies, however difficult, is equally triumphant. When it comes to equity literacy, ridding ourselves of biases and watching our relationships with students and families shift in response to our new insights might be the biggest possible triumph. No strategy is more clearly within our individual spheres of influence as that.

Next, in Chapter 10, we build on these relational commitments by considering leadership commitments and strategies. We ask, what does it mean to lead with equity literacy?

REFLECTION QUESTIONS AND EXERCISES

1. Considering schools where you have been a student, parent, or educator, how might opportunities for family involvement be made more accessible to families experiencing poverty? Make sure to focus on being responsive to the barriers they face and naming what the school could do differently.

2. In addition to examples discussed in this chapter and other parts of this book, what are classroom or school practices or policies that might force people experiencing poverty to "perform" their poverty at school? Try to think of at least one practice or policy ostensibly meant to support students experiencing poverty but that was executed in a way that forced them to perform their poverty. How could this policy or practice be changed to eliminate the forced performance?

3. What are some respectful, collaborative ways schools can elicit input from economically marginalized families?

CHAPTER 10

Cultivating School Change through Equity Literacy

Commitments and Strategies
for School and District Leaders

Principles of Equity Literacy discussed in this chapter include:

Principle 1: People experiencing poverty are the experts on their own experiences.

Principle 8: Educational outcome disparities are the result of inequities, of unjust distributions of access and opportunity, not the result of deficiencies in the mindsets, cultures, or grittiness of people experiencing poverty.

Principle 9: Equitable educators adopt a structural view rather than a deficit view of families experiencing poverty.

Principle 10: Strategies for creating and sustaining equitable classrooms, schools, and school systems must be based on evidence of what works.

Principle 12: There is no path to educational equity that does not involve a redistribution of access and opportunity.

During a recent workshop for school superintendents in Pennsylvania, a participant—I'll call him Mitchell—described a familiar equity conundrum. Parents at his wealthier schools were raising loads of money to mitigate the barrage of budget cuts. One year they raised so much at one high school that they funded the hiring of an additional science teacher. But parents at the higher-poverty schools, despite caring just as deeply about their children's education, did not have the time or resources to raise that kind of money. They usually managed to raise a couple thousand dollars—enough, perhaps, to support a few extracurriculars or student trips. It was a classic, chronic case of *privilege begets privilege*.

Mitchell was miffed. He wanted to run an equitable ship. He wanted to flex his equity literacy muscles and redistribute access and opportunity, but these fundraising disparities made resource equity impossible. He spent months meeting with various people about what to do.

Jaws dropped when Mitchell described what he eventually did. Modeling the will of equity literacy, he decided, against the school board's wishes and impassioned warnings from staff, that every penny raised through PTAs or other entities would be amassed into one district pot. A committee would disseminate it based on need.

If we look at this policy purely on its equity merits, on its commitment to a fairer distribution of access and opportunity, it's hard to imagine a compelling argument against it. As we learned in Chapter 2, this is how equity works. Access and opportunity are finite resources. When we redistribute them, it can feel like a loss to people accustomed to a disproportionate share. The *will* of equity literacy requires us to cultivate equity despite the blowback. That is what Mitchell did.

You can imagine the complaints, the political grandstanding of some school board members, the insistence from the most privileged families that Mitchell's policy victimized their children. Mitchell did the mental calculus and decided the blowback was worth the equity progress. Then he acted. He probably risked his job. But his district was making gains in graduation rates and shrinking other outcome disparities. The leverage helped.

Most fellow workshop attendees were incredulous. "We could never do that in my district. They'd have our heads," one exclaimed. "Oh no, I don't think so," another chuckled awkwardly. It was as though they were so strapped to the way things had been that they were incapable of even imagining a more equitable future.

In this chapter I challenge school and district leaders—principals, instructional coaches, department heads, professional development directors, anyone who is a positional or informal leader—to enact policy and practice changes that shift institutional culture toward equity. Perhaps some of us do not have the leverage or boldness to make the change Mitchell made—at least not yet. That is a lesson in itself: In this supposedly "great equalizer" system, there are moves many of us could never imagine making even though without question they would create more equity. What does that say about the system and whose interests it prioritizes? What does it say about us?

It is equally true that there is no blueprint, no infallible sequence of initiatives sure to land everyone at equity. Mitchell didn't begin the process with this funding initiative. He worked toward it with a sense of purpose, building momentum first.

Following his lead, I include here both momentum-building strategies and strategies that require bigger institutional shifts. They are drawn from two sources: (1) research on effective equity practices for leaders working in schools or districts with significant or growing numbers of students experiencing poverty, and (2) insights I've gained working with school and district leaders as they labor toward contextually sound solutions. As with all strategies, each will be more or less relevant to you based on contextual factors. It is up to you to decide what has the most transformative potential in your school or district. Remember, though, as I argue throughout this book, policy and practice shifts must be matched by understanding and ideological shifts. Your most important first strategy is to strengthen your equity literacy and the equity literacy of everybody in your building.

The strategies offered in this chapter are grouped around three big guiding commitments for educational leaders: (1) shaping institutional culture around an ethic of equity, (2) cultivating equity literacy in faculty and staff, and (3) creating policies and practices to redistribute access and opportunity.

SHAPING INSTITUTIONAL CULTURE AROUND AN ETHIC OF EQUITY

The most common mistake I observe as school leaders work toward institutional change for equity is not so much about strategy as about pacing. There's a common notion in the world of "diversity and inclusion" work that we should meet people where they are, that progress toward equity is developmental. This is true to some extent in the sense that all individual learning is developmental. However, development ought to connote forward movement; it should never become a justification for heel-dragging.

At an institutional level—a school or district level—some leaders have the mistaken idea that they must wait for the entire staff to catch up developmentally before fomenting change. I often hear comments like, "We're taking baby steps" or "We're not quite ready for that level of change." Over time, this approach prioritizes the comfort and safety of our most resistant colleagues over the comfort and safety of our most marginalized students (and colleagues). That is equity's opposite.

As we take stock of our potential for reshaping institutional culture for equity, we start with the realization that we can't wait for everybody to be on board. Multiple equity initiatives can happen simultaneously. We must change harmful policies and practices through our equity lenses *right now* as we identify them, even if some of our colleagues struggle to adapt to new ways of doing things. If we cultivate it mindfully, equity literacy gives us the knowledge and skills that allow us to naturally see the harmfulness and understand what needs to change. Students who are suffering right now under problematic practices cannot afford for us to wait until everybody buys in or for us to walk gingerly, hesitatingly, toward equity. We can start creating change now while also working to pull the hesitators along.

With this sense of urgency in mind, we begin the process of shaping institutional culture around an ethic of equity using these equity leadership actions:

Visibly and Vocally Embrace Equity. We must be vocal and visible in our equity advocacy: *This is who we are as an institution. This is where we are going. If you want to fit in here, you need to prioritize equity.*

Too many leaders pawn this responsibility off on people with less power in the school or district. Institutional change is not the responsibility of a student club or an ad hoc committee. It is up to leaders to set the equity tone by publicly flexing our equity literacy muscles. If we visibly and vocally make equity a priority, we send a message to others it should be a priority for them, too (Milner, 2015).

Unfortunately, the most common question I hear from teachers is, "What if I want to institute more equitable practices but I don't feel supported by leadership?" The commonness of this question reflects our failure, a failure of leadership. Similarly, in their research, William Parrett and Kathleen Budge (2012) found that school-level leaders often feel stymied by their district-level supervisors when it comes to instituting positive change for equity. This is how inequity persists in an institution where most people want equity.

Perhaps we cannot control the message or mandates coming down *to* us, but we can control the message and mandates coming *from* us. We can name inequity and advocate equity at every opportunity, wrapping it into the everyday conversations in our spheres of influence. We can make equity a central aspect of our institutional culture, even in an individual classroom. Our most important strategy is to do so through public displays of our commitment.

Publicly Support People Advocating Equity. If you want to assess your school or district's commitment to equity, consider how the people most vehement about equity are treated. In many schools—even those with a stated commitment to equity—the most vigorous equity advocates are marginalized, seen as troublemakers simply for pointing out inequitable practices or challenging institutional bias. They often are pushed so far to the margins of the institutional culture that, despite their equity expertise, they are omitted from committees or work groups assembled to craft diversity and equity policy. This is a sign of a sick institutional culture.

In a school or district committed to equity, the most vigorous advocates with the most equity expertise are at the center of institutional culture. As leaders, we publicly celebrate their commitment. We hold them up as examples. If they have deeper expertise than we do on an equity issue, we have the will to defer to their expertise, then champion their ideas. We protect them from the hostility many equity advocates feel from colleagues who prefer the old institutional culture.

By doing so, we ward off the threat of burnout (Gorski & Chen, 2015)—one of the conditions that drive many equity-oriented educators out of teaching careers because of how they are punished at every turn simply for advocating for the most marginalized families. As equity-oriented leaders, the last thing we want is to lose colleagues who will help us shift the institutional culture. After the families themselves, these colleagues are our greatest equity assets. Acknowledge and treat them in such a way that everybody will see this is true.

Challenge Deficit Views Directly. As I discussed in Chapter 4, progress toward equity for families experiencing poverty cannot occur through a deficit view, even at the individual classroom level. We are no threat to inequity if our energy is focused on fixing fictional mindset or grit deficiencies in students experiencing poverty rather than redressing the conditions that deny them an equitable distribution of access and opportunity (Gorski, 2016c). If we hope to make institutional progress, we must eliminate the deficit view from the institutional culture.

For school leaders, this means directly challenging the deficit view in our own minds and in the words and actions of colleagues (Shields, 2014). We can challenge them humbly, remembering that we're all on a path toward greater consciousness. But we can't allow public expressions of the deficit view or other negative attitudes toward students or families to go unchallenged (Parrett & Budge, 2012). Doing so is complicity.

In describing a principal who modeled an ethic of critical care, one building block of equity literacy, Camille Wilson (2016) pointed to his zero-tolerance approach to deficit views. Such an approach requires not just naming the deficit view when it crops up, but also providing learning opportunities that help shift people's thinking by bridging them from a personal failure view of poverty to a view that associates poverty with inequity and injustice (Jones & Vagle, 2013).

Demystify and Challenge Inequitable State or District Policy. A common strategy among people and organizations behind the spate of recent neoliberal school reforms—merit pay, school vouchers, and drastic increases in high-stakes testing, for example—is to frame their policy initiatives as *equity* initiatives. We mustn't be fooled. The consensus among people and organizations who study educational equity is clear: Despite being sold as increasing access and opportunity for racially, economically, linguistically, and otherwise marginalized students, these reforms roundly bolster the access and opportunity of families who already have the most access and opportunity. Charter schools have been no threat at all to educational outcome disparities and, it turns out, are more racially and economically segregated on average than neighborhood public schools (Orfield & Frankenberg, 2013; Rotberg, 2014). Vouchers might give middle-class families more options, but they generally don't help families experiencing poverty, and they pull much-needed resources out of high-poverty neighborhood public schools (Ravitch, 2016).

It can be a puzzle figuring out how to stave off the influences of these initiatives. In some cases we might not be able to stave them off completely, at least in the immediate term. Sometimes we are forced to follow mandates at least temporarily, even when we know they do damage, like just about every time we give a young child a high-stakes test. But one thing we can do, perhaps while we work toward the kinds of bigger change discussed in the next chapter, is to look deeply into how state and federal education policy impacts students and families experiencing poverty (Milner, 2015). We can cultivate our equity literacy to develop clearer understandings of how the ramifications of these policies in our schools—how the pressures of high-stakes testing can undermine students' access to engaging pedagogy and a robust education, for example—tend to have the most adverse impact on the most marginalized students. Then we can do everything in our power to mitigate the damage.

If we want to be credible leaders for equity, it is incumbent upon us to learn both how to see this reality clearly and how to demystify these policies in our spheres of influence (Wilson, 2016). Be honest and critical about the damage they're doing. We can commit to becoming *policy-fluent* (Miller, Pavlakis, Lac, & Hoffman, 2014), extending our equity literacy to understand how even noneducation state and federal policy related to health care, housing, and other areas harms students experiencing poverty, compromising their educational potentials. As mentioned previously, even if we don't have the power to overturn this policy in the immediate term, we can encourage conversations about how our schools or districts can mitigate their effects on the most marginalized families.

Hire with Equity Literacy in Mind. In a school or district committed to equity, the equity lens should be second nature. Every decision should be filtered through it. This includes hiring, even when we're not hiring somebody for a specific equity position.

A couple of fairly easy steps can help us reshape hiring practices with an eye on equity. First, consider all applicants' attitudes about families experiencing poverty (Djonko-Moore, 2016)—better yet, do this intersectionally, considering all applicants' attitudes about Students of Color, immigrant students, English language learners, and other disproportionately marginalized groups. You can begin by adding a single question to every interview protocol: *In your view, why do students experiencing poverty not do as well in school on average as their wealthier peers?* In the best-case scenario, the applicant responds with a structural equity view, pointing to the barriers with which students experiencing poverty contend. This applicant is likely to be an advocate for students experiencing poverty and an asset to our equity culture. If an applicant responds with a deficit view, a list of problems with the cultures, mindsets, or values of people experiencing poverty, we need to find a stronger applicant—one that meets our basic equity literacy requirement—or commit to providing intensive professional development.

We should remember, of course, that a deficit response to that question reflects the dominant perspective. We are all on a path toward consciousness. I am not advocating that we never hire somebody without a perfect equity-infused structural view; that would remove almost everybody from the applicant pool. But at least by asking this question, we position ourselves to assess what kind of professional development new staff need. On the other hand, if we see consistent signs of a deficit, stereotyped view in an applicant, it is not in the interests of students experiencing poverty or, really, of any students for us to hire that person. If we see this view consistently across applicants, we need to reconsider recruitment strategies.

Here is an example of why equity literacy starts with the ability to recognize bias and inequity: If I'm doing the hiring and can't distinguish a deficit, stereotyped view from a structural, equity view, I will be little help hiring with equity literacy in mind. Equity understanding drives equity action. If I don't have that understanding well enough developed, I should have the humility to hand the hiring responsibility to somebody who does. Also avoid burying one person with this ability on a hiring committee full of people without it, washing out the equity lens. This is one way to model an institutional commitment to equity.

Prioritize the Interests and Needs of Families Experiencing Poverty (and Other Marginalized Groups). If we had to synthesize strategies for shaping an institutional culture around equity into one overarching strategy, this would be it: Examine every policy and practice, every decision. Are we prioritizing the interests and needs of families experiencing poverty as a central institutional commitment, or keeping our existing priority structure and making small curricular or programmatic shifts to help people experiencing poverty get by? William Parrett and Kathleen Budge (2012) challenge us to embrace a commitment to social justice leadership in part by asking ourselves these sorts of questions. They argue, "Such leaders ask questions that cause themselves and others to assess and critique the current conditions in their schools. They identify whose interests are being served by the current conditions and whose are not" (p. 15).

This also means we must prioritize the interests and needs of families experiencing poverty over our own desires for quick, convenient practical solutions. We must prioritize their needs and interests over colleagues' desires to feel comfortable with their stereotyped views, over the pull of tradition. Leaders often respond to this challenge by trying to protect one or two precious policies or practices that have long histories at their schools. Longevity is not the same as equity. It never should be prioritized over the well-being of students and families.

CULTIVATING EQUITY LITERACY IN FACULTY AND STAFF

Bias and inequity reside in every crevice of institutional culture and practice: policies, curricula, communication practices, decisionmaking processes. As I explained earlier, in my experience, most of this bias and inequity is not mean-spirited and intentional, the result of rabidly bigoted administrators meeting in a conference room to discuss how to oppress "the poor kids." Unfortunately, when it comes to equity, intention is irrelevant. The absence of intention does not make a policy that unintentionally harms students experiencing poverty any less harmful.

This means that all of us, from those most dedicated to equity to those who can't imagine how matters of equity have anything to do with their work, perpetuate inequity in one way or another. Nobody is immune because nobody has perfect equity literacy. And because nobody has perfect equity literacy, a critical component in the process of creating more equitable schools and districts is developing a plan for cultivating equity literacy in everybody around us—not just teachers and counselors, but *everybody*.

The suggestions below offer points of departure for making this happen.

Build Professional Development (PD) Around the Knowledge and Skills of Equity Literacy. In most schools and districts with which I've worked, PD around equity (if it exists at all) is at best inconsistent and disjointed and at worst contradictory to equity philosophies. In many cases what passes for "inclusion" or "diversity" PD reflects what I call "equity light": a surface-level exploration of this or that culture or a list of simplistic practical strategies without any real equity substance, so participants leave with a misguided notion that we can eliminate, say, racial outcome disparities without mentioning the word "racism." (We can't.) Simply stated, when we adopt PD strategy based on an approach meant to help teachers understand poverty that fails to acknowledge the inequities that cause and sustain poverty, we undermine rather than cultivate equity literacy. Again, there is no path to equity that does not include a direct confrontation with inequity. We are complicit with the inequities we want to destroy when we spend time searching for that path.

There is a robust literature on what generally makes for effective professional development. For example, brief one-shot workshops during that 45-minute faculty meeting don't work (Stosich, 2016). Nor is the sampler approach, offering a series of workshops that feature different or even contradictory views on equity issues, effective.

By embracing a PD approach designed to strengthen the abilities of equity literacy—to (1) recognize inequity, (2) respond to inequity, (3) redress inequity, and (4) sustain equity—rather than approaches built to step carefully around matters of equity, we can optimize individual and institutional equity growth. Although there is no proscriptive PD plan for equity, we can look at PD approaches through an equity lens and assess whether they are designed to cultivate that growth. Start with the guidelines below.

First, choose a PD approach rooted first and foremost in supporting shifts in understanding, shifts in belief systems (Aragon, Culpepper, McKee, & Perkins, 2013). Be cautious of approaches that favor simple and detached practical strategies. Practical strategies should be informed by shifts in ideology and understanding.

Especially embrace a PD approach that reflects a structural view, helping educators understand inequities and barriers harming students in and out of school and how they impact school engagement (Shields, 2014). Even if we can't eliminate all out-of-school barriers, we can discuss ways to mitigate their effects through school policy and practice. In the spirit of equity literacy, this is the best way to nudge people out of their deficit views, which should be a core goal of PD on poverty and education (Gorski, 2016a). Meanwhile, be wary of approaches that even hint at a deficit view (Dudley-Marling, 2015). Does the approach you're considering focus on how to fix economically marginalized peoples' cultures, mindsets, grittiness, or values? Does it fail to strengthen participants' understandings of the inequities and biases with which people experiencing poverty contend both in and out of school? If so, it could deepen participants' stereotypes and false understandings of poverty (Smiley & Helfenbein, 2011), when equity PD ought to dislodge stereotypes and false understandings (Chandler, 2014; Jones, 2016).

Also be cautious of PD approaches that oversimplify educational outcome disparities to narrow causes. For example, the recent avalanche of brain research that links educational outcome disparities to disparities in brain development, the result of gaps in access to health care, nutritional foods, and other necessities, plays an important role in a robust equity view of poverty and education. But PD approaches focusing exclusively on brain research or on mitigating the effects of brain development disparities are too narrow; they generally fail to account for the long list of inequities in and out of schools not linked to brain development, like class bias in teachers and counselors.

The most important equity literacy skill educators can learn through PD is the ability to recognize even the subtlest biases and inequities. These include the biases that persist in our own views on poverty and people experiencing it (Lampert et al., 2016; Sallee & Boske, 2013). We know that teachers' attitudes about people experiencing poverty inform the way they teach and relate to students, so PD should include opportunities to reflect on these attitudes, where the attitudes come from, and why it can be so difficult to let go of them (Djonko-Moore, 2016). In my experience, helping educators to reflect critically on notions like meritocracy and how we're socialized to endorse them strengthens their abilities to see more clearly how bias and inequity operate in and around us (Gorski, 2012). Rich Milner (2015) suggests *color-blindness* (or *class-blindness*) as another notion PD should demystify because it masks inequity, which is the opposite of exposing and challenging inequity.

Once educators have learned to overcome bias, to recognize even the subtlest inequities, to see links between big structural conditions and educational outcome disparities, PD can incorporate strategies for putting educators' growing equity views into practice. This might include practice co-examining existing policy and practice, examining learning materials for bias, responding to bias incidents in the classroom or teacher lounge, strengthening relationships with families experiencing poverty, examining test score or behavior referral data through an equity lens, and other practical applications.

Finally, when we begin to see progress through a PD approach, we should stick with that approach. Reach for PD depth rather than PD breadth. While it is true that various PD approaches have various strengths, there is great value in sticking with an approach long enough that we develop shared institutional language and understandings.

Strengthen Structural Awareness to Foster Responsiveness to Bigger Social Conditions and Policy. As discussed throughout this book, equity literacy requires responsiveness even to the inequities we cannot fully eliminate. We cannot single-handedly ensure that every parent has living-wage work even if we know the scarcity of living-wage jobs has tremendous implications for students. But we can find ways to be *responsive* to these implications.

Of course, responsiveness relies on recognition. We can't be responsive to conditions we're incapable of seeing or unwilling to see. As leaders, we can foster this recognition by strengthening structural awareness in ourselves and our colleagues. We shouldn't rely solely on formal PD to do this. We can make awareness-raising part of our everyday conversations.

This requires challenging the deficit view at every turn, as mentioned earlier. But it also means actively fostering the structural view. A colleague says, *I'm so frustrated with those parents. If only they cared enough about their children to show up for parent–teacher conferences.* Enacting your equity literacy, you respond, *I wonder whether you've seen all the research showing that parents experiencing poverty have the exact same attitudes about their kids' education as wealthier parents. I wonder what sorts of barriers might make it harder for them to attend conferences.* You model shifting from a deficit to a structural view. *I wonder if there's something we can do differently as a school to help them bear the weight of these barriers.* I use a lot of "I wonder" statements. They allow me to invite colleagues into a reconsidering process. They also position me as a participant in that process rather than as a judge of their equity competence.

We can be proactive, not just reactive. Find ways to help colleagues exercise their equity literacy potency. Incorporate it into staff or department meetings. *I know parents experiencing poverty are not coming in for conferences at rates we wanted to see. Let's address this pattern by brain-storming the barriers they might experience inside and outside school that might make attendance harder for them than for wealthier parents.* Start the conversation at barriers. Return to Chapter 6 for examples you can intro-duce if participants don't name them. Divide responses into two categories: (1) barriers we can eliminate and (2) barriers we can mitigate. (Chapter 7 will be helpful here, too.) Then move to strategies. *We can* mitigate *some parents' lack of access to transportation by providing transportation. We can* eliminate *some parents' experiences of humiliation when they come into the school by strengthening our PD on poverty.* When somebody slips into a deficit view, invite them back to the structural view. *Okay, you've moved from talking about barriers to placing blame on our most marginalized fam-ilies. Let's stay focused on barriers.*

Practice Identifying Policies and Practices that Force Students to "Perform" Their Poverty.

In ways big and small, students experiencing poverty often are forced to "perform" their poverty publicly. That is, they are implicitly coerced into engaging or responding in ways that spotlight their econom-ic disadvantage. (Review Commitment 6 in Chapter 9 for a more detailed description.)

One way to help ourselves and our colleagues practice a structural view is to work on identifying the policies and practices that coerce this per-formance. We ask what they did on summer vacation. We charge fees for school-sponsored activities knowing it will force some students to have to identify themselves as unable to afford them. We march children through the Scholastic Book Fair so that lower-income youth can watch their class-mates purchase books. We host chocolate bar fundraiser competitions. We assign homework requiring technology some students don't have. The list goes on.

But rather than dumping this list onto our colleagues, we can challenge them to do the excavating, digging examples up themselves. The analytical work required to do this cultivates equity literacy.

Once we've identified the policies and practices, we can discuss how to modify them, moving from *recognize* to *respond* to *redress*. It's not always easy examining an institution we might love or classroom practices we've embraced enthusiastically for years. Watch for defensiveness. It can be a learning tool. *Why are we so tied to certain policies and practices that we'd argue to sustain them even if they could humiliate students?*

I suggest asking everybody in a workshop format to identify one way they force students or parents to perform their poverty. Model the process by naming your own complicities. Ask colleagues how they will commit to doing things differently in order to eliminate the inequitable practice. Celebrate their responses. This is the bridge from inequitable practice to equitable practice.

CREATING POLICIES AND PRACTICES
TO REDISTRIBUTE ACCESS AND OPPORTUNITY

If progress toward equity requires redistributions of opportunity, access, and resources, equity-minded policies and practices are the vehicles to ensure these redistributions. As stated earlier, we cannot wait, and our students cannot afford for us to wait, until everybody is on board philosophically before instituting equitable policy. We also should not presume that PD is sufficient. In the end, we strengthen our equity literacy because doing so equips us with the knowledge and skills to foster equity. Action without equity literacy is dangerous, guiding us to strategies that create the illusion of movement without ensuring that movement. Equity literacy without action—knowing the changes we should make but choosing not to at least try making them—is an expression of privilege. Both scenarios leave us at inequity.

We should prioritize recognizing and reshaping or redressing inequitable policies and practices. If we are committed to creating an equitable school, district, or school system, we should be able to explain precisely how each equity initiative, each shift in policy and practice, narrows the opportunity gap by redistributing access and opportunity (Lineburg & Ratliff, 2015). Some of the suggestions below will be more mitigative, such as partnering with local agencies to provide wraparound services like health screenings. Others will be more transformative. There is no shame in instituting mitigative change when the inequities to which we're responding are outside our spheres of influence. However, we should always challenge ourselves to resist limiting our initiatives, in Carolyn Shields's (2014) words, to "tinkering around the edges of change" (p. 128).

As with every recommendation in this book, these do not represent an exhaustive list, but instead a place to begin crafting equity-based policies and equity-informed practices.

Distribute the Most Experienced and Effective Teachers Equitably. As discussed in Chapter 7, the most effective and experienced teachers are underrepresented in high-poverty schools, in schools with large populations of Students of Color, and even in lower-tracked classes within individual schools (Glazerman & Max, 2011). These teachers should be distributed more equitably. We also should work on shifting the culture in education that places teaching jobs into a hierarchy of desirability based on who the students are. We can do this by acknowledging the hard work of teachers and administrators who choose to stay in high-poverty schools or to teach classes populated disproportionately by students experiencing poverty in mixed-class schools.

Partner with Local Organizations to Offer Wraparound Services. Even as we advocate bigger policy change related to disparities in health care and access to healthy food, we can mitigate the disparities' impact by partnering with local agencies and organizations to provide wraparound services to families who need them (Guinan & Hansell, 2014; Phillips & Putnam, 2016). We can start by reaching out to community organizations for advice on the sorts of services that would be most helpful (Kundu, 2014). These might include health care services like general health screenings and dental care, help accessing healthy foods like fresh fruit and vegetables, or even access to washing machines and dryers. Once we know which services we should offer, we can forge relationships with organizations working on those issues locally or even nationally. Do some research. You'll find, for example, that many health care associations, including the American Academy of Pediatrics, actively seek ways to partner with schools (Dreyer, 2016).

Identify and Eliminate Policies and Practices That Punish or Humiliate Students Experiencing Poverty Simply for Being Students Experiencing Poverty. In several chapters I have alluded to school policies and practices that punish students experiencing poverty for their poverty. One essential application of equity literacy is to identify and eliminate these policies and practices. Do this now.

Start by reviewing challenges that economically marginalized families experience in and out of school and then examining each policy and practice, formal and informal, assessing whether it exacerbates these barriers or humiliates people experiencing poverty in other ways. As we identify examples, remember that sometimes one example, one practice, might by itself seem like a small deal. Learn to consider each individual example as a symptom of a bigger issue so we can see how the accumulation of these sleights affects students. Nothing is too small to address:

- As mentioned earlier, in many schools we march students through Scholastic Book Fairs (or other shopping events) knowing that some cannot afford to purchase the books. Often we close the library during book fairs, cutting off access to books for students who have the least access to books so we can provide students with the most access to books more access to books.
- We might consider offering financial assistance or fee forgiveness for students who can't afford extra fees attached to educational experiences to be a good mitigative step. But it can be humiliating for students and families who must continuously perform their poverty by asking for help.
- Students should not be coerced, even implicitly, to raise money by competing with one another to sell bad chocolate, ugly candles, or other goods. This is a set-up for students experiencing poverty and can be humiliating for them and their families.

- Schools are infamous for instituting inflexible tardy and absentee policies grounded in principles of equality so that every student is punished the same way for not complying. Equality is not equity. This inflexibility might punish students experiencing poverty for their parents' lack of access to jobs with flexible hours and paid leave or even for their lack of access to preventive health care.
- Equitable policy should forbid homework assignments requiring pricey technologies or materials to which some students do not have access. No percentage of a student's grade should be determined by access to these resources.
- Many schools are moving to entirely online systems for communicating with families. Are we sure all families have consistent access to these systems? Based on whose standards was the decision to move to these online systems made?
- We never should host events that highlight families' economic standing or implicitly pressure them to spend money they might not have. Student art auctions are an especially egregious example of both. Are there ways this happens in your school or district? We should find more equitable ways to raise money.
- Never allow student photo companies or other companies to send goods home with students that aren't paid for already. Curtail the predatory practices of these companies that will send home entire packets of photos and require parents to send back the items they choose not to purchase.
- Review patterns of discipline. Are they applied equitably across race and class? Research has shown how teachers tend to punish Students of Color more harshly than White students for the same infractions. How is bias influencing discipline practices in your school or district?

Eliminate Fees Associated with Any Learning Opportunity. As previously stressed, students' access to learning opportunities should never depend upon families' abilities to pay extra fees. Any fee precluding some students from participating or forcing students to perform their poverty by asking for financial help should be eliminated (Cloutier-Bordeleau, 2015). In every way, every learning activity, including extracurriculars, should be economically and socially available to every student (Parrett & Budge, 2012).

De-Track. We have known since the mid-1980s that academic tracking benefits the 5% of highest-achieving students (when "achievement" is measured in traditional ways) and either has no benefit or causes harm to 95% of students (Oakes, 2005). This fact alone should make us wonder what drives this popular education practice.

As a mitigative step, we should examine our school's or district's practices for deciding who receives access to gifted education, honors classes, and Advanced Placement classes, as research shows that these decisions often are rife with class and race bias (Latz & Adams, 2011). A more transformative approach is to de-track altogether (Dudley-Marling, 2015), organizing students into mixed-ability groups, which research has shown to be more effective for students experiencing poverty (Fram, Miller-Cribbs, & van Horn, 2007).

Provide Strong, Options-Based College and Career Counseling with Equity-Literate Counselors. Strengthen counseling practice for students experiencing poverty (Kids Count, 2016; Suitts, 2016). I often feel demoralized by current or recently graduated high school students' stories about the lackluster or nonexistent college and career counseling at their schools. We can do better.

Although many high schools have interpreted "doing better" as embracing the "college for all" mantra, research shows that high schools need to do a better job helping students make sense of the pros and cons of the full spectrum of postsecondary pathways. Based on their longitudinal study of African American youth in Baltimore, Stefanie DeLuca, Susan Clampet-Lundquist, and Kathryn Edin (2016) explained,

> The dominant "college-for-all" norm that prevails in many high schools encourages students to aspire to a four-year degree, but it does little to prepare them to navigate other pathways, such as direct entry into the labor market, occupationally based community college programs, or trade schools. Most of the youth in our study who pursued post-secondary education chose for-profit trade schools. . . . High schools must deliver information about how various postsecondary options stack up against one another—including average time to completion, costs, job placement rates, and average wages in the occupation. The youth in our study were almost never given this information. (pp. 193–194)

One aspect of good college and career counseling is helping students make sense of these options and helping them navigate the predatory practices of many for-profit schools.

This is not a simple matter of training counselors to provide this information or let go of their biases. It is our responsibility as school leaders to make sure counselors at high-poverty schools are not overloaded with so many other tasks that we undermine their ability to provide the same level of college and career counseling offered as a matter of course in wealthier schools.

A Few Other Points of Departure. In other chapters we have explored additional examples of ways we might formulate policy and practice to redistribute access and opportunity. These include:

- Planning opportunities for family engagement with the lives of families experiencing poverty in mind;
- Protecting arts and physical education programs and protecting economically marginalized students' access to these programs;
- Interpreting data through an equity literacy lens; and
- Prioritizing literacy instruction across the curriculum.

CONCLUSION

Institutional change will not happen without an intense investment on the part of school and district leaders. The responsibility cannot be handed off to a student club, a diversity committee, or even an equity specialist. We have the accountability power, and our first responsibility is to hold ourselves accountable for taking the lead on equity.

In the next and final chapter we expand our spheres of influence to consider what sorts of larger-scale advocacy we might do in support of families experiencing poverty.

REFLECTION QUESTIONS AND EXERCISES

1. What measures can a school take to help ensure that hires are made with equity literacy in mind?

2. Think of a policy or practice that might punish students experiencing poverty for implications of their family's poverty. How would you change that policy or practice to be more equitable?

3. Identify three organizations in your local community to which you or your school could reach out in hopes of partnering on a wraparound service relevant to your students.

4. Starting as far back as you can remember, make a list of every school experience you had that required an extra fee or cost, whether your family could afford the fee or not. Include trips, materials required for particular classes (including art and music), extracurricular fees, and even costs associated with nonrequired but socially important items or events such as school dances and yearbooks. Reflect not just on the financial cost, but also the possible emotional and social cost the accumulation of these fees or expenses might have on families experiencing poverty.

CHAPTER 11

Expanding Our Spheres of Influence

Advocating Change for the Educational and Societal Good

> Principles of Equity Literacy discussed in this chapter include:
>
> *Principle 2:* The right to equitable educational opportunity is universal.
>
> *Principle 6:* We cannot understand the relationship between poverty and education without understanding the barriers and inequities that people experiencing poverty face in and out of schools.
>
> *Principle 11:* Simplistic instructional strategies, absent a commitment to more intensive institutional change, are no threat to inequities.
>
> *Principle 12:* There is no path to educational equity that does not involve a redistribution of access and opportunity.

All the way back in Chapter 1 I explained how, when I began writing this book, I struggled to decide on its focus. Initially I intended to write a book about the big social policies we need if we hope to realize equitable educational opportunity: access to living-wage work and other steps toward eliminating wealth and income disparities, equitable access to a health care system not controlled solely by people who profit from health care industries, better and more affordable housing initiatives. I remain committed to those changes. I ultimately decided, instead, to write a book mostly about what we can do in our spheres of influence to improve educational access and opportunity for students experiencing poverty—students who cannot afford to wait for larger societal changes. So I focused largely on classroom and school practices, on the attitudes and ideologies we carry or don't carry into classrooms and schools, and on what several decades' worth of scholarship indicates are key strategies for fostering equitable learning environments for economically marginalized families.

This is a central tenet of my work and how I make decisions about what sorts of change I support. We should start with our spheres of influence,

with what we can control. Another commitment is developing deep understandings of the barriers outside our spheres that impact students inside
them. Even if we can't eliminate those barriers, we can learn to be responsive to them, to mitigate them, to not replicate them unwittingly.

When we feel that we have our arms fairly wrapped around our current
spheres, we should challenge ourselves to find ways of growing our influence. Doing so expands our impact. Small steps are fine. We might start with
challenging a colleague's deficit views or raising questions about a long-
standing practice we know harms students experiencing poverty. Eventually
we might connect with a network of fellow educators working on bigger
educational or social policy issues. (See a list of some of these networks in
Chapter 7.) Any expansion of our spheres of influence is a good expansion
as long as we sustain our equity literacy and continue working to understand as deeply as possible the problems we are attempting to redress.

In this chapter I propose initiatives for addressing some of these problems. I offer only a starter list, not a comprehensive one. I know that some
readers will read these initiatives and still think, "That would be great, but
it's still a little outside my sphere of influence." I get it. Really, I do. There's
already a lot to do, and just being a strong advocate for students in our
own classrooms can be challenging. I hope that, as more of us adopt the
structural view described in Chapter 4 and embrace the instructional, relational, and leadership strategies described in Chapters 8, 9, and 10, we
will start finding opportunities to expand our spheres. More specifically,
I hope we will work together to influence bigger policy initiatives directly
affecting students experiencing poverty and their educational opportunities
and outcomes.

I divide my proposed initiatives into two categories: (1) policy advocacy
for educational equity and (2) policy advocacy for societal justice.

POLICY ADVOCACY FOR EDUCATIONAL EQUITY

Initiative One: Advocate for Universal Preschool and Kindergarten. Here's
a brief quiz. Of the following industrialized countries—the United States,
Cyprus, Lithuania, Iceland—which has the lowest percentage of eligible students in preschool?

If you guessed the United States, the wealthiest country in the world, you
are correct (Organisation for Economic Co-operation and Development,
2016). A+ for you, but not so much for the United States. Among industrialized countries, the United States ranks 23rd in preschool enrollment.

As covered in Chapter 7, even if families experiencing poverty can find
quality preschool programs in their communities (which is a pretty big "if"),
these programs almost always are too pricey for them to afford. Add to this

the long list of other challenges we explored in Chapters 6 and 7—lack of access to everything from preventive health care to libraries—and it should be little surprise that economically marginalized youth come to school on average with lower levels of the kinds of cognitive development that are rewarded in schools. To clarify, this doesn't mean they have less potential than wealthier peers. It only means they are less privileged.

Speaking broadly, research suggests that investments in early educational opportunities, like enrolling youth experiencing poverty in quality preschool programs, have greater long-term payoffs than any other single school-based strategy for addressing educational outcome disparities (Crosnoe, Wirth, Pianta, Leventhal, & Pierce, 2010). This is a critical link. It demonstrates that early childhood education can mitigate the risk students experiencing poverty have of falling behind wealthier peers by the end of elementary school. For example, Carla Peterson and her colleagues (2010) found that participation in Early Head Start, a prekindergarten program for economically marginalized families that focuses on child development literally beginning at the prenatal stage, significantly lowers the likelihood that children will have cognitive or language delays while increasing the likelihood that they will have access to necessary interventions for challenges that do arise. Of course, this does not replace universal health care as a critical point of advocacy, but it can be an important mitigation while we work on bigger issues.

The Head Start model combines access to a preschool environment with attention to a range of other needs, including nutrition and health services. To a large extent it works. In his analysis of the long-term effects of Head Start on students experiencing poverty, Myungkook Joo (2010) found that participation led to lower rates of grade repetition, school suspension, and expulsion throughout the rest of participating youths' educational careers.

Unfortunately, despite its potential to mitigate the effects of economic inequalities in the educational lives of youth, the quality of Head Start programs is famously inconsistent (Karoly & Gonzalez, 2011). Even more unfortunately, for a variety of reasons, not least of which is the capacity of Head Start sites themselves and the scarcity of such sites in rural areas, less than 40% of eligible children are enrolled in the program (Barnett & Friedman-Krauss, 2016).

But it's a start. It's something upon which to build until every young person has access to high-quality early childhood education. If we care about the education of youth experiencing poverty, we should be committed to this goal as a matter of federal policy. By "high-quality," I mean preschools that feature collaborative and cooperative learning, early exposure to learning technologies, and literacy development goals (Lineburg & Ratliff, 2015). Meanwhile, as Rich Milner (2015) argues, we also can bolster the quality of preschools by advocating higher pay for early childhood educators.

Initiative Two: Advocate for Smaller Class Sizes. Is it just me, or are the most visible people insisting that class size doesn't matter almost always politicians and pundits who send their children to pricey private schools? During the 2012 presidential race, Mitt Romney made the mistake of telling a school full of teachers in West Philadelphia that class size doesn't matter. He made that claim knowing that his children's educational experiences were not at stake. They all attended pricey independent schools, as did President Obama's children, as did President Trump's children. The teachers were not buying what he was selling, and they told him so. They know, as anybody knows who has experienced the difference between teaching 12 or 16 students (the average class sizes, respectively, at Belmont Hill School, where the Romneys sent their sons, and Sidwell Friends School, where the Obamas sent their daughters) and, say, 25 or 30 students.

Class size does matter, and despite the illusion of a debate on this point, research consistently has shown this to be the case, especially for students experiencing poverty (Schanzenbach, 2014). And, yes, one positive effect of small class sizes is higher standardized test scores (Shin & Chung, 2009). But reduced class sizes also result in more positive student and—big shocker! —*teacher* attitudes (Zahorick, Halbach, Ehrle, & Molnar, 2003) and higher levels of student engagement (Blatchford, Bassett, & Brown, 2011; Dee & West, 2011).

Initiative Three: Extend Health Services and Screenings at Schools. Due, in large part, to a lack of access to preventive health care, students experiencing poverty are much more likely than wealthier peers to have undiagnosed health concerns affecting even the most basic functions, like vision (Schmalzried, Gunning, & Platzer, 2014). When health services and screenings are available at schools, they tend to be extremely, and in some cases illogically, limited in scope. For instance, the vision screenings offered at many schools—you know, *Cover your right eye and read the third row of letters*—focus on nearsightedness, which affects the ability to read at a distance (as from a chalkboard), and not farsightedness, which affects up-close reading (as from a book). Far too often students whose families cannot afford regular health care are assumed to have a learning disability when they just need glasses, an expense that also might be difficult for families experiencing poverty to bear. Marge and Herman Gould (2003), in their landmark study of undiagnosed eye conditions, explain, "It is estimated that one out of four school-age children have undiagnosed vision problems" (p. 324). The rate is even higher for economically marginalized students. Unfortunately, as the Goulds lament, the lack of proper care can have implications beyond grades, including damaging students' self-esteem.

Vision problems are only the tip of the iceberg. As we explored in Chapter 6, youth experiencing poverty are more prone than wealthier peers to a host of health concerns that impact their school engagement whether or not they are diagnosed. Not the least of these is asthma, a near-chronic problem in high-poverty urban communities.

One sensible response is to advocate the protection of school nurse positions (Baisch et al., 2011), which, as we learned earlier, are slowly disappearing, especially from high-poverty schools. But we also must advocate for more and broader health care services in high-poverty schools. Obviously, schools cannot become full-service hospitals, but increased services and screenings for health risks like asthma, depression, or farsightedness, which are more common or more commonly undiagnosed in people experiencing poverty, would go a long way toward mitigating health care disparities that impede student engagement and learning (Council on Community Pediatrics, 2016).

Initiative Four: Protect Physical Education and Recess and Encourage Fitness. Even as we try to incorporate movement into our individual teaching, as recommended in Chapter 8, we should vigorously defend physical education programs and recess. Students learn better when they have access to regular exercise opportunities. Sadly, youth experiencing poverty are less likely than their peers to have these opportunities outside of school (Fahlman et al., 2006), whether because their families cannot afford to sign them up for organized sports, because their neighborhoods lack the sorts of recreational facilities that are common in wealthier communities, or because they are charged with caring for younger siblings while their parents work. They also are less likely to have these opportunities in school, as physical education and recess are cut with more frequency at high-poverty schools (Carlson et al., 2014).

Some schools have found creative ways to encourage more exercise among students. For example, several high-poverty elementary schools in Seattle have participated in a "walking school bus" wherein children and chaperones from the neighborhood walk to school together (Mendoza, Levinger, & Johnston, 2009). A similar program was instituted in Albuquerque, New Mexico, with an added dimension: The participating school partnered with a physician who met with participants before and after the program and a premedical student who walked with students and community members. They emphasized the importance of exercise and healthy eating. According to Alberta Kong and her colleagues (2010), participants reported increased levels of physical activity and healthier eating during the 10-week program.

As cool as they might sound, we certainly should not think of programs like the walking school bus as suitable replacements for physical education or recess. Our priority should be to protect physical education and recess from the school accountability chopping block.

Initiative Five: Protect Arts Programs. Students who have access to the arts do better academically and are more engaged in school (Dwyer, 2011). With this reality in mind, earlier I made a research-informed pitch for why we should mitigate the impact of disappearing art, music, and drama programs in our individual instructional practices. Even more, we should do what we can policy-wise to protect the arts in school. Kristen Engebretsen (2011), arts education policy manager for Americans for the Arts, outlines a variety of strategies for our arts-protecting advocacy, such as familiarizing ourselves with the research about the importance of arts education (see Chapter 8), identifying allies and forging partnerships with supportive people in and out of schools, and offering concrete solutions that tie arts education to student engagement.

Initiative Six: Protect School and Local Libraries in High-Poverty Neighborhoods. Increased access to books is directly related to higher reading proficiency (Krashen, 2013). This, you might think, is reason enough to protect *all* school and local libraries from losing funding or being shuttered altogether. And it might be reason enough to advocate for better libraries in high-poverty schools, which have significantly fewer resources on average than libraries at wealthier schools (Pribesh, Gavigan, & Dickinson, 2011).

We should feel a special sense of urgency to protect local and school libraries and their funding in high-poverty and mixed-class communities. Public and school libraries can play mitigating roles in disparities between economically marginalized and wealthier youth when it comes to having access to a wide variety of books and other media as well as computers and the Internet. Also, public libraries are among the few public spaces and resources available for many people in high-poverty communities, where they can host neighborhood meetings or classes, find tutoring services, and search for jobs (Horrigan, 2015).

Unfortunately, socioeconomic disparities in access to books and the Internet are replicated almost exactly in school and public libraries (Pribesh et al., 2011). As a result, disparities in access to well-stocked libraries in high-poverty neighborhoods and schools are *widening* the literacy gap between economically marginalized and wealthier students. We should do anything we can to disrupt these disparities, including lobbying local legislators when library hours are slashed.

Initiative Seven: Resist Neoliberal School Reform Initiatives. In Chapter 7 we covered the growing influence of neoliberal school reform initiatives designed to take the "public" out of public education: voucher programs, hyperstandardization, significant portions of the charter school movement. One thing most of these initiatives have in common is that they have the harshest impact on the most marginalized students and families. Anything we can do to stem the neoliberal tide and resist these initiatives is good for students experiencing poverty and the future of public education.

POLICY ADVOCACY FOR SOCIETAL JUSTICE

Initiative One: Advocate for Living-Wage Laws. As long as we have more working-age adults looking for work than living-wage jobs, poverty will persist. As long as poverty persists, educational outcome disparities will exist. We can mitigate those disparities—some schools are doing an admirable job of it—but we cannot eliminate them.

Many parents experiencing poverty must work multiple jobs because of the scarcity of full-time living-wage work, especially in high-poverty communities. The result is less time to read to their children, to visit their children's schools, and to just *be* with their families. How can we at once insist parents be more involved in their children's learning and ignore the biggest barrier to that involvement?

This is the most important big-level social policy issue when it comes to educational outcome disparities (Berliner, 2013). Notably, in many ways *living wages* are, themselves, just a mitigation, a subsistence stopgap. It is a low plateau on our way toward *fair wages* and stemming the growing wealth and income gaps that make the United States among the most economically unequal industrialized countries in the world. Want to get involved? Visit these organizations:

- Economic Policy Institute: epi.org
- National Employment Law Project: nelp.org
- United for a Fair Economy: faireconomy.org

Initiative Two: Advocate for Affordable Housing Policies and Tenant Rights. In societies that can afford to provide stable, affordable housing to all people, homelessness and housing instability should be nonissues. Unfortunately, they remain significant challenges in the lives of economically marginalized people and, as a result, have a significant impact on the school lives of youth. If we care about maximizing the educational experiences of all students, we also must care about affordable housing policies and tenants' rights.

Housing stability is key (Coulton et al., 2016), but it requires attention to a lot of interlocking concerns. The scarcity of affordable quality housing is the most significant of these concerns. It underlies high rates of transience in families experiencing poverty, which might mean changing schools and a bevy of other distractions. One of the most important ways we can chip away at educational outcome disparities is by advocating for affordable housing policies (DeLuca et al., 2016; Sharkey, Putnam, & Turner, 2016). But we also should advocate for tenants' rights, understanding patterns of tenant neglect by too many low-income housing management companies.

Organizations working on these issues include:

- National Coalition for the Homeless: nationalhomeless.org
- National Housing Law Project: nhlp.org
- National Low Income Housing Coalition: nlihc.org

Initiative Three: Advocate for Universal Health Care. As a U.S. citizen, I'm embarrassed about having to write about each item in this section. But I'm especially embarrassed and confounded by the idea that any educator with a commitment to equity would argue against universal health care, at the very least for minors who have no say in what level of medical coverage their parents can afford. We are putting children at a disadvantage before they are even born based on how we tie high-quality prenatal care access to wealth. Then the disparities compound every year—every day, really—throughout children's lives. We can mitigate the effects of these atrocities with wraparound services and school nurses, but we cannot eliminate them if we continue to prioritize the wealth of insurance, pharmaceutical, and other health care–related corporations over the health of children.

Reactive health care—waiting until somebody becomes sick and then providing a subsistence level of care—will not do. Preventive health care is essential (Suitts, 2016). Students experiencing poverty miss too much school and develop long-term health problems from preventable diseases because we as a country don't care enough about them to ensure that they have ongoing health care. No amount of grit or growth mindset can make up for these entirely avoidable health problems. We should stand up as a collective of educators and insist on universal high-quality health care.

We can join with organizations already fighting this battle:

- Physicians for a National Health Program: pnhp.org
- Universal Health Care Action Network: uhcan.org

Initiative Four: Advocate for Environmental Justice. Despite all the talk about conservation and sustainability these days, we seem to forget that environmental degradation has the most immediate and violent impact on people experiencing poverty. Economically marginalized students, especially if they also are People of Color, are much, much more likely than their wealthier peers to live near environmental hazard sites, to be exposed to dangerous levels of radon and carbon monoxide, and to be subject to water contamination from mining operations, industrialized farms, and factory runoffs. We can join local communities in the battle against these environmental injustices.

These organizations can help us get started:

- Earth Justice: earthjustice.org
- Indigenous Environmental Network: ienearth.org
- National Resources Defense Council: nrdc.org/

CONCLUSION

Sounds like a lot of heavy lifting, right? When it comes to creating equitable educational opportunity, there is much work to be done and many spheres in which to do it. I'm reminded of one of my favorite quotes by Edward Everett Hale, a late 19th- and early 20th-century U.S. author and Unitarian clergyman: "I am only one; but still I am one. I cannot do everything; but still I can do something; and because I cannot do everything, I will not refuse to do something that I can do."

Maybe for you that something is advocating for a schoolwide commitment to higher-order pedagogy. Maybe it's initiating a working group to explore offering more health screenings at your school. Or maybe it's joining a movement to address issues like food deserts, the scarcity of living wage jobs, or disparities in access to preventive health care.

Maybe, for now, you will choose to focus on your classroom or department, and that's all right, too. The challenge is to begin with our immediate spheres of influence. Then, when we've made good equity progress and exercised our equity literacy sufficiently there, we can find ways to stretch our spheres.

If you do choose to take on any of these bigger concerns, find ways to do so collaboratively, with colleagues or friends with similar passions. There is power in numbers.

REFLECTION QUESTIONS AND EXERCISES

1. Identify a local or regional organization or network in your area that is working on one of the "policy advocacy for educational equity" initiatives. What is that organization or network doing? What role could you play in the initiative?

2. Which of the "policy advocacy for societal justice" initiatives do you find most compelling? How would that initiative support the educational success of students experiencing poverty at your school?

Conclusion

Recently a colleague and I took a group of students, mostly future teachers, to visit 110 6th-graders at a high-poverty middle school. "If you could offer one piece of advice to these future teachers," I asked the 6th-graders, "what would it be?" They were sitting on the cafeteria floor, the only space in the building big enough to seat them all, fidgety with curiosity about the strangers in their presence.

The few requisite responses about eliminating homework and extending recess induced giggles from both groups of students. "What else?" I asked. The cafeteria grew quiet.

"Respect us," a young woman said softly, then repeated forcefully: "Respect your students!" Several of her classmates nodded. I asked her name. "I'm Tanya," she said.

"How many of you agree with Tanya?" I asked her peers. "How many of you wish your teachers respected you more?" Nearly every hand shot up.

"That would be nice," a young man shared, sounding exasperated. His name was Tyrique.

It comes down to that in many ways, I thought. It comes down to respect. This sounds simple, I know, but it's not. Respecting students would be easy if respect were measured by intentions. After all, who among us doesn't want to respect students? Who among us doesn't *intend* respect? Unfortunately, respect is not about intentions. It's about actions.

Respect and the extent to which we demonstrate it in our teaching is tied up in those things, those at times little bitty things, we do or don't do, say or don't say, think or don't think. And it's about our willingness to take a stand when students are being shortchanged—not standing *in front of* or standing *in place of*, but standing *next to*, standing *with* students and families experiencing poverty. If students know they're being cheated out of the kind of education wealthier or Whiter or more English-proficient students are receiving, and if they know that we know they're being cheated, and if we're not responding with our equity literacy, then how can we say we respect students? Of course, we all know that students who are being cheated *do* know full well they're being cheated. They might not say so out loud, because there's always a price to pay for speaking up. There's the shushing, labeling, and ostracizing.

The good news is, we do have the power to stand up. We can start by standing up to our own biases and ideologies about people experiencing poverty, even if it means ditching the deficit view, quitting grit, and embracing the oddly unpopular structural view that economically marginalized people are not the problem we need to fix, that something bigger is amiss. Then we can do everything possible in our spheres of influence to align our actions—our teaching, leading, and relationship-building—with our good intentions.

We can listen.

"What does respect mean," I prodded the 6th-graders, "and how do you know when a teacher respects you?"

I glanced at the 6th-graders' teachers. They stood in a small cluster behind their students. *They look a little perplexed,* I remember thinking. Later that day one of them, Ms. Morrison, confided that she was, in fact, perplexed, never having seen "the kids" so attentive and respectful of one another in such a large group.

Hands flew up.

"Get to know me, don't treat me based on who you think I am," one student shared. "Get to know my interests."

Another student pleaded, "Make class fun instead of boring and hands-on like Ms. Greene's science class."

"Believe in us!" and "Don't get mad when I need help!" and "Remember that sometimes when I'm tardy or don't finish my homework it's not my fault!" they exclaimed.

"Be flexible, but also have rules," a young woman suggested.

Then a young man sitting all the way in the back shouted, "Let me spend time with my friends!" His peers roared with laughter.

It is tempting to read that comment—"Let me spend time with my friends!"—and think, *I knew that was coming. Here is a student who doesn't take school seriously.* A version of that thought popped into my mind for a moment. I looked at my teacher education students and noticed that several were laughing. I looked at the 6th-graders' teachers. One half-buried her head in her hands as though she was embarrassed.

"What's your name?" I asked the young man.

"Jonathan," he answered, appearing confused about why his peers were laughing.

"And why would you like your teachers to let you spend more time with your friends?" I probed.

Grinning, he threw his hands in the air. And then, as if it was the most obvious thing in the world, he replied, "Because we study together. They help me with my math."

I learned several important lessons from that visit with 110 6th-graders. First, it cemented for me why cultural competence, cultural proficiency, and especially the culture or mindset of poverty frameworks are insufficient guides for turning the tide of inequity in schools. Sure, the students wanted teachers to learn about their cultures, but they saw themselves as individuals, not as one giant cultural group. "Don't treat me based on who you think I am." They wanted equity-literate, not just culturally competent, teachers.

Second, although they didn't use the word *equity,* the students in that high-poverty school demanded it. They demanded the sorts of educational experiences they knew their peers at wealthier schools were getting. Respect, to them, meant high expectations. "Believe in us!" It also meant higher-order "hands-on" pedagogy.

Third, the most well-meaning of us can communicate low expectations in the most implicit, unintentional ways. It might be a perplexed look, presumptuous giggle, or throwaway comment we wouldn't even remember five minutes later. Here I am, writing a book about poverty and education, and occasionally I catch myself thinking thoughts, if only for a moment, that ought not to still be in my head. The problem is, those biases *are* still there, hiding, and making themselves known at the most inopportune times. The other problem is, the students notice, and they don't forget five minutes later.

We need to have high expectations for ourselves—expectations that we will be vigilant about identifying and squashing our biases, our deficit views, our attachment to grit or to practical strategies designed to excuse us from the difficult ideological work of equity literacy. It's not enough to pretend we have transcended these inner challenges or that we can hide their implications. Students are way too smart for that.

In order to reflect on my own equity efforts, inspired in large part by lessons I learned from students I have met all over the world, I crafted four questions—I call them *equity literacy accountability questions*—against which I try to hold myself accountable:

1. Are my equity efforts focused on fixing marginalized people or fixing the conditions that marginalize people? This question keeps me accountable to a structural view rather than a deficit view.
2. Are my equity efforts, again in Carolyn Shields's (2014) words, "tinkering around the edges of change" (p. 128), leaving the current distribution of access and opportunity unchanged, or are they supporting a permanent redistribution of access and opportunity? This question keeps me accountable to the redistributive principle of equity literacy.
3. Are my equity efforts designed to help students experiencing poverty overcome biases and inequities, or are they designed to root inequitable policy and practice out of my spheres of influence? This question helps ensure that I do not even implicitly replace my equity commitment with troublesome workarounds like grit.

4. Are my equity efforts positioning me as the expert of other people's experiences, or are they built on the recognition that people experiencing poverty are the experts of their own experience? This question is a constant reminder that I am a servant to equity work—that my decisions as an agent of change must always be informed by the people who have the most expertise.

As with the strategies, initiatives, and commitments discussed throughout this book, the idea is not to be perfect. Nobody is perfect. The idea is to aspire to something close to perfection, and then work toward that aspiration as vigilantly as possible.

It is my hope that, with this book and the equity literacy framework, I have helped you, as those 6th-graders helped me, to think in more complex, holistic ways about students and families experiencing poverty and what it means to create an equitable classroom, school, or district. I also hope that the strategies in Chapters 8 through 11 and sprinkled throughout the other chapters equip you with ample practical ways to bolster the important, incredible work you're already doing. Finally, I hope all the contextual stuff in the other chapters is useful grounding as you continue seeking ways to understand and support economically marginalized youth.

I end, then, where I began, with an unbending faith in educators, in all you underpaid and underappreciated civil servants who care deeply enough about youth to build your lives around educating, mentoring, and advocating for them. We are in a unique position as educators. Even if we focus only on creating change within our spheres of influence, we can't help but pay that change forward by a factor of the number of students whose lives we touch. We have no choice in that matter, any more than those celebrities who insist that they're not role models have a choice in *that* matter.

I suppose the only question is, What would we like to pay forward?

References

Abell, T., & Lyon, L. (1979). Do the differences make a difference? An empirical evaluation of the culture of poverty in the United States. *American Anthropologist, 6*(3), 602–621.

Alexander, M. (2012). *The new Jim Crow: Mass incarceration in the age of colorblindness.* New York, NY: The New Press.

Alexander, R. J. (2006). *Education as dialogue: Moral and pedagogical choices for a runaway world.* Hong Kong: Hong Kong Institute of Education with Dialogos.

Allard, S. W., & Roth, B. (2010). *Strained suburbs: The social service challenges of rising suburban poverty.* Washington, DC: Brookings Institute.

Allington, D., & McGill-Franzen, A. (2015). The reading achievement gap: Why do poor students lag behind rich students in reading development? *BookSource.* Retrieved from booksourcebanter.com/2015/05/08/reading-achievement-gap/

Amatea, E. S., & West-Olatunji, C. A. (2007). Joining the conversation about educating our poorest children: Emerging leadership roles for school counselors in high-poverty schools. *Professional School Counseling, 11*(2), 81–89.

American Association of University Women. (2017). *The simple truth about the gender pay gap: Spring 2017 edition.* Washington, DC: Author.

Andress, L., & Fitch, C. (2016). Juggling the five dimensions of food access: Perceptions of rural low-income residents. *Appetite, 105,* 151–155.

Aragon, A., Culpepper, S. A., McKee, M. W., & Perkins, M. (2013). Understanding profiles of preservice teachers with different levels of commitment to teaching in urban schools. *Urban Education, 49,* 543–573.

Au, W. (2013). Hiding behind high-stakes testing: Meritocracy, objectivity, and inequality in U.S. education. *The International Education Journal, 12*(2), 7–19.

Babic, M. (2016). 5 myths about the working poor in America. *Oxfam America.* Retrieved from politicsofpoverty.oxfamamerica.org/2016/09/5-myths-about-the-working-poor-in-america/

Baetan, G. (2004). Inner-city misery. *City, 8*(2), 235–241.

Baisch, M. J., Lundeen, S. P., & Murphy, M. K. (2011). Evidence-based research on the value of school nurses in an urban school system. *Journal of School Health, 81*(2), 74–80.

Baker, B. D., Farrie, D., & Sciarra, D. G. (2016). *Mind the gap: 20 years of progress and retrenchment in school funding and achievement gaps.* Princeton, NJ: Policy Information Center.

Baldwin, P. (2007). In and out of roles, stories and buckets! *English 4-11, 30,* 3–6.

Balfanz, R., & Byrnes, V. (2006). Closing the mathematics achievement gap in high-poverty middle schools: Enablers and constraints. *Journal of Education for Students Placed at Risk, 11*(2), 143–159.

Barnett, W. S., & Friedman-Krauss, A. H. (2016). *State(s) of Head Start.* New Brunswick, NJ: The National Institute for Early Childhood Education.

Barr, R. D., & Parrett, W. H. (2007). *The kids left behind: Catching up the underachieving children of poverty.* Bloomington, IN: Solution Tree Press.

Barshay, J. (2014). Why Hoboken is throwing away all of its student laptops. *WNYC News.* Retrieved from wnyc.org/story/why-hoboken-throwing-away-all-its-student-laptops/

Barton, P. E. (2004). Why does the gap persist? *Educational Leadership, 62*(3), 8–13.

Basch, C. (2011). Physical activity and the achievement gap among urban minority youth. *Journal of School Health, 81*(10), 626–634.

Bassok, D., & Galdo, E. (2016). Inequality in preschool quality? Community-level disparities in access to high-quality learning environments. *Early Education and Development, 27*(1), 128–144.

Battey, D. (2013). "Good" mathematics teaching for students of color and those in poverty: The importance of relational interactions within instruction. *Educational Studies in Mathematics, 82*, 125–144.

Baugh, J. (1983). *Black street speech.* Austin, TX: University of Texas Press.

Berliner, D. (2009). *Poverty and potential: Out-of school factors and school success.* Tempe, AZ: Education and the Public Interest Center & Education Policy Research Unit.

Berliner, D. C. (2013). Effects of inequality and poverty vs. teachers and schooling on America's youth. *Teachers College Record, 115*, 1–26.

Bernhard, J. K., Winsler, A., Bleiker, C., Ginieniewicz, J., & Madigan, A. L. (2008). "Read my story!" Using the early authors program to promote early literacy among diverse, urban, preschool children in poverty. *Journal of Education for Students Placed at Risk, 13*, 76–105.

Bertrand, M., & Mullainathan, S. (2003). *Are Emily and Greg more employable than Lakisha and Jamal?: Experiment on labor market discrimination.* Cambridge, MA: National Bureau of Economic Research.

Billings, D. (1974). Culture and poverty in Appalachia: A theoretical discussion and empirical analysis. *Social Forces, 53*(2), 315–323.

Blank, R. M., & Greenberg, M. (2008). *Improving the measurement of poverty.* Washington, DC: Brookings Institution.

Blatchford, P., Bassett, P., & Brown, P. (2011). Examining the effect of class size on classroom engagement and teacher-pupil interaction: Differences in relation to pupil prior attainment and primary vs. secondary schools. *Learning and Instruction, 21*(6), 715–730.

Boas, F. (1911). Introduction. In F. Boas (Ed.), *Handbook of American Indian languages* (pp. 1–79). Washington, DC: U.S. Government Printing Office.

Boggs, C. (2007). Corporate power, ecological crisis, and animal rights. *Fast Capitalism, 2*(2). Retrieved from fastcapitalism.com/

Bonilla-Silva, J. (2018). *Racism without racists: Color-blind racism and the persistence of racial inequality in America.* Lanham, MD: Rowman & Littlefield.

Books, S. (2004). *Poverty and schooling in the U.S.: Context and consequences.* New York, NY: Lawrence Erlbaum Associates.

Borrego, S. (2008). Class on campus: Breaking the silence surrounding socioeconomics. *Diversity &Democracy, 11*(3), 1–2.

Boser, U., Wilhelm, M., & Hanna, R. (2014). *The power of the Pygmalion effect*. Washington, DC: Center for American Progress.

Bourdieu, P. (1982). *Language and symbolic power*. Cambridge, MA: Harvard University Press.

Bracey, G. W. (2006). Poverty's infernal mechanism. *Principal Leadership, 6*(6), 60.

Bradshaw, T. K. (2007). Theories of poverty and anti-poverty programs in community development. *Community Development, 38*(1), 7–25.

Brann-Barrett, M. T. (2010). Same landscape, different lens: Variations in young people's socio-economic experiences and perceptions in their disadvantaged working-class community. *Journal of Youth Studies, 14*(3), 261–278.

Bray, M. (2013). Shadow education: Comparative perspectives on the expansion and implications of private tutoring. *Procedia, 77*, 412–420.

Bray, S. S., & Schommer-Aikins, M. (2014). School counselors' ways of knowing and social orientation in relationship to poverty beliefs. *Journal of Counseling & Development, 93*, 312–320.

Bridges, L. (2013). *Make every student count: How collaboration among families, schools, and communities ensures student success*. New York, NY: Scholastic.

Brizuela, M., Andersen, E., & Stallings, L. (1999). Discourse markers as indicators of register. *Hispania, 82*(1), 128–141.

Brown, D. L. (2009, May 18). The high cost of poverty: Why the poor pay more. *The Washington Post*. Retrieved from washingtonpost.com/wp-dyn/content/article/2009/05/17/AR2009051702053.html?sid=ST2009051801162

Buchmann, C., Condron, D. J., & Roscigno, V. J. (2010). Shadow education, American style: Test preparation, the SAT, and college enrollment. *Social Forces, 89*(2), 435–462.

Burling, R. (1973). *English in black and white*. New York, NY: Holt, Rinehart & Winston

Byrd-Blake, M., Afolayan, M. O., Hunt, J. W., Fabunmi, M., Pryor, B. W., & Leander, R. (2010). Morale of teachers in high poverty schools: A post-NCLB mixed methods analysis. *Education and Urban Society, 42*(4), 450–472.

Carbis, G. (2015). I want to challenge people's assumptions about poverty. *Our Schools/Our Selves, 24*(2), 29–30.

Carlson, J. A., Mignano, A. M., Norman, G. J., McKenzie, T. L., Kerr, J., Arredondo, E. M., Madanat, H., Cain, K. L., Elder, J. P., Saelens, B. E., & Sallis, J. F. (2014). Socioeconomic disparities in elementary school practices and children's physical activity during school. *American Journal of Health Promotion, 28* (Supplement), S47–S53.

Carmon, N. (1985). Poverty and culture. *Sociological Perspectives, 28*(4), 403–418.

Carreiro, J. L., & Kapitulik, B. P. (2010). Budgets, board games, and make believe: The challenge of teaching social class inequality with nontraditional students. *The American Sociologist, 41*, 232–248.

Center for American Progress (CAP). (2007). *From poverty to prosperity: A national strategy to cut poverty in half*. Washington, DC: Author.

Centers for Disease Control. (2017). *Health, United States, 2016*. Washington, DC: Author.

Chafel, J. A., Flint, A. S., Hammel, J., & Pomeroy, K. H. (2007). Young children, social issues, and critical literacy stories of teachers and researchers. *Young Children, 62*(1), 73–82.

Chandler, R. (2014). Teachers' beliefs about poverty and the impact on learning disabilities identification in a poor, rural school district. *Rural Educator, 35*(3), 31–39.

Chenoweth, K. (2009). It can be done, it's being done, and here's how. *Phi Delta Kappan, 91*(1), 38–43.

Chenoweth, K., & Theokas, C. (2013). How high-poverty schools are getting it done. *Educational Leadership, 70*(7), 56–59.

Chetty, R., Grusky, D., Hell, M., Hendren, N., Manduca, R., & Narang, J. (2016). *The fading American dream: Trends in absolute mobility since 1940.* Cambridge, MA: The National Bureau of Economic Research.

Child Trends. (2014). *Early childhood program enrollment.* Bethesda, MD: Author.

Children First for Oregon. (2016). *Status of Oregon's children and families: 2016 county databook.* Portland, OR: Author.

Children's Defense Fund (CDF). (2008). *Child poverty in America.* Retrieved from childrensdefense.org/child-research-data-publications/data/child-poverty-in-america.pdf

Children's Defense Fund. (2015). *Ending child poverty now.* Washington, DC: Author.

Chomsky, N. (1965). *The theory of syntax.* Cambridge, MA: MIT Press.

Christensen, L. (2008). Welcoming all languages. *Educational Leadership, 66*(1), 59–62.

Christian, R., & Mukarji-Connolly, A. (2012). What's home got to do with it? Unsheltered queer youth. *A New Queer Agenda: The Scholar and Feminist Online, 10*(1–2).

Clark, L. P., Millett, D. B., & Marshall, J. D. (2014). National patterns in environmental injustice and inequality: Outdoor NO_2 air pollution in the United States. *PLoS One, 9*(4), 1–8.

Cloutier-Bordeleau, M. (2015). Considering poverty: Reconstructing the discourse of socio-economic status in our schools. *Our Schools/Our Selves, 24*(2), 97–104.

Cohen, R., & Wardrip, K. (2011). *Should I stay or should I go? Exploring the effects of housing instability and mobility on children.* Washington, DC: Center for Housing Policy.

Collins, J. (1988). Language and class in minority education. *Anthropology & Education Quarterly, 19*(4), 299–326.

Comber, B. (2016). Poverty, place and pedagogy in education: Research stories from front-line workers. *The Australian Educational Researcher, 43*, 393–417.

Comber, B., Nixon, H., Ashmore, L., Loo, S., & Cook, J. (2006). Urban renewal from the inside out: Spatial and critical literacies in a low socioeconomic school community. *Mind, Culture, and Activity, 13*(3), 228–246.

Constantino, R. (2005). Print environments between high and low socioeconomic status communities. *Teacher Librarian, 32*(3), 22–25.

Cookson, P. W. (2013). *Class rules: Exposing inequality in American public schools.* New York, NY: Teachers College Press.

Cooper, C. E. (2010). Family poverty, school-based parental involvement, and policy-focused protective factors in kindergarten. *Early Childhood Research Quarterly, 25*, 480–492.

Cooper, C. E., Crosnoe, R., Suizzo, M., & Pituch, K. (2010). Poverty, race, and parental involvement during the transition to elementary school. *Journal of Family Issues, 31*(7), 859–883.

Cooter, K. (2006). When mama can't read: Counteracting intergenerational illiteracy. *Reading Teacher, 59,* 698–702.

Coulton, C., Richter, F., Kim, S., Fischer, R., & Cho, Y. (2016). Temporal effects of distressed housing on early childhood risk factors and kindergarten readiness. *Children and Youth Services Review, 68,* 59–72.

Coulton, C., Theodos, B., Turner, M. A. (2012). Residential mobility and neighborhood change: Real neighborhoods under the microscope. *Cityscape, 14*(3), 55–89.

Council of Graduate Schools. (2011). *Graduate enrollment and degrees—U.S. and Canadian comparisons.* Washington, DC: Author.

Council on Community Pediatrics. (2016). Poverty and child health in the United States. *Pediatrics, 137*(4), 1–14.

Crawford, E., Wright, M., & Masten, O. (2006). Resilience and spirituality in youth. In E. Roehlkepartain, P. King, L. Wagener, & P. Benson (Eds.), *The handbook of spiritual development in childhood and adolescence* (pp. 355–370). Thousand Oaks, CA: Sage.

Croft, S. J., Roberts, M. A., & Stenhouse, V. (2016). The perfect storm of education reform: High-stakes testing and teacher evaluation. *Social Justice, 42*(1), 70–92.

Cronin, D., & Lewin, B. (2000). *Click, clack, moo.* New York: Simon & Schuster

Crosnoe, R., Wirth, R. J., Pianta, R. C., Leventhal, T., & Pierce, K. M. (2010). Family socioeconomic status and consistent environmental stimulation in early childhood. *Child Development, 81*(3), 972–987.

Curry, K. A., Jean-Marie, G., & Adams, C. A. (2016). Social networks and parental motivational beliefs: Evidence from an urban school district. *Educational Administration Quarterly, 52*(5), 841–877.

Cutler, D. M., & Lleras-Muney, A. (2010). Understanding differences in health behaviors by education. *Journal of Health Economics, 29*(1), 1–28.

D'Amico, D., Pawlewicz, R. J., Earley, P. M., & McGeehan, A. P. (2017). Where are the black teachers?: Discrimination in the teacher labor market. *Harvard Educational Review, 87*(1), 26–49.

Darling-Hammond, L. (2013). "Test-and-punish" sabotages quality of children's education. *Stanford Center for Opportunity Policy in Education Blog.* Retrieved from edpolicy.stanford.edu/blog/entry/753

Davis, D. W., Gordon, M. K., & Burns, B. M. (2011). Educational interventions for childhood asthma: A review and integrative model for preschoolers from low-income families. *Pediatric Nursing, 37*(1), 31–38.

Dee, T., & West, M. (2011). The non-cognitive returns to class size. *Educational Evaluation and Policy Analysis, 33*(1), 23–46.

DeFilippis, J. N. (2016). "What about the rest of us?": An overview of LGBT poverty issues and a call to action. *Journal of Progressive Human Services, 27*(3), 143–174.

DeLuca, S., Clampet-Lundquist, S., & Edin, K. (2016). *Coming of age in the other America.* New York, NY: Sage.

DeSocio, J., & Hootman, J. (2004). Children's mental health and school success. *Journal of School Nursing, 20*(4), 189–196.

Djonko-Moore, C. M. (2016). An exploration of teacher attrition and mobility in high poverty schools. *Race, Ethnicity and Education, 19*(5), 1063–1087.

Domhoff, G. W. (2012). *Wealth, income, and power: Who rules America?* Retrieved from.ucsc.edu/whorulesamerica/power/wealth.html.

Dotterer, A. M., & Wehrspann, E. (2015). Parent involvement and academic outcomes among urban adolescents: Examining the role of school engagement. *Educational Psychology, 36*(4), 812–830.

Dreyer, B. P. (2016). Poverty and child health in the United States: Addressing the social determinants of health in the medical home. *Social Policy Report, 29*(4), 18–20.

Dube, A., Lester, T. W., & Reich, M. (2010). *Minimum wage effects across state borders: Estimates using contiguous counties.* Berkeley, CA: Institute for Research on Labor and Employment.

Duckworth, A. L., Peterson, C., Matthews, M. D., & Kelly, D. R. (2007). Grit: Perseverance and passion for long-term goals. *Journal of Personality and Social Psychology, 92*(6), 1087–1101.

Dudley-Marling, C. (2015). The resilience of deficit thinking. *Journal of Teaching and Learning, 10*(1), 1–11.

Dudley-Marling, C., & Lucas, K. (2009). Pathologizing the language and culture of poor children. *Language Arts, 86*(5), 362–370.

Duncan, G. J., Magnuson, K., Kalil, A., & Ziol-Guest, K. (2012). The importance of early childhood poverty. *Social Indicators Research, 108*(1), 87–98.

Dupere, V., Leventhal, T., Crosnoe, R., & Dion, E. (2010). Understanding the positive role of neighborhood socioeconomic advantage in achievement: The contribution of home, child care, and school environments. *Developmental Psychology, 46*(5), 1227–1244.

Durso, L., & Gates, G. (2012). *Serving our youth: Findings from a national survey of service providers working with lesbian, gay, bisexual, and transgender youth who are homeless or at risk of becoming homeless.* Los Angeles, CA: The William Institute, True Colors Fund, and The Palette Fund.

Dutro, E. (2009). Children writing "hard times": Lived experiences of poverty and the class-privileged assumptions of a mandated curriculum. *Language Arts, 87*(2), 89–98.

Dweck, C. S. (2010). Even geniuses work hard. *Educational Leadership, 68*(1), 16–20.

Dwyer, M. C. (2011). *Reinvesting in arts education.* Washington, DC: President's Committee on the Arts and the Humanities.

Dynarski, M., & Kainz, K. (2015). Why federal spending on disadvantaged students (Title I) doesn't work. *Evidence Speaks, 1*(7), 1–5.

Eberstadt, N. (2006). The mismeasure of poverty. *Policy Review, 138*, 19–51.

Engebretsen, K. (2011, August 26). The top 10 ways to support arts education. *Artsblog.* Retrieved from blog.americansforthearts.org/2011/08/26/the-top-10-ways-to-support-arts-education

Eichner, A., & Robbins, G. (2015). *National snapshot: Poverty among women & families, 2014.* Washington, DC: National Women's Law Center.

Elkin, A. (2012). Students hop, skip, and jump their way to understanding. *Teaching Children Mathematics, 18*(9), 524.

Erickson, W., Lee, C., & von Schrader, S. (2016). *2015 Disability Status Report: United States.* Ithaca, NY: Yang Tan Institute on Employment and Disability.

Evans, G. W. (2004). The environment of childhood poverty. *American Psychologist, 59*(2), 77–92.

Evans, G. W., Wells, N. M., & Schamberg, M. A. (2010). The role of the environment in SES and obesity. In L. Dube, A. Behara, D. Dagher, J. Drewnowski, J. P. LeBel, J. D. Richard, & R. Y. Yada (Eds.), *Obesity prevention: The role of society and brain on individual behavior* (pp. 713–725). New York, NY: Elsevier.

Evans, W., Harris, P., Sethuraman, S., Thiruvaiyaru, D., Pendergraft, E., Cliett, K., & Cato, V. (2016). Empowering young children in poverty by improving their home literacy environments. *Journal of Research in Childhood Education, 30*(2), 211–225.

Fahlman, M. M., Hall, H. L., & Lock, R. (2006). Ethnic and socioeconomic comparisons of fitness, activity levels, and barriers to exercise in high school females. *Journal of School Health, 76*(1), 12–17.

Falls, S. (2010). American dreams: Class in the United States. In D. E. Chapman (Ed.), *Examining social theory: Crossing borders/reflecting back* (pp. 19–35). New York, NY: Peter Lang.

Fernald, A., Marchman, V. A., & Weisleder, A. (2013). SES differences in language processing skill and vocabulary are evident at 18 months. *Developmental Science, 16*(2), 234–248.

Fiarman, S. E. (2016). Unconscious bias: When good intentions aren't enough. *Educational Leadership, 74*(3), 10–15.

Figlio, D. N. (2005). *Names, expectations, and the black-white achievement gap.* Cambridge, MA: National Bureau of Economic Research.

File, T., & Ryan, C. (2014). *Computer and Internet use in the United States: 2013.* Washington, DC: United States Census Bureau.

Fine, M., Greene, C., & Sanchez, S. (2016). Neoliberal blues and prec(ar)ious knowledge. *Urban Review, 48*, 499–519.

Finley, S., & Diversi, M. (2010). Critical homelessness: Expanding narratives of inclusive democracy. *Cultural Studies–Critical Methodologies, 10*(1), 4–13.

Flessa, J. J. (2007). *Poverty and education: Toward effective action.* Toronto, Ontario, Canada: Elementary Teachers Federation of Ontario.

Fram, M. S., Miller-Cribbs, J. E., & van Horn, L. (2007). Poverty, race, and the contexts of achievement: Examining educational experiences of children in the U.S. south. *Social Work, 52*(4), 309–319.

Freeman, E. (2010). The shifting geography of urban education. *Education and Urban Society, 42*(6), 674–704.

Fuentes-Nieva, R., & Galasso, N. (2014). *Working for the few: Political capture and economic inequality.* Oxford, UK: Oxfam GB.

Fulda, K. G., Lykens, K. K., Bae, S., & Singh, K. P. (2009). Unmet health care needs for children with special health care needs stratified by socioeconomic status. *Child and Adolescent Mental Health, 14*(4), 190–199.

Gabe, T. (2012). *Poverty in the United States: 2011.* Washington, DC: Congressional Research Service.

Gagnon, D., & Mattingly, M. J. (2012). *Beginning teachers are more common in rural, high-poverty, racially diverse schools.* Durham, NH: Carsey Institute.

Galbraith, J., & Winterbottom, M. (2011). Peer-tutoring: What's in it for the tutor? *Educational Studies, 37*(3), 321–332.

Gándara, P. (2010). Overcoming triple segregation. *Educational Leadership, 68*(3), 60–64.

Gans, H. J. (1996). *The war against the poor.* New York: Basic Books.

Garfinkel, I., Harris, D., Waldfogel, J., & Wimer, C. (2016). *Doing more for our children: Modeling a universal child allowance or more generous child tax credit.* Washington, DC: The Century Foundation.

Garza, R. E., & Garza, E. (2010). Successful white female teachers of Mexican American students of low socioeconomic status. *Journal of Latinos in Education, 9*(3), 189–206.

Gelatt, J., Adams, G., & Huerta, S. (2014). *Supporting immigrant families' access to prekindergarten.* Washington, DC: Urban Institute.

Georges, A. (2009). Relation of instruction and poverty to mathematics achievement gains during kindergarten. *Teachers College Record, 111*(9), 2148–2178.

Ghosh-Dastidar, B., Cohen, D., Hunter, G., Zenk, S. M., Huang, C., Beckman, R., & Dubowitz, T. (2014). Distance to store, food prices, and obesity in urban food deserts. *American Journal of Preventive Medicine, 47*(5), 587–595.

Gilliam, W., Maupin, A., Reyes, C., Accavitti, M., & Shic, F. (2016). *Do early educators' implicit biases regarding sex and race relate to behavior expectations and recommendations of preschool expulsions and suspensions?* New Haven, CT: Yale Child Study Center.

Glazerman, S., & Max, J. (2011). *Do low-income students have equal access to the highest-performing teachers?* Washington, DC: Institute of Education Sciences.

Glynn, S. J., Boushey, H., & Berg, P. (2016). *Who gets time off?: Predicting access to paid leave and workplace flexibility.* Washington, DC: Center for American Progress.

Godfrey, E. B., & Cherng, H. S. (2016). The kids are all right? Income inequality and civic engagement among our nation's youth. *Journal of Youth Adolescence, 45,* 2218–2232.

Goldring, R., Taie, S., & Riddles, M. (2014). *Teacher attrition and mobility: Results from the 2012–13 teacher follow-up survey.* Washington, DC: Institute of Education Sciences.

Gonzalez, N., Moll, L. C., & Amanti, C. (Eds.). (2005). *Funds of knowledge: Theorizing practices in households, communities, and classrooms.* Mahwah, NJ: Lawrence Erlbaum Associates.

Gorski, P. (2008). The myth of the "culture of poverty." *Educational Leadership, 65*(7), 32–35.

Gorski, P. (2009). Insisting on digital equity: Reframing the dominant discourse on multicultural education and technology. *Urban Education, 44,* 348–364.

Gorski, P. (2012). Perceiving the problem of poverty and schooling: Deconstructing the class stereotypes that mis-shape education policy and practice. *Equity & Excellence in Education, 45*(2), 302–319.

Gorski, P. (2013). Building a pedagogy of engagement for students in poverty. *Phi Delta Kappan, 95*(1), 48–52.

Gorski, P. (2016a). Rethinking the role of "culture" in educational equity: From cultural competence to equity literacy. *Multicultural Perspectives, 18*(4), 221–226.

Gorski, P. (2016b). Poverty and the ideological imperative: A call to unhook from deficit and grit ideology and to strive for structural ideology in teacher education. *Journal of Education for Teaching, 42*(4), 378–386.

Gorski, P. (2016c). Equity literacy: More than celebrating diversity. *Diversity in Education, 11*(1), 12–15.

Gorski, P., & Chen, C. (2015). "Frayed all over": The causes and consequences of activist burnout among social justice education activists. *Educational Studies, 51*(5), 385–405.

Gorski, P., & Swalwell, K. (2015). Equity literacy for all. *Educational Leadership, 72*(6), 34–40.

Gould, E., Davis, A., & Kimball, W. (2015). *Broad-based wage growth is a key tool in the fight against poverty.* Washington, DC: Economic Policy Institute.

Gould, M. C., & Gould, H. (2003). A clear vision for equity and opportunity. *Phi Delta Kappan, 85*(4), 324–328.

Graham, M. A. (2009, February). Focus on "culture of poverty" misses the mark. *Counseling Today,* 45–48.

Grant, S. D., Oka, E. R., & Baker, J. A. (2009). The culturally relevant assessment of Ebonics-speaking children. *Journal of Applied School Psychology, 25*(3), 113–127.

Greenwald, A. G., & Pettigrew, T. F. (2014). With malice toward none and charity for some: Ingroup favoritism enables discrimination. *American Psychologist, 69*(7), 669–684.

Greenwood, C. R., & Delquari, J. (1995). Classwide peer tutoring and the prevention of school failure. *Preventing School Failure, 39*(4), 21–25.

Greve, F. (2009, May 23). America's poor are its most generous. *The Seattle Times.* Retrieved from seattletimes.com/nation-world/americas-poor-are-its-most-generous-donors/

Gruber, M. (1972). The nonculture of poverty among black youths. *Social Work, 17*(3), 50–58.

Grusky, D. B., & Ryo, E. (2006). Did Katrina recalibrate attitudes toward poverty and inequality? A test of the "dirty little secret" hypothesis. *Du Bois Review, 3*(1), 59–82.

Guinan, K., & Hansell, L. (2014). Applying Montessori theory to break the cycle of poverty: A unique multi-generational model of transforming housing, education, and community for at-risk families. *North American Montessori Teachers Association Journal, 39*(2), 103–110.

Haberman, M. (1991). The pedagogy of poverty versus good teaching. *Phi Delta Kappan, 73,* 290–294.

Haine, D. (2010). Introducing students to environmental justice: A North Carolina case study. *Learn NC.* Retrieved from learnnc.org/lp/pages/6968

Hair, N. L., Hanson, J. L., Wolfe, B. L., & Pollack, S. D. (2015). Association of child poverty, brain development, and academic achievement. *JAME Pediatrics, 169*(9), 822–829.

Hamovitch, B. (1996). Socialization without voice: An ideology of hope for at-risk students. *Teachers College Record, 98*(2), 286–306.

Hart, B., & Risley, T. R. (1995). *Meaningful differences in the everyday experiences of young American children.* Baltimore, MD: Brookes.

Hatch, G., & Smith, D. (2004). Integrating physical education, math, and physics. *Journal of Physical Education, Recreation & Dance, 75*(1), 42–50.

Heberle, A. E., & Carter, A. S. (2015). Cognitive aspects of young children's experience of economic disadvantage. *Psychological Bulletin, 141*(4), 723–746.

Henry, B., & Fredericksen, A. (2015). *Low wage nation: Nearly half of new jobs don't pay enough to make ends meet.* Seattle, WA: Alliance for a Just Society.

Henry, M., Watt, R., Rosenthal, L., & Shivji, A. (2016). *The 2016 annual homeless assessment report.* Washington, DC: U.S. Department of Housing and Urban Development.

Hill, N. E., & Craft, S. A. (2003). Parent-school involvement and school performance: Mediated pathways among socioeconomically comparable African American and Euro-American families. *Journal of Educational Psychology, 91,* 74–83.

Hillemeier, M. M., Morgan, P. L., Farkas, G., & Maczuga, S. A. (2013). Quality disparities in child care for at-risk children: Comparing Head Start and non–Head Start settings. *Maternal and Child Health Journal, 17*(1), 180–188.

Hillier, A., Chilton, M., Zhao, Q., Szymkowiak, D., Coffman, R., & Mallya, G. (2015). *Concentration of tobacco advertisements at SNAP and WIC stores.* Atlanta, GA: Centers for Disease Control and Prevention.

Hindman, A. H., Wasik, B. A., & Snell, E. K. (2016). Closing the 30 million word gap: Next steps in designing research to inform practice. *Child Development Perspectives, 10*(2), 134–139.

Holme, J. J., & Wells, A. S. (2008). School choice beyond district borders: Lessons for the reauthorization of NCLB from interdistrict desegregation and open enrollment plans. In R. Kahlenberg (Ed.), *Improving on No Child Left Behind* (pp. 139–215). Washington, DC: Century Foundation Press.

Holmes, A., Fox, E. B., Wieder, B., & Zubak-Skees, C. (2016). *Rich people have high-speed Internet; many poor people still don't.* Washington, DC: Center for Public Integrity.

Holtzman, C., & Susholtz, L. (2011). *Object lessons: Teaching math through the visual arts.* Portland, ME: Stenhouse Publishers.

hooks, b. (2000). *Where we stand: Class matters.* New York, NY: Routledge.

Hopkins, D. J. (2009). Partisan reinforcement and the poor: The impact of context on explanations for poverty. *Social Science Quarterly, 90*(3), 744–764.

Hornsey, M. J. (2008). Social identity and self-categorization theory: A historical review. *Social and Personality Psychology Compass, 2*(1), 204–222.

Horrigan, J. B. (2015). *Libraries at the crossroads.* Washington, DC: Pew Research Center.

Hout, M. (2008). How class works: Objective and subjective aspects of class since the 1970s. In A. Lareau & D. Conley (Eds.), *Social class: How does it work?* (pp. 25–64). New York, NY: Sage.

Howard, L. (2007). How exemplary teachers educate children of poverty, having low school readiness skills, without referrals to special education. Unpublished doctoral dissertation, George Mason University.

Howard, T., Dresser, S. G., & Dunklee, D. R. (2009). *Poverty is not a learning disability: Equalizing opportunities for low SES students.* Thousand Oaks, CA: Corwin.

Hoy, W. K., Tarter, C. J., & Hoy, A. W. (2006). Academic optimism in schools: A force for student achievement. *American Educational Research Journal, 43,* 425–446.

Hughes, C., Newkirk, R., & Stenhjem, P. H. (2010). Addressing the challenge of disenfranchisement of youth: Poverty and racism in the schools. *Reclaiming Children and Youth, 19*(1), 22–26.

Hughes, J. (2010). What teacher preparation programs can do to better prepare teachers to meet the challenges of educating students living in poverty. *Action in Teacher Education, 32*(1), 54–64.

Humensky, J. L. (2010). Are adolescents with high socioeconomic status more likely to engage in alcohol and illicit drug use in early adulthood? *Substance Abuse Treatment, Prevention, and Policy, 5,* 1–10.

Jackson, C. K., Johnson, R., & Persico, C. (2015). *The effects of school spending on educational and economic outcomes: Evidence from school finance reforms* (NBER Working Paper No. 20847). Cambridge, MA: National Bureau of Economic Research.

James, R. N. III, & Sharpe, D. L. (2007). The nature and causes of the U-shaped charitable giving profile. *Nonprofit and Voluntary Sector Quarterly, 36,* 218–238.

Jaramillo, J., Mello, Z. R., & Worrell, F. Z. (2016). Ethnic identity, stereotype threat, and perceived discrimination among Native American adolescents. *Journal of Research on Adolescents, 26*(4), 769–775.

Jarrett, R. J., & Coba-Rodriguez, S. (2015). "My mother didn't play about education": Low-income, African American mothers' early school experiences and their impact on school involvement for preschoolers transitioning to Kindergarten. *The Journal of Negro Education, 84*(3), 457–473.

Jensen, E. (2009). *Teaching with poverty in mind.* Alexandria, VA: Association for Supervision and Curriculum Development.

Jervis, R. (2006). Understanding beliefs. *Political Psychology, 27*(5), 641–663.

Jessim, L., & Harber, K. D. (2005). Teacher expectations and self-fulfilling prophecies: Knowns and unknowns, resolved and unresolved controversies. *Personality and Social Psychology Review, 9*(2), 131–155.

Jeynes, W. (2011). *Parent involvement and academic success.* New York, NY: Routledge.

Jiang, Y., Granja, M. R., & Koball, H. (2017). *Basic facts about low-income children.* New York, NY: National Center for Children in Poverty.

Johnson, J. W. (2016). "All I do is win . . . no matter what": Low-income, African American single mothers and their collegiate daughters' unrelenting academic achievement. *The Journal of Negro Education, 85*(2), 156–171.

Johnson, S. B., Arevalo, J., Cates, C. B., Weisleder, A., Dreyer, B. P., & Mendelsohn, A. L. (2016). Perceptions about parental engagement among Hispanic immigrant mothers of first graders from low-income backgrounds. *Early Childhood Education Journal, 44,* 445–452.

Jones, H. (2016). Discussing poverty with student teachers: The realities of dialogue. *Journal of Education for Teaching, 42*(4), 468–482.

Jones, R. K., & Luo, Y. (1999). The culture of poverty and African American culture: An empirical assessment. *Sociological Perspectives, 42*(3), 439–458.

Jones, S. (2008). Grass houses: Representations and reinventions of social class through children's literature. *Journal of Language and Literacy Education, 4*(2), 40–58.

Jones, S. (2012). Critical literacies in the making: Social class and identities in the early reading classroom. *Journal of Early Childhood Literacy, 13*(2), 197–224.

Jones, S., & Vagle, M. D. (2013). Living contradictions and working for change: Toward a theory of social class-sensitive pedagogy. *Educational Researcher, 42*(3), 129–141.

Joo, M. (2010). Long-term effects of Head Start on academic and school outcomes of children in persistent poverty: Girls vs. boys. *Children & Youth Services Review, 32*(6), 807–814.

Joyner, S., & Molina, C. (2012). *Impact of class time on student learning*. Austin, TX: Texas Comprehensive Center.

Judge, S. (2005). Resilient and vulnerable at-risk children: Protective factors affecting early school competence. *Journal of Children & Poverty, 11*(2), 149–168.

Kahn, M., & Gorski, P. C. (2016). The gendered and heterosexist evolution of the teacher exemplar in the United States and its equity implications for LGBTQ and gender non-conforming teachers. *The International Journal of Multicultural Education, 18*(2), 15–38.

Kannapel, P. J., & Clements, S. K. (2005). *Inside the black box of high-performing, high-poverty schools: A report from the Pritchard Committee for Academic Excellence*. Lexington, KY: Pritchard Commission for Academic Excellence.

Karemaker, A., Pitchford, N., & O'Malley, C. (2010). Enhanced recognition of written words and enjoyment of reading in struggling beginner readers through whole-word multimedia software. *Computers & Education, 54*(1), 199–208.

Karoly, L. A., & Gonzalez, G. C. (2011). Early care and education for children in immigrant families. *Future of Children, 21*(1), 70–101.

Katz, M. B. (2015). What kind of a problem is poverty? The archeology of an idea. In A. Roy & E. S. Crane (Eds.), *Territories of poverty* (pp. 39–78). Athens, GA: University of Georgia Press.

Kellett, M. (2009). Children as researchers: What we can learn from them about the impact of poverty on literacy opportunities. *International Journal of Inclusive Education, 13*(4), 395–408.

Kelley, J. E., & Darragh, J. J. (2011). Depictions and gaps: Portrayal of U.S. poverty in realistic fiction children's picture books. *Reading Horizons, 50*(4), 263–282.

Kelly, M. (2010). Regulating the reproduction and mothering of poor women: The controlling image of the welfare mother in television news coverage of welfare reform. *Journal of Poverty, 14*, 76–96.

Kendall, D. E. (2011). *Media representations of wealth and poverty in America*. Lanham, MD: Rowman & Littlefield.

Kennedy, E. (2010). Improving literacy achievement in a high-poverty school: Empowering classroom teachers through professional development. *Reading Research Quarterly, 45*(4), 384–387.

Kids Count. (2016). *Data book: State trends in child well-being*. Baltimore, MD: Annie E. Casey Foundation.

Kim, M. (1999). Problems facing the working poor. *Proceedings of the Economic Policy Institute Symposium*. Retrieved from dol.gov/oasam/programs/history/herman/reports/futurework/conference/workingpoor/workingpoor_toc.htm

King, M. L. (1967, August). *Where do we go from here?* Speech presented at the Southern Christian Leadership Conference, Atlanta, Georgia.

Kiyama, J. M., Harper, C. E., Ramos, D., Aguayo, D., Page, L. A., & Riester, K. A. (2015). *Parent and family engagement in higher education*. New York, NY: Wiley.

Klebanov, P. K., Evans, G. W., & Brooks-Gunn, J. (2014). Poverty, ethnicity, and the risk of obesity among low birth weight infants. *Journal of Applied Developmental Psychology, 35*, 245–253.

Kneebone, E. (2016). Suburban poverty is missing from the conversation about America's future. *Brookings Institution*. Retrieved from brookings.edu/articles/suburban-poverty-is-missing-from-the-conversation-about-americas-future/

Kneebone, E., & Berube, A. (2013). *Confronting suburban poverty in America.* Washington, DC: Brookings Institution.

Kochhar, R., & Fry, R. (2014). Wealth inequality has widened along racial, ethnic lines since end of Great Recession. *Pew Research Center Fact Tank*. Retrieved from pewresearch.org/fact-tank/2014/12/12/racial-wealth-gaps-great-recession/

Kohn, A. (2014). Grit? A skeptical look at the latest educational fad. *Educational Leadership, 74*, 104–108.

Kong, A., Burks, N., Conklin, C., Roldan, C., Skipper, B., Scott, S., Sussman, A., & Leggot, J. (2010). A pilot walking school bus program to prevent obesity in Hispanic elementary school children: Role of physician involvement in the school community. *Clinical Pediatrics, 49*(1), 989–991.

Kozol, J. (2012). *Savage inequalities: Children in America's schools*. New York, NY: HarperPerennial.

Krashen, S. (2013). Access to books and time to read versus the Common Core state standards and tests. *English Journal, 103*(2), 21–29.

Krashen, S., Lee, S., & McQuillan, J. (2010). An analysis of the PIRLS (2006) data: Can the school library reduce the effect of poverty on reaching achievement? *CSLA Journal, 34*(1), 26–28.

Kraus, M. W., & Keltner, D. (2009). Signs of socioeconomic status: A thin-slicing approach. *Psychological Science, 20*, 99–106.

Kundu, A. (2014). Grit, overemphasized; Agency, overlooked. *Phi Delta Kappan, 96*, 80.

Labadie, M., Pole, K., & Rogers, R. (2013). How kindergarten students connect and critically respond to themes of social class in children's literature. *Literacy Research and Instruction, 52*, 312–338.

Labov, W. (1972). *Sociolinguistic patterns*. Philadelphia, PA: University of Pennsylvania Press.

Ladson-Billings, G. (2006). It's not the culture of poverty, it's the poverty of culture: The problem with teacher education. *Anthropology and Education Quarterly, 37*(2), 104–109.

LaGue, K., & Wilson, K. (2010). Using peer tutors to improve reading comprehension. *Kappa Delta Pi Record, 46*(4), 182–186.

Lampert, J., Burnett, B., & Lebhers, S. (2016). "More like the kids than the other teachers": One working class pre-service teacher's experiences in a middle-class profession. *Teaching and Teacher Education, 58*, 35–42.

Landsman, J., & Gorski, P. C. (2007). Countering standardization. *Educational Leadership, 64*(8), 40–44.

Lareau, A. (1994). Parent involvement in schooling: A dissenting view. In C. Fagano & B. Z. Werber (Eds.), *School, family, and community interaction: A view from the firing lines* (pp. 61–73). Boulder, CO: Westview Press.

Lareau, A., & Weininger, E. B. (2008). Class and the transition to adulthood. In A. Lareau & D. Conley (Eds.), *Social class: How does it work?* (pp. 118–151). New York, NY: Sage.

Latz, A. O., & Adams, C. M. (2011). Critical differentiation and the twice oppressed: Social class and giftedness. *Journal for the Education of the Gifted,
34*(5), 773–789.

Lee, C. D. (1995). A culturally based cognitive apprenticeship: Teaching African
American high school students skills in literary interpretation. *Reading Research Quarterly, 30*(4), 608–630.

Lee, J.-S., & Bowen, N. K. (2006). Parent involvement, cultural capital, and the
achievement gap among elementary school children. *American Educational Research Journal, 43*(2), 193–218.

Lee, S. G., & Jeon, S. Y. (2005). The relations of socioeconomic status to health status, health behaviors in the elderly. *Journal of Preventive Medicine and Public
Health, 38*(2), 154–162.

Lee, V., & Burkam, D. (2003). Dropping out of high school: The role of school organization and structure. *American Educational Research Journal, 40*(2), 353–393.

Lefmann, T., & Combs-Orme, T. (2014). Prenatal stress, poverty, and child outcomes. *Child & Adolescent Social Work Journal, 31*, 577–590.

Leonardo, Z., & Grubb, W. N. (2013). *Education and racism: A primer on issues
and dilemmas.* New York, NY: Routledge.

Levitan, J. (2016). The difference between educational equality, equity, and justice.
American Journal of Education Forum. Retrieved from ajeforum.com/the-
difference-between-educational-equality-equity-and-justice-and-why-it-
matters-by-joseph-levitan/

Lewis, O. (1959). *Five families: Mexican case studies in the culture of poverty.* New
York, NY: Basic Books.

Li, G. (2010). Race, class, and schooling: Multicultural families doing the hard work of
home literacy in America's inner city. *Reading & Writing Quarterly, 26*, 140–165.

Lindsey, R. B., Karns, M. S., & Myatt, K. (2010). *Culturally proficient education:
An asset-based response to conditions of poverty.* Thousand Oaks, CA: Corwin.

Lindsey, R. B., Robins, K. N., & Terrell, R. D. (2009). *Cultural proficiency: A manual for school leaders.* Thousand Oaks, CA: Corwin.

Lineburg, M. Y., & Gearheart, R. (2013). *Educating students in poverty: Effective
practices for leadership and teaching.* New York, NY: Routledge.

Lineburg, M. Y., & Ratliff, B. C. (2015). Teaching students in poverty in small and
mid-sized urban school districts. *Advances in Educational Administration, 22*,
85–108.

Lipman, P. (2011). Neoliberal education restructuring: Dangers and opportunities of
the present crisis. *Monthly Review, 63*(3), 114–127.

Lippi-Green, R. (1994). Standard language ideology, and discriminatory pretext in
the courts. *Language in Society, 23*(2), 163–198.

Liu, G. (2008). Improving Title I funding equity across states, districts, and schools.
Iowa Law Review, 93(3), 973–1013.

Loughan, A., & Perna, R. (2012). Neurocognitive impacts for children of poverty
and neglect. *American Psychological Association's Children, Youth, and Family News.* Retrieved from apa.org/pi/families/resources/newsletter/2012/07/
neurocognitive-impacts.aspx

Lucio, J., Jefferson, A., & Peck, L. (2016). Dreaming the impossible dream: Low-income families and their hopes for the future. *Journal of Poverty, 20*, 359–379.

Luhby, T. (2012a). American's near poor: 30 million and struggling. *CNNMoney*. Retrieved from money.cnn.com/2012/10/24/news/economy/americans-poverty/index.html.

Luhby, T. (2012b). Median income falls, but so does poverty. *CNNMoney*. Retrieved from money.cnn.com/2012/09/12/news/economy/median-income-poverty/index.html?iid=EL.

Luhman, R. (1990). Appalachian English stereotypes: Language attitudes in Kentucky. *Language in Society, 19*(3), 331–348.

Luke, A. (2010). Documenting reproduction and inequality: Revisiting Jean Anyon's "Social Class and School Knowledge." *Curriculum Inquiry, 40*(1), 167–182.

MacLeod, K. E., Gee, G. C., Crawford, P., & Wang, M. C. (2008). Neighborhood environment as a predictor of television viewing among girls. *Journal of Epidemiology & Community Health, 62*, 288–292.

Macpherson, A. K., Jones, J., Rothman, L., Macarthur, C., & Howard, A. W. (2010). Safety standards and socioeconomic disparities in school playground injuries: A retrospective cohort study. *BMC Public Health, 10*, 542–547.

Maheady, L., Mallette, B., & Harper, G. F. (2006). Four classwide peer tutoring models: Similarities, differences, and implications for research and practice. *Reading & Writing Quarterly, 22*, 65–89.

Mann, B. (2014). Equity and equality are not equal. *The Education Trust*. Retrieved from edtrust.org/the-equity-line/equity-and-equality-are-not-equal/

Marcella, J., Howes, C., & Fuligni, A. S. (2014). Exploring cumulative risk and family literacy practices in low-income Latino Families. *Early Childhood and Development, 25*, 36–55.

Marsh, J. (2011). *Class dismissed: Why we cannot teach or learn our way out of inequality*. New York, NY: Monthly Review Press.

Maughan, E. D. (2016). Building strong children: Why we need nurses in schools. *American Educator, 40*(1), 19–25.

McDermott, N. (2014). The myth of gay affluence. *The Atlantic*. Retrieved from theatlantic.com/business/archive/2014/03/the-myth-of-gay-affluence/284570/

McGill-Franzen, A., & Allington, D. (2014). Won't read much if I don't have many books: Poverty, access to books, and the rich/poor reading achievement gap. *Heinemann Digital Campus*. Retrieved from heinemann.com/blog/wont-read-much-if-i-dont-have-any-books-poverty-access-to-books-and-the-richpoor-reading-achievement-gap/

Meade, E. E. (2014). *Overview of community characteristics in areas with concentrated poverty*. Washington, DC: Department of Health and Human Services.

Meisenheimer, M. (2015). *Food insecurity in early childhood*. Washington, DC: Center for the Study of Social Policy.

Meiser, T., & Hewstone, M. (2004). Cognitive processes in stereotype formation: The role of correct contingency learning for biased group judgments. *Journal of Personality and Social Psychology, 87*(5), 599–614.

Mendoza, J. A., Levinger, D. D., & Johnston, B. D. (2009). Pilot evaluation of a walking school bus program in a low-income urban community. *BMC Public Health, 9*, 122–129.

Messacar, D., & Oreopoulos, P. (2012). *Staying in school: A proposal to raise high school graduation rates*. Washington, DC: The Hamilton Project.

Meyer, B., & Sullivan, J. (2012). Identifying the disadvantaged: Official poverty, consumption poverty, and the new supplemental poverty measure. *Journal of Economic Perspectives, 3*, 111–136.

Milbourne, P. (2010). Putting poverty and welfare in place. *Policy & Politics, 38*(1), 153–169.

Miller, P., Pavlakis, A., Lac, V., & Hoffman, D. (2014). Responding to poverty and its complex challenges: The importance of poverty fluency for educational leaders. *Theory into Practice, 53*, 131–138.

Miller, P. J., Cho, G. E., & Bracey, J. R. (2005). Working-class children's experience through the prism of personal storytelling. *Human Development, 48*, 115–135.

Milner, H. R. (2015). *Rac(e)ing to class: Confronting poverty and race in schools and classrooms*. Cambridge, MA: Harvard University Press.

Mistry, R. S., Brown, C., Chow, K., & Collins, G. (2012). Increasing the complexity of young adolescents' beliefs about poverty and inequality: Results of an 8th grade social studies curriculum intervention. *Journal of Youth and Adolescence, 41*, 704–716.

Mitra, S., Findley, P. A., & Sambamoorthi, U. (2009). Healthcare expenditures of living with a disability: Total expenditures, out of pocket expenses and burden, 1996–2004. *Archives of Physical Medicine and Rehabilitation, 90*, 1532–1540.

Mohai, P., & Saha, R. (2015). Which came first, people or pollution? Assessing the disparate siting and post-siting demographic change hypotheses of environmental justice. *Environmental Research Letters, 10*, 1–17.

Moll, L. C., Amanti, C., Neff, D., & Gonzalez, N. (1992). Funds of knowledge for teaching: Using a qualitative approach to connect homes and classrooms. *Theory into Practice, 31*, 132–141.

Morrissey, T. W., Oellerich, D., Meade, E., Simms, J., & Stock, A. (2016). Neighborhood poverty and children's food insecurity. *Children and Youth Services Review, 66*, 85–93.

Moses, J. (2012). *Moving away from racial stereotypes in poverty policy*. Washington, DC: Center for American Progress.

Moynihan, D. (1965). *The negro family: The case for national action*. Washington, DC: U. S. Department of Labor.

Mulvihill, T. M., & Swaminathan, R. (2006). "I fight poverty. I work!": Examining discourses of poverty and their impact on pre-service teachers. *International Journal of Teaching and Learning in Higher Education, 18*(2), 97–111.

Mundy, C. A., & Leko, M. M. (2015). Uncovering and informing preservice teachers' prior knowledge about poverty. *Networks, 17*(1), 1–10.

National Alliance on Mental Illness. (2011). *State mental health cuts: A national crisis*. Arlington, VA: Author.

National Association for the Teaching of English Working Party on Social Class and English Teaching. (1982). Checklist for class bias and some recommended books. *English in Education, 16*(2), 34–37.

National Center for Education Statistics (NCES). (2005). *Parent and family involvement in education: 2002–2003*. Washington, DC: U.S. Department of Education.

National Coalition for the Homeless. (2009). Homeless veterans. *National Coalition for the Homeless*. Retrieved from nationalhomeless.org/factsheets/veterans.html

National Council of Teachers of Mathematics. (2000). *Principles and standards for school mathematics.* Reston, VA: Author.

National Employment Law Project. (2016). *City minimum wage laws: Recent trends and economic evidence.* New York, NY: Author.

National Low Income Housing Coalition. (2016). *The gap: The affordable housing gap analysis 2016.* Washington, DC: Author.

Nesdale, D., & Flesser, D. (2001). Social identity and the development of children's group attitudes. *Child Development, 72*(2), 506.

Neuman, S. B. (2009). Use the science of what works to change the odds for children at risk. *Phi Delta Kappan, 90*(8), 582–587.

Newmeyer, F. (1985). *Grammatical theory: Its limits and possibilities.* Chicago, IL: University of Chicago Press.

Noel, A., Stark, P., Redford, J., & Zukerberg, A. (2013). *Parent and family involvement in education, from the National Household Education Surveys Program of 2012.* Washington, DC: U.S. Department of Education.

Noguera, P. (2011). A broader and bolder approach uses education to break the cycle of poverty. *Phi Delta Kappan, 93*(3), 8–14.

Noguera, P., & Akom, A. (2000, June 5). Disparities demystified. *The Nation,* 29–31.

Norton, M. I., & Ariely, D. (2011). Building a better America—one wealth quintile at a time. *Perspectives on Psychological Science, 6*(1), 9–12.

Oakes, J. (2005). *Keeping track: How schools structure inequality* (2nd ed.). New Haven, CT: Yale University Press.

Ohmer, M. L., Warner, B. D., & Beck, E. (2010). Preventing violence in low-income communities: Facilitating residents' ability to intervene in neighborhood problems. *Journal of Sociology & Social Welfare, 37*(2), 161–181.

Orfield, G., & Frankenberg, E. (2013). *Educational delusions? Why choice can deepen inequality and how to make schools fair.* Berkeley, CA: University of California Press.

Organisation for Economic Co-operation and Development. (2016). *Enrollment in childcare and pre-school.* Paris, France: Author.

Owens, A., Reardon, S. F., & Jencks, C. (2016). Income segregation between schools and school districts. *American Education Research Journal, 53*(4), 1159–1197.

Palmer, M. (2011). Disability and poverty: A conceptual overview. *Journal of Disability Policy Studies, 21*(4), 210–218.

Pampel, F. C., Krueger, P. M., & Denney, J. T. (2010). Socioeconomic disparities in health behaviors. *Annual Review of Sociology, 36,* 349–370.

Papageorge, N. W., Gershenson, S., & Kang, K. (2016). *Teacher expectations matter.* Bonn, Germany: Institute for the Study of Labor.

Parrett, W. H., & Budge, K. M. (2012). *Turning high-poverty schools into high-performing schools.* Alexandria, VA: Association for Supervision and Curriculum Development.

Patrick, M. E., Wightman, P., Schoeni, R. F., & Schulenberg, J. E. (2012). Socioeconomic status and substance use among young adults: A comparison across constructs and drugs. *Journal of Studies on Alcohol and Drugs, 73*(5), 772–782.

Patterson, J. A., Hale, D., & Stessman, M. (2008). Cultural contradictions and school leaving: A case study of an urban high school. *The High School Journal, 91*(2), 1–16.

Payne, R. K. (2005). *A framework for understanding poverty*. Highlands, TX: *aha!* Process.

Payne, R. K. (2006). *Reflections on Katrina and the role of poverty in the Gulf Coast crisis*. Retrieved from ahaprocess.com/files/Hurricane_Katrina_ reflections.pdf

Perrin, J. M., Boat, T. F., & Kelleher, K. (2016). The influence of health care policies on children's health and development. *Social Policy Report, 29*(4), 3–17.

Peterson, C., Mayer, L., Summers, J., & Luze, G. (2010). Meeting needs of young children at high risk for or having a disability. *Early Childhood Education Journal, 37*(6), 509–517.

Pew Charitable Trusts. (2012). *Pursuing the American dream: Economic mobility across generations*. Washington, DC: Author.

Pew Research Center. (2016). *On views of race and inequality, Blacks and Whites are worlds apart*. Washington, DC: Author. Retrieved from pewsocialtrends.org/2016/06/27/on-views-of-race-and-inequality-blacks-and-whites-are-worlds-apart/

Phillips, M., & Putnam, R. D. (2016). Increasing equality of opportunity in and out of schools, grades K–12. In The Saguaro Seminar (Ed.), *Closing the opportunity gap* (pp. 36–49). Cambridge, MA: Harvard Kennedy School.

Piff, P. K., Kraus, M. W., Cote, S., Cheng, B. H., & Keltner, D. (2010). Having less, giving more: The influence of social class on prosocial behavior. *Journal of Personality and Social Psychology, 99*(5), 771–784.

Pinto, L., & Cresnik, L. (2014). Mythology, moral panic, and the Ruby Payne bandwagon. *Our Schools/Our Selves, 24*(1), 43–54.

Pogrow, S. (2006). Restructuring high-poverty elementary schools for success: A description of the Hi-Perform school design. *Phi Delta Kappan, 88*(3), 223–229.

Pribesh, S., Gavigan, K., & Dickinson, G. (2011). The access gap: Poverty and characteristics of school library media centers. *The Library Quarterly, 81*(2), 143–160.

Prins, E., & Schafft, K. A. (2009). Individual and structural attributions for poverty and persistence in family literacy programs: The resurgence of the culture of poverty. *Teachers College Record, 111*(9), 2280–2310.

Proctor, B. D., Semega, J. L., & Kollar, M. A. (2016). *Income and poverty in the United States: 2015*. Washington, DC: U.S. Census Bureau.

Pullum, G. K. (1999). African American Vernacular English is not standard English with mistakes. In R. S. Wheeler (Ed.), *The workings of language* (pp. 39–58). Westport, CT: Praeger.

Radford, A. (2013). 'No point in applying': Why poor students are missing at top colleges. *The Atlantic Online.* Retrieved from theatlantic.com/education/archive/2013/09/no-point-in-applying-why-poor-students-are-missing-at-top-colleges/279699/

Ramalho, E. M., Garza, E., & Merchant, B. (2010). Successful school leadership in socioeconomically challenging contexts: School principals creating and sustaining successful school improvement. *International Studies in Educational Administration, 38*(3), 35–56.

Ravitch, D. (2016). *The death and life of the great American school system*. New York, NY: Basic Books.

Ray, N. (2006). *Lesbian, gay, bisexual, and transgender youth: An epidemic of homelessness*. New York, NY: National Gay and Lesbian Task Force Policy Institute and the National Coalition for the Homeless.

Reardon, S. F. (2013). The widening income achievement gap. *Educational Leadership, 70*(8), 10–16.

Reed, M. (2015). To find solutions, look inward. *Educational Leadership, 72,* 80–85.

Reich, M., Jacobs, K., & Berhardt, A. (2014). *Local minimum wage laws: Impacts on workers, families, and businesses.* Berkeley, CA: Center for Labor Research and Education.

Reis, S., & Fogarty, E. (2006). Savoring reading schoolwide. *Educational Leadership, 64*(2), 32–36.

Rios, E., & Gilson, D. (2016, December 22). 11 charts that show income inequality isn't getting better anytime soon. *Mother Jones Online.* Retrieved from motherjones. com/politics/2016/12/america-income-inequality-wealth-net-worth-charts

Rivera, L. A., & Tilcsik, A. (2016). Class advantage, commitment penalty: The gendered effect of social class signals in an elite labor market. *American Sociological Review, 81*(6), 1097–1131.

Robinson, J. G. (2007). Presence and persistence: Poverty ideology and inner-city teaching. *Urban Review, 39,* 541–565.

Robinson, D. V., & Volpé, L. (2015). Navigating the parent involvement terrain— The engagement of high poverty parents in a rural school district. *Journal of Family Diversity in Education, 1*(4), 66–85.

Rodman, R. (1977). Culture of poverty: The rise and fall of a concept. *Sociological Review, 25*(4), 867–876.

Rosemblatt, K. A. (2009). Other Americas: Transnationalism, scholarship, and the culture of poverty in Mexico and the United States. *Hispanic American Historical Review, 89*(4), 603–641.

Rosner, D., & Markowitz, G. (2016, February 13). It's not just Flint: There's an ugly history of lead poisoning and the poor in the United States. *Mother Jones Online.* Retrieved from motherjones.com/environment/2016/02/flint-lead-poisoning-america-toxic-crisis/

Rotberg, I. C. (2014). Charter schools and the risk of increased segregation. *Phi Delta Kappan, 95*(5), 26–31.

Rothstein, R. (2013). *For public schools, segregation then, segregation since.* Washington, DC: Economic Policy Institute.

Rouse, C. E., & Barrow, L. (2006). U.S. elementary and secondary schools: Equalizing opportunity or replacing the status quo? *The Future of Children, 16*(2), 99–123.

Rugh, J. S., Albright, L., & Massey, D. S. (2015). Race, space, and cumulative disadvantage: A case study of the subprime lending collapse. *Social Problems, 62*(2), 186–218.

Rushe, D. (November 1, 2012). US has added 1.1m new millionaires under Obama, says study. Retrieved from guardian.co.uk/business/2012/nov/01/us-new-millionaires-obama

Ryan, W. (1971). *Blaming the victim.* New York, NY: Vintage Books.

Sallee, M., & Boske, C. (2013). There are no children here: The case of an inner-city school addressing issues facing children and families living in poverty. *Journal of Cases in Educational Leadership, 16*(2), 61–70.

Sánchez , L. (2014). Fostering wideawakeness: Third grade children researching their community. In J. Landsman & P. Gorski (Eds.), *The poor are not the problem: Insisting on class equity in schools* (pp. 183–194). Sterling, VA: Stylus.

Sano, J. (2009). Farmhands and factory workers, honesty and humility: The portrayal of social class and morals in English language learner children's books. *Teachers College Record, 111*(11), 2560–2588.

Sato, M., & Lensmire, T. J. (2009). Poverty and Payne: Supporting teachers to work with children of poverty. *Phi Delta Kappan, 90*(5), 365–370.

Schanzenbach, D. W. (2014). *Does class size matter?* Boulder, CO: National Education Policy Center.

Schmalzried, H. D., Gunning, B., & Platzer, T. (2014). Creating a school-based eye care program. *Journal of School Health, 85*, 341–345.

Schmitt, S. A., & Lipscomb, S. T. (2016). Longitudinal associations between residential mobility and early academic skills among low-income children. *Early Childhood Research Quarterly, 36*, 190–200.

Schuchart, C., Buch, S., & Piel, S. (2015). Characteristics of mathematical tasks and social class-related achievement differences among primary school children. *International Journal of Educational Research, 70*, 1–15.

Sen, A. (1992). *Inequality reexamined.* Oxford, UK: Clarendon Press.

Sharkey, P., Putnam, R. D., & Turner, M. (2016). Rebuilding communities to help close the opportunity gap. In The Saguaro Seminar (Ed.), *Closing the opportunity gap* (pp. 50–61). Cambridge, MA: Harvard Kennedy School.

Sheets, R. H. (2009). What is diversity pedagogy? *Multicultural Education, 16*(3), 11–17.

Shields, C. M. (2014). The war on poverty must be won: Transformative leaders can make a difference. *International Journal of Educational Leadership and Management, 2*(2), 124–146.

Shier, M., Jones, M., & Graham, J. (2010). Perspectives of employed people experiencing homelessness of self and being homeless: Challenging socially constructed perceptions and stereotypes. *Journal of Sociology & Social Welfare, 37*(4), 13–37.

Shin, I., & Chung, J. (2009). Class size and student achievement in the United States: A meta-analysis. *Journal of Educational Policy, 6*(2), 3–19.

Siapush, M., McNeil, A., Hammond, D., & Fong, G. T. (2006). Socioeconomic and country variations in knowledge of health risks of tobacco smoking and toxic constituents of smoke: Results from the 2002 International Tobacco Control Four Country Survey. *Tobacco Control, 15*, 65–70.

Simon, N. S., & Johnson, S. M. (2015). Teacher turnover in high-poverty schools: What we know and can do. *Teachers College Record, 177*(3), 1–36.

Skalicky, A., Meyers, A. F., Adams, W. G., Yang, Z., Cook, J. T., & Frank, D. A. (2006). Child food insecurity and iron deficiency anemia in low-income infants and toddlers in the United States. *Maternal and Child Health Journal, 10*(2), 177–185.

Slavin, R. E., Lake, C., & Groff, C. (2009). Effective programs in middle and high school mathematics: A best evidence synthesis. *Review of Educational Research, 79*(2), 839–911.

Sleeter, C. (2004). Context-conscious portraits and context-blind policy. *Anthropology and Education Quarterly, 35*(1), 132–136.

Smiley, A. D., & Helfenbein, R. J. (2011). Becoming teachers: The Payne effect. *Multicultural Perspectives, 13*(1), 5–15.

Solari, C. D., Morris, S., Shivji, A., & de Souza, T. (2016). *The 2015 annual homeless report to Congress.* Washington, DC: U.S. Department of Housing and Urban Development.

Southeast Asia Resource Action Center. (2011). *Southeast Asian Americans at a glance.* Washington, DC: Author.

Spatig-Amerikaner, A. (2012). *Unequal education: Federal loophole enables lower spending on students of color.* Washington, DC: Center for American Progress.

Spencer, B., & Castano, E. (2007). Social class is dead! Long live social class! Stereotype threat among low socioeconomic status individuals. *Social Justice Research, 20,* 418–432.

St. Denis, V. (2009). Rethinking cultural theory in Aboriginal education. In C. Levine-Rasky (Ed.), *Canadian perspectives on the sociology of education* (pp. 163–182). Don Mills, England: Oxford University Press.

Steele, C. M. (2010). *Whistling Vivaldi and other clues to how stereotypes affect us.* New York, NY: W.W. Norton & Company.

Stokas, A. G. (2015). A genealogy of grit: Education in the new gilded age. *Educational Theory, 65*(5), 513–528.

Stosich, E. L. (2016). Building teacher and school capacity to teach ambitious standards in high-poverty schools. *Teaching and Teacher Education, 58,* 43–53.

Strange, M. (2011). Finding fairness for rural schools. *Phi Delta Kappan, 92*(6), 8–15.

Streib, J. (2011). Class reproduction by four year olds. *Qualitative Sociology, 34,* 337–352.

Streib, J. (2012). Class reproduction by four year olds. *Classism Exposed Blog.* Retrieved from classism.org/class-reproduction-year-olds

Suitts, S. (2013). *Update: A new majority: Low income students in the south and nation.* Atlanta, GA: Southern Education Foundation.

Suitts, S. (2016). Students facing poverty: The new majority. *Educational Leadership, 74*(3), 36–40.

Sullivan, J., & Lloyd, R. S. (2006). The Forum Theatre of Augusto Boal: A dramatic model for dialogue and community-based environmental science. *The International Journal of Justice and Sustainability, 11*(6), 627–646.

Swalwell, K. (2011). Why our students need "equity literacy." *Teaching Tolerance Blog.* Retrieved from tolerance.org/blog/why-our-students-need-equity-literacy

Swalwell, K. (2015). Mind the civic empowerment gap: Economically elite students and critical civic education. *Curriculum Inquiry, 45*(5), 491–512.

Taylor, P., Kochhar, R., Dockterman, D., & Motel, S. (2011). *In two years of economic recovery, women lost jobs, men found them.* Washington, DC: Pew Research Center.

Taylor, P., Kochhar, R., Fry, R., Velasco, G., & Motel, S. (2011). *Wealth gaps rise to record highs between Whites, Blacks and Hispanics.* Washington, DC: Pew Research Center.

Temple, J. A., Reynolds, A. J., & Arteaga, I. (2010). Low birth weight, preschool education, and school remediation. *Education & Urban Society, 42*(6), 705–729.

Templeton, B. L. (2011). *Understanding poverty in the classroom.* New York, NY: Rowman & Littlefield.

Terry, N. P., Connor, C. M., Thomas-Tate, S., & Love, M. (2010). Examining relationships among dialect variation, literacy skills, and school context in first grade. *Journal of Speech, Language, and Hearing Research, 53,* 126–145.

Thurston, L. P., & Berkeley, T. R. (2010). Morality and the ethic of care: Peaceable rural schools, caring rural communities. *Rural Special Education Quarterly, 29*(2), 25–31.

Toch, T. (2011). Beyond basic skills. *Phi Delta Kappan, 92*(6), 72–73.

Tranter, R., & Palin, N. (2004) Including the excluded: An art in itself. *Support for Learning, 19*(2), 88–95.

Tucker, J., & Lowell, C. (2016). *National snapshot: Poverty among women and families, 2015.* Washington, DC: National Women's Law Center.

Ullicci, K., & Howard, T. (2015). Pathologizing the poor: Implications for preparing teachers to work in high-poverty schools. *Urban Education, 50*(2), 170–193.

UNICEF. (2015). *Assistive technology for children with disabilities: Creating opportunities for education, inclusion and participation.* New York, NY: Author.

United Nations Inter-Agency Group for Child Mortality Estimation. (2014). *Committing to child survival: A promise renewed.* New York, NY: UNICEF.

U.S. Census Bureau. (2012). *Current population survey: Annual social and economic supplements.* Washington, DC: Author.

U.S. Census Bureau. (2013). *Northern Virginia dominates list of highest-income counties.* Washington, DC: Author.

U.S. Census Bureau. (2015). *Public education finances: 2013.* Washington, DC: Author.

U.S. Census Bureau. (2016). *March 2016 current population survey.* Washington, DC: Author.

U.S. Department of Education. (2001). *The longitudinal evaluation of school change and performance in Title I schools.* Washington, DC: Author.

U.S. Department of Education. (2003). *President's commission on excellence in education.* Washington, DC: Author.

U.S. Department of Education (2017). *Reimagining the role of technology in education.* Washington, DC: Author.

U.S. Department of Health and Human Services. (2017). Annual update of the HHS poverty guidelines. *Federal Register, 82*(19), 8831–8832.

Ushomirsky, N., & Williams, D. (2015). *Funding gaps 2015.* Washington, DC: The Education Trust.

Valencia, R. R. (2009). A response to Ruby Payne's claim that the deficit thinking model has no scholarly utility. *Teachers College Record.* Retrieved from tcrecord.org

Valentine, C. (1968). *Culture and poverty: Critique and counter-proposal.* Chicago, IL: University of Chicago Press.

Van de Walle, J. (2006). *Elementary and middle school mathematics.* Boston, MA: Pearson.

van Doorn, B. W. (2015). Pre- and post-welfare reform media portrayals of poverty in the United States: The continuing importance of race and ethnicity. *Politics & Policy, 43,* 142–162.

Van Galen, J. (2007). Late to class: Social class and schooling in the new economy. *Educational Horizon, 85,* 156–167.

Vera, D. (2011). Using popular culture print to increase emergent literary skills in one high-poverty school district. *Journal of Early Childhood Literacy, 11*(3), 307–330.

Waldfogel, J., & Putnam, R. D. (2016). Promoting opportunity in early childhood. In The Saguaro Seminar (Ed.), *Closing the opportunity gap* (pp. 24–35). Cambridge, MA: Harvard Kennedy School.

Wang, W., & Parker, K. (2011). *Women see value and benefits of college; men lag on both fronts*. Washington, DC: Pew Social and Demographic Trends.

Wasserberg, M. J. (2014). Stereotype threat effects on African American children in an urban elementary school. *Journal of Experimental Education, 82*(4), 502–517.

Weiner, L. (2003). Why is classroom management so vexing to urban teachers? *Theory into Practice, 42*(4), 305–312.

Weiner, B., Osborne, D., & Rudolph, U. (2011). An attributional analysis of reactions to poverty: The political ideology of the giver and the perceived morality of the receiver. *Personality and Social Psychology Review, 15*(2), 199–213.

West, R., & Odum, J. (2016). *Poverty and opportunity in the states: The good, the bad, and the ugly*. Washington, DC: Center for American Progress.

West-Olatunji, C., Sanders, T., Mehta, S., & Behar-Horenstein, L. (2010). Parenting practices among low-income parents/guardians of academically successful fifth grade African American children. *Multicultural Perspectives, 12*(3), 138–144.

Western Regional Advocacy Project (2010). *Without housing: Decades of federal housing cutbacks, massive homelessness, and policy failures*. San Francisco, CA: Author.

Wheeler, R., & Thomas, J. (2013). And "still" the children suffer: The dilemma of standard English, social justice, and social access. *JAC: A Journal of Rhetoric, Culture, and Politics, 33*(1/2), 363–396.

Whittaker, C. (2012). Integrating literature circles into a cotaught inclusive classroom. *Intervention in School & Clinic, 47*(4), 214–223.

Williams, J. R., Masuda, Y. J., & Tallis, H. (2016). A measure whose time has come: Formalizing time poverty. *Social Indicators Research, 128*, 265–283.

Williams, T. T., & Sánchez, B. (2012). Parental involvement (and uninvolvement) at an inner-city high school. *Urban Education, 47*, 625–652.

Williams, W. R. (2009). Struggling with poverty: Implications for theory and policy of increasing research on social class-based stigma. *Analyses of Social Issues and Public Policy, 9*(1), 37–56.

Wilson, C. M. (2016). Enacting critical care and transformative leadership in schools highly impacted by poverty: An African-American principal's counter narrative. *International Journal of Educational Leadership in Education, 19*(5), 557–577.

Wilson, W. J. (1996). *When work disappears: The world of the new urban poor*. New York, NY: Vintage Books.

Wolff, E. N. (2012). *The asset price meltdown and the wealth of the middle class*. New York, NY: National Bureau of Economic Research.

Wolff, E. N. (2014, December). *Household wealth trends in the United States, 1962–2013*. NBER Working Paper no. 20733. Retrieved from nber.org/papers/w20733.pdf

Worpole, K. (2000). *In our backyard: The social promise of environmentalism*. London, UK: Green Alliance.

Wright, T. (2011). Countering the politics of class, race, gender, and geography in early childhood education. *Educational Policy, 25*(1), 240–261.

Yeager, D. S., & Walton, G. M. (2011). Social-psychological interventions in education: They're not magic. *Review of Educational Research, 81*(2), 267–301.

Yin, M., Shaewitz, D., & Megra, M. (2014). *An uneven playing field: The lack of equal pay for people with disabilities.* Washington, DC: American Institutes for Research.

Yollis, L. (2012). Blogging helps students learn key literacy skills and more. *Curriculum Review, 52*(2), 7.

Zahorik, J., Halbach, A., Ehrle, K., & Molnar, A. (2003). Teaching practices for smaller classes. *Educational Leadership, 61*(1), 75–77.

Zhang, H., & Cowen, D. J. (2009). Mapping academic achievement and public school choice under the No Child Left Behind legislation. *Southeastern Geographer, 49*(1), 24–40.

Ziol-Guest, K. M., & McKenna, C. C. (2014). Early childhood housing instability and school readiness. *Child Development, 85*(1), 103–113.

Name Index

Subject Index

Haberman, Martin, 138
Handbook of Research on Multicultural Education (Banks), xiv
Head Start, 179
Health care
  access to, 2–3, 89–90, 120, 124, 180–181
  advocacy for universal, 184
  prenatal care, 2, 51–52, 89, 97, 179, 184
  preventive screenings, 2–3, 89, 92, 157, 172, 180–181, 184
  reactive versus preventive, 184
  school nurses and, 108–109, 181, 184
  vision screenings, 180, 181
Higher-order pedagogies. *See also* Instructional/curricular strategies
  access to, 1, 112–114, 129–132
High-poverty schools, 1–2, 28–29, 33, 104, 105–109, 112–113, 116–120, 124, 128, 129, 133, 140, 172, 175, 181–182
High school
  college and career counseling, 108, 175
  college preparation, 99–100, 107, 111, 112, 175
  graduation rates, xi, 101
High-stakes/standardized testing
  class size and, 180
  collaborative examination of assessment data, 126
  evidence of what works and, 25, 33–34
  higher-order pedagogies and, 130–131
  hyperfocus on, 114, 165–166, 182
  literacy enjoyment and, 127–128
  in measuring achievement gap, 101
  in neoliberal school reform, 117–120
  test scores as inadequate measures of equity, 24–25, 30, 99–100, 149
Homelessness, 42–43, 51, 53, 183–184
Homework, 16, 39, 73, 74, 100, 152, 157, 171, 174
hooks, bell, 148

Housing
  affordability of. *See* Affordable housing
  discrimination in, 50
  homelessness and, 42–43, 51, 53, 183–184
Howard, Lizette, 131, 149, 151
Humiliation of students, 22–23, 85–87, 109–110, 150
  identifying and eliminating policies and practices, 173–174
  "performing" poverty, 154–156, 171, 173–174
  school activity fees, 19, 34, 156, 157, 171, 173, 174
  school supplies and, 85–86, 154–155, 157
Humility, in relationships with students, 150–151
Hurricane Katrina, 40–41

"I Have a Dream" speech (King), 133–134
Immigrant families, xiv, 53, 76, 95, 103–104
Income
  defined, 9
  growing inequality of, 8, 37–38, 44–46, 52, 183
  as societal barrier, 24, 29–30
  wealth versus, 9, 44–46
Inequality Reexamined (Sen), 52
Inequity
  as cause of educational outcomes, 25, 30–31, 57, 67, 87–96, 99
  challenging inequitable policies, 165–166
  defined, 19
  in equity literacy, 25, 30–31, 87–96, 124
  multiple layers of instructional strategy for, 25, 34, 123
Inequity-responsiveness, 156–157
In-group bias, 71–73
Injustice, generational, 8, 65
Institutional culture, 34. *See also* Leadership strategies; Policy advocacy

About the Author

Paul C. Gorski is an associate professor of Integrative Studies and a senior research fellow at the Center for the Advancement of Well-Being at George Mason University. He is the founder of EdChange and the Equity Literacy Institute. Paul's passions include all matters of educational justice, the relationship between equity literacy and equity action, and the intersection of racial and economic justice. He has written, co-written, or co-edited 10 books, including *Case Studies on Diversity and Social Justice Education* (with Seema Pothini), *Cultivating Social Justice Teachers* (with Kristien Zenkov, Nana Osei-Kofi, and Jeff Sapp), and *The Poverty and Education Reader* (with Julie Landsman). His articles have appeared in *Educational Leadership*, *Kappan*, *Teaching Tolerance*, *Rethinking Schools*, *School Administrator*, and a wide variety of other practitioner publications, as well as dozens of research journals. He lives in Virginia with his cat, Buster.